Informed Agitation

Informed Agitation

Library and Information Skills in Social Justice Movements and Beyond

Edited by Melissa Morrone

Library Juice Press
Sacramento, CA

Library of Congress Cataloging-in-Publication Data

Informed agitation : library and information skills in social justice movements and beyond / edited by Melissa Morrone.
      pages cm
Includes bibliographical references and index.
Summary: "Explores activist librarianship in the early 21st century"-- Provided by publisher.
   ISBN 978-1-936117-87-1 (alk. paper)
   1. Libraries and society. 2. Library science--Social aspects. 3. Library science--Political
aspects. 4. Librarians--Political activity. 5. Librarians--Professional ethics. 6. Freedom of
information. 7. Intellectual freedom. 8. Social justice. 9. Information policy. I. Morrone,
Melissa, editor of compilation. II. Title: Library and information skills in social justice movements and beyond.
   Z716.4I55 2013
   021.2--dc23
                          2013042417

Table of Contents

Introduction

Our specific skill is making information accessible to the common-wealth—of which we are members. Thus, objectivity is no more than a useful abstraction—like the line of the equator. [...] The Good News is Advocacy! Participation! Librarians can *generate* information. Why watch it congeal on a 3x5 world? (West, 1972, p. [i]; emphasis in original)

Twice in one day, I am in conversations with people who say, almost verba-tim, "I thought librarians were at least *liberal*—until I went to library school."

"Do you think that there's a core of inherently progressive values in librari-anship?" I ask a friend getting her doctorate in library and information science. She stares at me. "I hope so!"

Another librarian friend reads me part of a letter from her former philoso-phy professor in which he declares, unbidden, that libraries are "the only admi-rable, non-coercive, non-competitive institution in our society."

After a ballet class, a professional modern dancer and I chat about our work. "Wow, a librarian!" she says. "I've always thought librarians are so cool. I mean, librarians are pretty radical, right?"

The visiting father of a fellow member of our books-to-prisoners group, Books Through Bars, is introduced to me and another librarian. "Oh, the radical librarians!" he exclaims. "Well," we say, after a pause. "Mostly we just go to work."

* * *

I don't know of any polls conducted on the political views of librarians, but I think it is fair to say that we have a reputation (and frequently a reality) for liberalism. After all, aren't our field's core values infused with progressive values at some level, as is so vivid to my friend with the Ph.D.? But no matter how much of a spirit of egalitarian access, critical thought, self-education, preservation of cultural memory, intellectual freedom, and other noble values animates librarianship—or how committed an individual library worker may be to these values—our everyday jobs don't necessarily rise above the mundane and, well, frustrating. (As I write this, a PUBLIB posting asks what to do about a patron who regularly tears pages out of their cooking magazines.) And regarding the personalities in librarianship, I think we can agree that library workers in general—including degreed librarians—are, strangely enough, a representative swath of humanity, with disparate motivations and political leanings. Some are incurious, unimaginative, ill-informed, even racist. Some embrace the weird pseudo-corporate practice of referring to public library users as "customers." Some don't even seem to like literature, or people.

Part of what makes librarianship so exciting is this ontological question about its politics. The library is so mainstream, yet also so...socialist. As one English librarian said (quoted in a particularly lovely piece in the non-library press about the value of libraries):

> If someone suggested the idea of public libraries now, they'd be considered insane[...] If you said you were going to take a little bit of money from every taxpayer, buy a whole load of books and music and games, stick them on a shelf and tell everyone, "These are yours to borrow and all you've got to do is bring them back," they'd be laughed out of government. (Bathurst, 2011)

And the library makes an appearance in a book introducing anarchism:

> A library is a good present-day instance of this ethic [of mutual aid] [...] Communities see libraries as something necessary and valuable to everyday life, as something that should be freely available to all. Anyone can use the library as much or as little as they see fit, with no sense of scarcity. People can borrow what they want, with no judgment (in the ideal) about the quantity or quality of their usage. They can enjoy the library space itself, on their own or with the assistance of a librarian. They can use it without offering anything in return, or if desired, freely

give back by donating books or volunteering time to reshel[ve] them. Imagine if everything from energy to education was such a "from each, to each" institution. (Milstein, 2010, p. 55)

Despite all its utopian flare, the metaphoric book of U.S. librarianship includes collaborations with state repression (as during World War I and the Cold War), bureaucratization resulting in homogenous and conventional collections, dubious relationships with municipal power, a conservative drive to socialize its users to the dominant culture, and other transgressions. On the other hand, ours is also a field that—at least some of the time—is a locus of popular education; connects with the "underserved" and other societal underdogs including queer teenagers, homeless people, newcomers to the country, and the lonely; links militarism and imperialism to austerity at home; facilitates scholarship both institutional and independent; and takes a feminized and very pale profession as the basis for a broader analysis of patriarchy and white privilege. On an individual level, librarianship has produced E. J. Josey, Eric Moon, Zoia Horn, Elizabeth Martinez, Sandy Berman, Celeste West, and other outspoken social justice-minded personalities of the 1960s (and beyond). During the 2012 symposium called "Practical Choices for Powerful Impacts: Realizing the Activist Potential of Librarians," organized by the Boston Radical Reference collective, academic librarian Alana Kumbier posited that many of us get into librarianship because we have activist backgrounds and a commitment to democratic goals. She went on: "All librarians are engaged in political work. But [...] I don't know that it's inherently activist. But what I would say is, I think a lot of the work that we do is, especially if we're intentionally thinking about the goals of social justice movements as we're doing our jobs" (Critical Librarianship Symposium Boston - live recording).

This attitude fits how I've approached librarianship. I first got involved in books-to-prisoners work when I was twenty-two, not long after deciding that I would one day become a librarian. The ability to combine my interest in literature and reading with ideals of justice was appealing and seemed to fit with my career plans. I've also been an active member of Radical Reference from right around the time when the project first formed (see Lia Friedman's essay for more details), especially with training and outreach. Personally, I find meaning from both the work I do at my place of employment and the related work I do as part of social movements. When I've helped give a research workshop at the Grassroots Media Conference or the US Social Forum, or compiled incarceration statistics for a Books Through Bars fact sheet, or investigated the history of a financial services company for a local Palestine solidarity group, I've felt that these activities are a necessary (and, I hope, useful) complement to what I do at my job. They remind me that the world is a bigger place than my immediate workaday routines, and that there are ways to bring my training into the movements I care about.

I'm not the first to observe that people outside of librarianship tend to have positive feelings about us, and I don't mean just like when I went to a party at the home of a sound designer and an actor, and all their theater world guests were totally charmed to hear I was a librarian. When I was at a planning meeting of the opposition before the 2004 Republican National Convention in New York City, I introduced myself as a librarian, and mine was the only introduction that got any reaction—applause—from the crowd. The challenge is how to channel this often fuzzy goodwill from activists and mainstream society alike into stronger support for public spaces, open access scholarship, open technological platforms, high-quality research instruction, preservation of marginalized communities' heritage, and other information issues that fall into our purview.

So what defines a radical librarian—an informed agitator, if you will, who wants to create other informed agitators? Public librarian Ann Sparanese (2008) has described her growing commitment to serving her entire New Jersey community, which led to vigorous collection development, grantwriting, and other undertakings: "With each new project, the idea of library activism—in this case, the idea of community outreach and service—informed my work. Although it seems so obvious to me and maybe it does to you too, you would be amazed at how it often just is not done" (p. 74). And in a seminal text in radical librarianship, the collection *Revolting Librarians*, Celeste West (1972) argued that some type of library activism is in fact a foundation for being a good professional: "True professionalism implies evolution, if not revolution; those who 'profess' a calling have certain goals and standards for improving existence, which necessarily means moving, shaking, transforming it" (p. [i]).

When I, a public librarian, demonstrate how to attach a resume to an email message, someone's existence is improved. But I wouldn't call that much of a movement or a transformation. Indeed, a lot of what I do at work is pretty quotidian. But I'm never unaware of the big picture—the "free"[1] resources, both material and intangible, that assist people going through major life changes of all sorts; the opportunities for community members to be teachers and creators as well as students and cultural consumers; and, overall, the environment of learning, self-actualization, and even caring (for oneself and also for other library users). Some of these elements are at the heart of any library, and others I deliberately bring in, for example enabling patrons and friends to lead workshops on subjects they're knowledgeable about. Outside of my job, too, I know that showing someone how to use the top level domain limiter in Google's advanced

---

1. Scare quotes because of the tax money involved.

search is not in and of itself a political act. But doing it for a working group of Occupy Wall Street, as part of a training on strategic business research, is another story. Context and vision matter.

I'm leery of getting too caught up in definitions. There is great fun and great value that come from being part of that community of self-selecting "radical" librarians. But I also think about the non-self-selectors, who make up the bulk of our colleagues and neighbors and include other smart, dedicated folks who question authority and try innovative things in the service of their publics (but may not call themselves activists). How do we take our political insights and use them in the workplace and beyond to speak truth to power, to push for rigorous thinking on policies, to address systemic inequalities, to improve service to *all* of our users? Activist and academic Chris Dixon expresses what some organizers on the left are grappling with generally: "From my perspective, [the] challenge is to move beyond self-selected radical scenes, and build broad-based movements rooted in the lives and struggles of ordinary, non-activist people. [...] We have to build alliances across differences" in hierarchies of race, class, gender, sexuality, citizenship, and ability (Soong, 2013). We know that those "ordinary, non-activist people" are in our classes, in our workrooms, at our reference desks, in our towns and cities. Unlike other activists who may spend the bulk of their time in radical silos, we are fortunate enough to be part of heterogeneous communities. What does alliance-building in the service of justice and equality in a library context look like?

Which brings us to this book. It follows such collections as *Activism in American Librarianship, 1962-1973; Revolting Librarians;* and *Revolting Librarians Redux*, which brought out some of the progressive voices and activist histories of the library sphere. As such, one of *Informed Agitation's* goals is to serve as documentation of a particular moment in the timeline of librarianship and social movements. It's also a moment when the tumultuous shifts in the publishing world and the ever-evolving online environment have made discussion of libraries' and librarians' "relevance" increasingly pronounced, and when austerity measures in the public sector, higher education, and elsewhere are strangling the future of library work itself. The essays here are also articulations of library activism outside of significant associations such as the Social Responsibilities Round Table of ALA and the Progressive Librarians Guild.

You'll encounter librarians who are fighting against the fears that lead us to hide behind so-called neutrality, "bringing us full circle back to our roots, as servants to power" (Harger, 2010, p. 62). The people in this book are fighting *against* the fear of ruffling the feathers of managers and colleagues, the fear of subsuming their identities to mainstream "3x5" library culture, the fear of taking to the streets in protest. They are struggling against the idea that neutrality covers all aspects of our work equally. They are also wrestling with the ideals, not always realized, of autonomy from institutional control—a key theme in grassroots activism of all kinds.

Several chapters are about archives, perhaps reflecting the ease with which this area of librarianship lends itself to social movement work. What better way to support marginalized communities than to document and preserve their materials and (in some cases literally) their voices? Other chapters address the importance of physical venues in which people gather, from the neighborhood public library branch (a site of multicultural, intergenerational, cross-class interactions) to explicitly radical spaces. You'll also read about ecological sustainability and one role for information workers in this area; identity and setting boundaries to "community"; librarians' responsibility to international solidarity; personal histories; digitization; prisons; healthcare; Occupy Wall Street; and, of course, information literacy, zines, and other issues related to instruction and collections.

And what's in your hands is just part of it all. Librarians (and others!) are out there being activists with data, literature, archives, instruction, and more. DuckDuckGo it. Talk to your favorite librarian over tea or beer about information work in social movements. Discuss some of the other important and contentious topics in our field, such as e-books and digital rights management; privacy concerns, from government surveillance of patrons' borrowing records to "Big Data"; threats to net neutrality; unequal access to broadband Internet; copyright and open access; legislative efforts to restrict online activity; labor struggles in library workplaces; and the state of library and information science education. Look at organizations and projects in your area that could use some experienced research assistance. Make a resource guide about something that affects you personally and distribute it around your city. As Bathurst (2011) says, "The great untold truth of libraries is that people need them not because they're about study and solitude, but because they're about connection." And making a connection can be the start of something that transforms the world.

~Melissa Morrone

References

Bathurst, B. (2011, April 30). The secret life of libraries. *The Guardian*. Retrieved from http://www.guardian.co.uk/books/2011/may/01/the-secret-life-of-libraries

Critical Librarianship Symposium Boston - live recording. Part two [Video file]. Retrieved from http://radicalreference.info/content/critical-librarianship-symposium-boston-live-recording

Harger, E. (2010). Looking backward, imagining forward: Celebrating 20 years of *Progressive Librarian*. *Progressive Librarian* 34-35, 58-71.

Milstein, C. (2010). *Anarchism and its aspirations*. Oakland, CA: AK Press.

Soong, C.S. (2013, May 1). May Day meanings. *Against the Grain*. Podcast retrieved from http://www.againstthegrain.org/program/708/wed-50113-may-day-meanings

Sparanese, A. (2008). Activist librarianship: Heritage or heresy? In A. Lewis (Ed.), *Questioning library neutrality: Essays from Progressive Librarian* (pp. 67-81). Duluth, MN: Library Juice Press.

West, C. (1972). Introduction. In C. West & E. Katz (Eds.), *Revolting librarians* (pp. [i-iv]). San Francisco, CA: Booklegger Press.

In the City

Documenting the Untold Stories of Feminist Activists at Welfare Rights Initiative: A Digital Oral History Archive Project

Cynthia Tobar

People had internalized all the bad things they hear about women on welfare, and so they started to realize that these problems that seemed so deeply and uniquely personal were actually not; there were bigger issues at play. And their harsh life experience gave them expertise that was missing in the decision-making that frames those policies. So that's a real transformation to take that leap, that shift in how you see yourself and how you see the world, from believing that you're the reason for the world's problems, you're the reason for poverty, and to instead realizing you've got some experience and expertise, in fact, that needs to be shared. And that if people understood how incredibly committed you are to getting off welfare, how you want nothing more than to be self-sufficient or self-sustaining for your family. And if they knew about the obstacles that you were encountering each day, exactly the nature of those obstacles, maybe some of those obstacles could be removed.

~Melinda Lackey, Co-founder, WRI, January 2012 (Tobar, 2012a)

Introduction

As an archivist/activist, I wish to incorporate multiple voices, reach diverse audiences, and encourage popular participation in presenting and preserving the history of the Welfare Rights Initiative (WRI), a grassroots student activist and community leadership training organization located at Hunter College. I wish to examine, via oral history interviews, social movement activity at the level of a grassroots organization as embodied by WRI, which was developed to aid student welfare recipients to become agents of social change and actively involve them with policymaking. I believe this social justice organization exemplifies not only grassroots organizing efforts in New York City, but also the history of working-class feminist activism in the United States.

The digital oral history archive of WRI is targeted at researchers, students, activists, and historians as a tool to enhance research and teaching in social protest movements and feminist activism. Consequently, this project seeks to fill in gaps in the research on this topic and capture the experiences of how the founders and participants of this largely woman-led organization came together to implement social change.

This archive documents WRI's progression from a student- and faculty-led grassroots movement to its present incarnation as a student advocacy organization. WRI seeks to serve under-served populations citywide, primarily women and girls, via its outreach programs that are designed to encourage those who are economically disadvantaged to study and obtain higher education and/or job training. This oral history project will give a platform to those who generally have little voice in the public debate on welfare reform: former and/or current welfare recipients—WRI's founders and membership base. It will provide students and scholars of social movements a positive working example of how women from various backgrounds can band together and enact social change.

Background: Welfare Rights Movement

When you have a reality, when you see the impact of policy right before you, and you see not only the impact of policy, but how women are penalized for the fact that they're—for example, couple years back I had a student, and when she came in she was explaining that, "Well, I wanna be in school. But my benefits were cut because I'm in school. And now I don't even have enough to feed my kid. So I'm trying to get food to feed my kid."[...] So here we are in a situation where here she was as a mom trying to get an education. They cut her food stamps because she's trying to get an education. So she's not able to give her kid what she was able to before. Another branch of that same larger agency then comes in and say, "You're not being a good mother because you're not feeding your child properly. So we have to come in and see if you're fit enough to keep that child." Well, that doesn't make sense. So did you realize, policy maker, that this was going to be the outcome of what you were designing?

~Dillonna Lewis, Co-Executive Director, WRI, August 2011 (Tobar, 2011a)

Scholars such as Guida West (Rutgers), Mimi Abramovitz (Hunter School of Social Work), and Premilla Nadasen (Queens College) have examined the role of gender bias in the establishment of social policy governing the eligibility for welfare benefits and the distribution of provisions between men and women. Many advocate for the involvement of welfare recipients in social policy to address the institutional resources that need to be in place in order to insure recipients of economic mobility once they are off welfare. These scholars have produced a rich body of work that makes the case for understanding and correcting a train of exclusions, prejudices, and hierarchies that adversely affect women in the social welfare system.

Almost from the start of the welfare rights movement, scholars have noted that differences among women, especially differences of race, class, and sexuality, frequently led to ruptures within grassroots activist groups.[1] Guida West's pioneering account, *The National Welfare Rights Organization: The Social Protest of Poor Women,* chronicles the rise and fall of the National Welfare Rights Organization, or NWRO. West's account, which was culled from her time as an active member of NWRO, illustrates the discrepancy between its formal principles and organizational structure (with membership and leadership theoretically confined to the welfare poor), and the daily reality of decision-making by primarily white, male, middle-class organizers.[2] The insights gained through West's own experience with the movement are evident again in her discussion of the difficulties in forming coalitions across class lines.

Mimi Abramovitz's *Under Attack, Fighting Back: Women and Welfare in the United States* examines the long-standing relationship between welfare and gender inequality. She asserts that sexism, patriarchy, and the gender division of labor and social reproduction have shaped the welfare state, and that traditional studies of social welfare that considered only class struggles and economic

---

1. Second wave feminist scholarship has suggested that conflicts over race, class, and sexuality were often irreconcilable, leading to many separate identity-based women's groups. Alice Echols shows how radical feminists in the post-1960s era placed consciousness-raising, such as critiquing beauty culture, sexual abuse, and power structures, above building organizing protests for social change (Echols, 1989).

2. See: Evans, 2008, and Rosen, 2000. Both Evans and Rosen also attribute outside forces, such as the rise of the religious right and the conservative movement, to the downswing in feminist organizing from the early 1980s.

production failed to regard these essential issues. Further, she examines welfare policies from the three main theoretical perspectives—liberal, social citizenship, and Marxist—and offers four feminist critiques to these traditional views (Abramovitz, 1996, p. 93).

The dominant narrative of the women's movement, which was composed almost entirely of white women, burst onto the scene in the late '60s. For a variety of reasons, black women (and other women of color) came late to organized feminism, not forming their own groups until the '70s. Black women who had been active participants in the previous decades' civil rights movement were subjected to ferocious demands that they step back into "traditional" gender roles. Most women of color remained hostile to feminism. Premilla Nadasen (2005), however, challenges this assumption in *Welfare Warriors: The Welfare Rights Movement in the United States*, stating that the welfare rights movement of the '60s and '70s articulated a new black feminism:

> The welfare rights movement has to be viewed as an integral part of the black freedom movement [...] It did not emerge simply as a frustrated response to the loss of direction by black activists and a desire to focus more attention on economic issues [...] Although support from middle-class activists [...] aided tremendously in the formation of the national movement, the impetus for organizing came from the women themselves and was rooted in their experiences. (p. 233)

Mobilizing CUNY Students for Welfare Rights

When I was on public assistance they were like, "What do you want to do?" I said, "Well, I'm going to go back to school." And they looked at me and they were like, "Oh, okay, so you're going to go get a two-year degree." I'm like, "No, I'm going to get a four-year degree." And they said, "You can't get a four-year degree on public assistance." "Can't? Why not?" You know, what is that about? And, I started to read. And, like, I'm entitled to go to school, and I'm going to go to school, and I'm not going to go to a two-year school, I'm going to go to a four-year school. And, I think at that time—yeah, I did, I had my associate's degree already from New York Technical College, and I was going to go to a four-year school now. So they were like, "Well, no, you can go and be a home health aid, or you can go and get a clerical position. These are the things that you can do." And they had a list of positions that I could have, like, kind of on a sheet. And they're like, "Okay." I'm like, "Well, this isn't going to work."

~Vanessa Lyles, WRI Alumni, September 2011 (Tobar, 2011b)

14

Previous welfare regulations made it relatively easy for recipients to go to college. But in 1995, New York City instituted the Work Experience Program (WEP), which required welfare recipients to perform unpaid labor for the city. WEP was created in tandem with the 1996 federal welfare reform legislation turning welfare funds and jurisdiction primarily over to individual states.[3] Hundreds of thousands of people were removed from the welfare rolls with no guarantee of employment training or education. At CUNY, enrollment of welfare recipients fell from 28,000 to 10,000 (Golden, 1999) as students dropped out to fulfill their workfare obligations. WRI aims to help students on public assistance throughout the CUNY system remain in college despite time-consuming, dead-end workfare requirements as well as other roadblocks the system puts in their way (Weikart, 2005).

"These students were targeted as the most able-bodied population that if put into a workfare program might give the workfare program good numbers and have it look successful," according to Melinda Lackey, founding director of WRI. In exchange for giving up their studies, these students were being offered workfare positions, which at the time consisted of working for the parks department or the sanitation department. Supposedly this was training for work in the real world, but most often people were given menial tasks such as cleaning bathrooms or subway platforms. For these former college students, this type of "work" experience was not going to propel them out of poverty.

A year later, in 1997, the Economic Justice Project (EJP) was formed. Through a collaboration with CUNY Law School, the EJP paired second-year CUNY law students with students from across CUNY who were fighting to keep their public assistance benefits and stay in school. In 2000, a coalition that included WRI and EJP was able to get New York State to pass the Work-Study and Internship Law, which allows work-study and internship hours to count toward a college student's public assistance work requirement and prohibits welfare officials from unreasonably interfering with the student's ability to attend classes.

WRI has evolved over the years, from its beginnings as an awareness-building course to an overall community leadership program. Dillonna Lewis, Co-Executive Director of WRI, has witnessed much of this change, saying:

3. By the '90s, centrist social policy took hold with the Personal Responsibility Work Opportunity Reconciliation Act (PRWOR). President Clinton signed it into law in 1996, making good on his 1992 campaign promise to "end welfare as we know it." The PRWOR's aim was to discourage illegitimacy and teen pregnancy by denying benefits to mothers with additional children while on welfare and mandating work requirements within two years of receiving benefits to promote individual responsibility.

I think in the early years of WRI, it was about training students to be more involved. Not so much that students started off being involved. With the students it was a first time experience. One of the things that I realized is that when someone comes to you, before you say, 'Here is the ticket, get on that bus and go to Albany and advocate for your rights,' you have to make sure that students feel confident and prepared to self-advocate. If someone can't feed their kids, and I don't feel empowered, they won't feel eager to jump on a bus to Albany [...] I always tell students, 'We don't give you strength. You don't come to WRI and we give you voice. You always had a voice, but it's just that now you can see different ways to make your voice more effective.' (Tobar, 2011a)

Community-Based Archiving

I think that everybody has to be in this for the long haul. I think everybody has to know that if we're ever going to treat people who are living below the poverty line, near the poverty line, just above the poverty line—the poverty line being a ridiculous number anyway—that it is a long, long haul and that we have to use every method we have, whether it be writing, speaking, organizing, whatever, and know that it will take us the people after us, and the people before us to do it.

~Ruth Sidel, Faculty advisory committee, WRI, February 2012 (Tobar, 2012b)

This notion of community-based archiving describes the methodology behind archival practice that directly involves the communities being documented in organizing their records for community intent. In an effort to give a "voice to the voiceless," there are various tactics an archivist can employ to include materials in their collections that would document the history of traditionally underrepresented people or organizations.

Archivists such as Randall Jimerson (2009) suggest four approaches that I believe directly co-relate to community-based archiving: 1) reconsider the principal of provenance in light of unequal power relationships; 2) "seek opportunities to preserve records of those often overlooked by their collecting strategies and recognize the broader concept of provenance for an entire community"; 3) consider going beyond our "custodial role to fill in the gaps, to ensure that documentation is created where it is missing"; and 4) recognize the value of "oral transmission" by both recognizing the "primacy of oral tradition in some cultures," and seeking to add to the completeness of the archival record by proactively creating oral histories (Theimer, 2010). The first two points concentrate on the challenges surrounding provenance of selected items for a collection, which addresses concerns about how we as archivists determine historical accuracy. The last two points refer to the importance of looking outside traditional archival practice and recognizing the value of emotional accuracy provided from unwritten accounts of the past.

In the context of community-based archiving and its demand that we all acknowledge the reality of growing disparities in the historical record and their social consequences, an inability to access scholarship is a symptom of a much larger issue. Thankfully, a growing number of activists, archivists, and scholars in many fields are waking up to the problem of open access to scholarship and are looking for ways to solve it. For some—as is illustrated by WRI—the limit to access is recognized as a troubling component within a larger network of socioeconomic factors that include the inequities and systematic impoverishment of the public education system and the "disruption" of higher education.

We have unprecedented need for this type of scholarship to be widely and freely available. As an open access activist, I felt that providing a Web-based portal for WRI's story was a key element in addressing this problem, and this principle provided the foundational basis for this project.

Some organizations, such as Groundswell—an activist network that consists of sixteen oral historians, community organizers, and cultural workers—were formed out of a desire to tackle the unique challenges that activists/archivists face as they work to "[preserve] oral histories for future generations of movement leaders," while also emphasizing the need to "[respect] community control and ownership" of these histories. For Sarah Loose, one of Groundswell's founders, the distinction for this type of activist oral history lies in its use towards facilitating movement building:

> What distinguishes "activist oral history" from most oral history work is its explicit aim of social transformation and its direct connection to or active, intentional use by social movement actors to further their organizing efforts and campaigns. Many oral history projects and archives contain or collect interviews that relate to controversial social issues and explore the dynamics of social movements. But unless and until these interviews are mobilized by and for the protagonists of social movements, they are unlikely to directly lead to social change in a meaningful and significant way. (Loose, 2011)

Ultimately, I'm interested in exploring how this form of community-based archiving can move beyond the academic to mobilize for social change and bolster WRI's movement-building efforts. Community-based archiving, as exemplified by this digital oral history archive, sustains the idea of online communities as a medium for transforming space, playing a vital role in uncovering human networks that have been overlooked in the past. Archives are arsenals of history, of law, and of democratic accountability. They can provide a corrective action in support of justice by documenting under-served communities. As citizen archivists, we can co-create with those affected communities, ensuring that there is equal representation of the needs, interests, and perspectives of all citizens.

Digital Framework and Access

For the digital framework, this project was modeled after a similar documentary project in 2006, undertaken by Tamar Carroll (College of the Holy Cross), that focused on documenting the National Congress of Neighborhood Women (NCNW). Taking the form of an electronic resource and providing an in-depth introduction, primary documents, and oral history interviews, Carroll chronicled how working-class women were able to form cross-racial partnerships to work for women's empowerment. The one drawback, however, is that this project is accessible only via the "Women and Social Movements in the United States, 1600-2000" database, which is available only to paid subscribers.

There have been other oral history projects that have focused on working-class feminist grassroots organizations and activists, such as the New York City Women Community Activists Oral History Project (located at Smith College), and documentary projects that have aimed at collecting primary source material specific to welfare programs in the United States, such as *Welfare in the United States: A History with Documents, 1935-1996* (Nadasen, Mittelstadt, & Chappell, 2009). None, however, has attempted to transform this type of research into a freely accessible, Web-based oral history digital archive.

The WRI Oral History Project consists of audio files of personal narratives as well as transcripts. In July 2011, I requested a brief informational interview with the executive directors, and, initially, this was the way narrators were solicited. Through their help, I was able to reach out to the founders of WRI via email invitations, introducing them to the project's goals and encouraging them to participate. The reaction was overwhelmingly positive: not one potential narrator turned down a request to be interviewed. I was also invited to join WRI on its annual retreat for students in October 2011, where I was able to reach out to current students and solicit student narrators for the project. I handled all the interviewing for the project, and, spanning an eight-month period beginning in August 2011, acquired key interviews with WRI's leadership, founders, and a few student alumni. My hope is that documenting the participation of WRI alumni, students, and leaders in oral histories available in an openly accessible online format will encourage the active use of their stories in scholarship, activism, and policymaking. Digital technologies such as social media and Semantic

Web markup, which have been incorporated in each individual interview's record in the archive, increase the findability of these interviews with an underrepresented portion of the community and present a more vital role in framing the historical record. One of the advantages of using born-digital oral history interviews in a free, Web-based format is their usability from a remote location. Even casual perusal by an interested Internet user fulfills the purpose of the digital archive: to offer the widest possible access to everyone.

Changes in metadata standards and Semantic Web technologies have an immense impact on resource discovery, increasing access to digital oral histories. In the spirit of new metadata standards that explore distributed, collaborative approaches to "finding stuff," I decided to implement Schema.org, a microdata standard that seeks to work seamlessly among the Google, Yahoo!, and Bing search engines, Schema.org provides a way to include structured data in webpages. Since its introduction in June 2011, the Schema.org vocabulary has grown to cover descriptive terms for content such as movies, music, organizations, locations, and news items. The mission of Schema.org is "to improve the display of search results, making it easier for people to find the right web pages." The initiative has emerged as a focal point for publishers of structured data in webpages, and this standard has been applied to the WRI Oral History Project site.

My goal was to provide cross-referencing and searchability within and across audio interviews so that scholars and researchers could conveniently study them, as well as to analyze whether the user-centric interface can in fact offer the most worthwhile access to this digital collection. Future considerations will involve preservation efforts for these born-digital interviews, as well as to digitally archive the project site. Currently, I am also exploring options such as using the Internet Archive's Archive-It service, which allows subscribers to archive website content that is then hosted and stored by the Internet Archive.

Conclusion

It is essential to capture the first-person memories of grassroots feminist activism, in the case of WRI within CUNY—and in New York City in general—before the women who founded and developed this organization move on. The historical importance of documenting oral history interviews of feminist activist grassroots organizations is difficult to estimate. CUNY has long been influenced by a strong activist spirit, a spirit that is prevalent among its faculty and student body and emblematic of dramatic demographic, social, economic, technological, and political shifts in New York City that have fundamentally altered the nature of both social welfare and workforce development. This sentiment is echoed in CUNY's libraries and its library faculty, who have become ardent advocates for open access and a quality higher education for all students. This trend is evident in recent Library Association of CUNY conferences, which have focused on the "past, present, and future of library activism" (Adams, 2012) as well as exploring how librarians are moving beyond being gatekeepers of knowledge and "becoming engaged in communities' production of knowledge" (Litwin, 2012).

Many people have strong opinions on the issue of social welfare, either demonstrating their full support of or opposition to welfare programs aimed at reducing poverty, hardship, and inequality. Because of this dichotomy, it is difficult to develop opportunities that promote open dialogue between supporters and opponents of welfare reform and its effect on welfare recipients' access to higher education. My hope is to address this issue by working with other activist organizations, such as Groundswell, as well as forming partnerships with schools beyond Hunter College and CUNY to host programs where the debate about welfare reform is active and contentious. These programs would use the recorded oral history interviews collected by the WRI Oral History Project to explore the themes and history behind the stereotypes of the welfare system in the U.S., as well as their function in regulating the social, political, and economic behavior of welfare recipients. Via this digital oral history, we can create an environment where people with different viewpoints might feel comfortable sharing their opinions about welfare and access to higher education and thereby want to find solutions. As a result, this project can use oral history and its future public programs to inspire welfare recipients to mobilize and add their collective voices to the debate in social policymaking.

Librarians and archivists aim to share knowledge and help locate and improve the discoverability of archival content. But outside of these traditional roles, we can play new roles in supporting the usability of archival content— such as oral history interviews—as evidence in social research as well as to better inform activism. We can help create new public spaces, both virtual and physical, that ensure that the rights and intentions of creators of community archives are respected, preserving the legacy of social movements for future generations while giving a voice to those who have traditionally been left out of our historical narrative. With these actions, we create a vital and participatory "living archive."

Documenting this type of activism in the digital realm is essential in order to improve the discoverability of these interviews, as well as to ensure that the legacy of WRI persists through open access. This is what begins dialogue, not politics as usual. And this is what's needed to mobilize community organizations and movements, empowering the community, and helping co-create solutions.

References

Abramovitz, M. (1996). Under attack, fighting back: Women and welfare in the United States. New York, NY: *Monthly Review Press.*

Adams, M. (2012, April 15). *2012 LACUNY dialogues: Libraries, librarians, and advocacy.* Retrieved from http://lacuny.org/news/winter11/2012/04/15/2012-lacuny-dialogues-libraries-librarians-and-advocacy/

Carroll, T.W. (2006). *How did working-class feminists meet the challenges of working across differences? The National Congress of Neighborhood Women, 1974-2006.* Binghamton, NY: State University of New York.

Echols, A. (1989). *Daring to be bad: Radical feminism in America, 1967-1975.* Minneapolis, MN: University of Minnesota Press.

Evans, S.M. (2008). *Tidal wave: How women changed America at century's end.* Paw Prints.

Golden, K. (1999). Head of the class. *Ms, 9,* 32-35.

Jimerson, R.C. (2009). *Archives power: Memory, accountability, and social justice.* Chicago, IL: Society of American Archivists.

Litwin, R. (2012, October 24). The 2013 LACUNY Institute: Libraries, Information, and the Right to the City [Blog post]. Retrieved from http://libraryjuicepress.com/blog/?p=3678

Loose, S.K. (2011). Oral history for movement building: Moments of power and possibility. In Groundswell 2011: A synthesis. Retrieved from http://www.oralhistoryforsocialchange.org/events/2011-gathering/ohformb/

Nadasen, P. (2005). *Welfare warriors: The welfare rights movement in the United States.* New York, NY: Routledge.

Nadasen, P., Mittelstadt, J., & Chappell, M. (2009). *Welfare in the United States: A history with documents, 1935-1996.* New York, NY: Routledge.

Rosen, R. (2000). *The world split open: How the modern women's movement changed America.* New York, NY: Viking.

Theimer, K. (2010, February 22). Chapter 6: Capturing the voices of the "voiceless populations," pp. 298-309 [Blog post]. Retrieved from http://readingarchivespower.wordpress.com/2010/02/22/capturing-the-voices-of-the-voiceless-populations-pp-298-309/

Tobar, C. (Interviewer) & Lewis, D. (Interviewee). (2011a). Interview with Dillonna Lewis [Interview transcript]. Retrieved from Welfare Rights Initiative Oral History Project website: http://wri-voices.org/interview/dillonna-lewis-interview

Tobar, C. (Interviewer) & Lyles, V. (Interviewee). (2011b). Interview with Vanessa Lyles [Interview transcript]. Retrieved from Welfare Rights Initiative Oral History Project website: http://wri-voices.org/interview/vanessa-lyles-interview

Tobar, C. (Interviewer) & Lackey, M. (Interviewee). (2012a). Interview with Melinda Lackey [Interview transcript]. Retrieved from Welfare Rights Initiative Oral History Project website: http://wri-voices.org/interview/melinda-lackey-interview

Tobar, C. (Interviewer) & Sidel, R. (Interviewee). (2012b). Interview with Ruth Sidel [Interview transcript]. Retrieved from Welfare Rights Initiative Oral History Project website: http://wri-voices.org/interview/ruth-sidel-interview

West, G. (1981). *The National Welfare Rights Organization: The social protest of poor women*. New York, NY: Praeger.

Weikart, L. (2005). The era of meanness: Welfare reform and barriers to a college degree. Affilia 20(4), 416-433.

threeSOURCE: Reimagining How We Collect and Share Information about Social Issues

Jen Hoyer and Stephen MacDonald

Introduction

This chapter examines management of information about social justice issues through a discussion of the development and implementation of three-SOURCE (www.threesource.ca). Managed by the Resource Coordinator (RC) at the Edmonton Social Planning Council, threeSOURCE is an online research database and library catalog that was created to help community organizations in the Canadian province of Alberta retrieve information about local social issues that they work to address.

The authors of this paper have been involved with threeSOURCE from its inception to the present. Jen Hoyer worked as RC at the Edmonton Social Planning Council from 2009 to 2011, launching threeSOURCE in October 2010. When Jen took off for the African bush in 2011, Stephen MacDonald took over the RC position and has worked to promote threeSOURCE, expanding the size and diversity of threeSOURCE's user base.

Our reflections on the creation, design, and implementation of three-SOURCE highlight exciting new ways to think about information delivery. As librarians working in a position that was not advertised exclusively to information professionals, we reflect on how our profession should look for new places for our skills to be used. Finally, we discuss how the work we do can reflect and challenge the core values of our profession.

A Library for Social Issues

While librarians and the many types of libraries they work in often care deeply about social justice issues, those working in the social services sector as researchers or practitioners tend not to maximize library resources relevant to their work. Reasons for this are beyond the scope of this chapter, but they include factors such as a limited amount of time to conduct research, accessibility to research that impacts their sector, and the relevance of collections that are available to them (Krekoski, 2008).

As a social justice research agency with over seventy years' history providing information about social issues in the community, the Edmonton Social Planning Council (ESPC) finds itself in a unique position to capture and provide access to resources about social issues in the province that are relevant to researchers, students, practitioners, and the general public. The ESPC has for decades maintained its library as a means of providing space for important resources that might not find a home in other library collections.

Much of the literature produced by social justice organizations is classified as grey literature. Grey literature refers to documents in any format and in any sector that are produced outside the realm of commercial publishing (Grey Literature Network Service, 2012). In the social services sector, this includes but is not limited to policy documents, operational plans, and program reviews. In traditional libraries, grey literature often falls through the cracks. It can be difficult to shelve, classify, and provide access to these types of publications. At the Edmonton Social Planning Council, in an environment dedicated to the use of such information, these documents were a natural fit. Over the history of the ESPC, countless stories have been told of policy makers and agency directors searching tirelessly for an important document—even one that their own organization had authored—and discovering that the only publicly available copy of the publication was sitting on a shelf of the library at the ESPC Resource Library. The significance of this small resource library collection cannot be understated; it has served as a unique and important repository of research publications on local social issues that support the work of Edmonton's social services sector.

Context Matters: Social Issues in the City of Edmonton and the Province of Alberta

Located in the central area of the province of Alberta, Edmonton is a growing, medium-sized city of 817,498 people (City of Edmonton, 2012). The city is located near Alberta's large oil sand reserves. The oil industry in Alberta is a major employer, creating spin-off jobs in the Edmonton area that fuel the city economy. In recent years, the city has attracted people from across Canada and from other countries in search of employment. Because of the city's strong economic standing, it has one of the lowest unemployment rates in the country. With that said, Edmonton is not immune from major social problems, including poverty, homelessness, and related issues:

- In 2010, there were over 91,000 children under the age of 18 living below the low income measure (Statistics Canada, 2012).
- Research has also found that there is a significant number of low-income employees working in the city. According to Statistics Canada data purchased by Public Interest Alberta, 418,900 workers in the province of Alberta (or 23.8% of the workforce) are making below $15 an hour. Most of these workers (77%) are at least 20 years old and are in the prime wage earning years. Research has also shown that more women than men are employed in low-wage positions in Alberta. Of all low-wage workers in Alberta, 60.8% (or 254,700) of these individuals are women (Public Interest Alberta, 2012).
- Similar trends are occurring in Edmonton. 139,900 workers in Edmonton are making below $15 an hour. Almost a quarter of these individuals (23.9%) are over 20 years of age. As in the province as a whole, more women than men are employed in low-wage positions. In Edmonton, 61.1% of low wage workers are women (Public Interest Alberta, 2012).
- Homelessness is a continuing problem in the province. According to the 2010 Edmonton Homeless Count, 2421 homeless individuals were counted in Edmonton. A significant percentage of these individuals (36%) appeared to be Aboriginal (Homeward Trust Edmonton, 2012). The number of homeless individuals seems to have dropped between 2008 and 2010, when volunteers counted 3079 homeless Edmontonians (Homeward Trust Edmonton, 2012). In Calgary, the January 2012 homeless count found 3190 homeless individuals in the city (Calgary Homeless Foundation, 2012).

This brief discussion about poverty and homelessness shows that Edmonton is dealing with related social issues as well, such as systemic racism and gender inequality. Fortunately, Edmonton has a swath of social service agencies that exist to fight social inequality and help vulnerable groups of people live a better life. threeSOURCE was designed to keep the social services sector informed about statistical trends related to social issues and new research that can help these organizations develop solutions to the problems they are addressing in the community.

Improving Access: Finding a Way Forward

Aware of the value of its library collection, and equally aware of the fact that a room full of books and reports in the offices of a small social justice think tank is not the first stop for researchers and policy makers in their search for the information they need, the ESPC decided to improve access and increase use of its resource collection. In 2009, funds were sought from a grant under the Government of Alberta's Community Initiatives Program to take the library online.

With a little software and some computer know-how, setting up a Web-based library system is a fairly easy venture. Doing a good job of it, however, can be tricky business. The unique nature of the ESPC's resource collection, combined with the distinctive information behavior of its targeted user community within the field of social justice researchers and practitioners, called for a thoughtful approach to the system design and implementation of this proposed digital library. The body of literature about the information behavior of practitioners and researchers in the fields of social policy and social justice is, to be generous, quite limited. A lengthy attempt at a literature review turned up nothing that could directly inform the development of a system for this specific context.

Meet the User

In 2008, the ESPC created the position of Resource Coordinator (RC), whose main role would be to spearhead library-related projects in the organization. A social science practitioner was hired to take on this position and was made responsible for reviving the oft-neglected physical library and bringing the library online. The first major project was to conduct a series of community consultations with organizations in the community that would benefit from resources in the library. "Community partners" were identified as organizations working in the community to achieve a more socially and economically just Edmonton (Krekoski, 2008).

Leaders of these organizations—which included social service agencies, think tanks, and activist groups—sat around the table to discuss the types of research information they need and the information that is necessary to carry out their role in the community. The diverse community leaders identified a wide range of pressing social issues that their respective organizations needed current information about. Poverty was referenced as a central theme that other issues stemmed from; other major concerns related to the actions of elected officials regarding social issues, the support systems in place for social issues, and the impact of the economic climate on social conditions. Participants discussed the types of research or policy publications that would be useful to their work in relation to these issues (Krekoski, 2008).

Participants also identified the following six reasons why they need access to current research and policy publications in their field: advocating for the issues that their organization addresses, demonstrating the role that their organization plays, building capacity within their sector, facilitating collaboration, undertaking education and awareness initiatives, and informing service delivery by their organization to the community.

This community consultation process had two immediate results. It sparked new research projects by the ESPC that would address social issues highlighted by participants. With regard to the library, it helped the ESPC investigate more deeply the ways it could provide community partners with better access to current information and research.

Designing the Right System: Asking the Right Questions

Understanding the information behavior of a library's projected users is the first crucial step towards finding the best solution for user needs. The community consultations described above provided basic information on what type of information the ESPC library's user community is looking for and how they intend to use it. At the same time, these discussions raised further questions about the information-seeking behavior of these community organizations. While agency executive directors might want more information on homelessness statistics and program implementation, where would they go to find this information if it existed? How would they prefer to access it? If policy makers are desperate to find documents from other jurisdictions, what is their first port of call? Is an online library system the best answer for their information needs?

In 2009, when the original RC left the position to follow new opportunities, the RC job advertisement for a social science graduate who could assist with research in a social justice think tank and also set up an online database of research materials caught the eye of an information professional. Fresh out of an MLIS degree program, and with a background working in public and school libraries, Jen Hoyer explained to the ESPC hiring committee that they didn't need an expert in the field, they needed an expert on information. With a librarian now at the helm, and as applications for funding to build an online library system were being submitted, the focus of community consultations switched to user behavior. A series of phone calls and face-to-face conversations broached new topics: *"What kind of information do you need to do your work? When you try to stay up-to-date in your field, who do you talk to first? If we have a great collection of resources on the shelf at our office, would you come look at them? Where do you go online to find the information you need?"*

Their answers to these questions were unanimous: Practitioners need the latest (and possibly most difficult to find) reports published by small think tanks scattered across the country. They want research that is relevant to their specialized field of work as soon it is published. Current information is shared by talking with colleagues. Going to a room full of books and reports doesn't fit in the schedule of a busy researcher, program planner, or executive director. An unfamiliar online tool would take time to learn. Many of these individuals do not have enough time to muddle through complex search interfaces. Although Google might not be the best research tool available, it usually helps them find the information they need to answer their research questions.

Evaluating the Real Need

Creating a relevant and effective online library tool for this audience became daunting: in a classic case of "the consumers do not actually know what they want," the projected user group did not want an online library—they were happy enough with Google. They didn't have time to search for new resources; they just wanted to have immediate access to this information so they could talk about it with their colleagues as soon as possible. Designing a system to meet the information needs of the social services sector would require thinking outside the box—or, outside the Web portal.

In light of this, we outlined what the user community needed, how this fit with subject scope and document formats in the resource collection, and how information behavior could fit with information delivery models.

What do our users want? Social service practitioners, researchers, and policy makers want current and timely information that is precisely relevant to their field of work or study. Collection development should rely on constantly monitoring collection use, attentively following appropriate authors and publishers, and delivering new information as soon as possible.

How do our users want it? They want to have a conversation. Users want to sit around their offices and ask colleagues what the newest and most relevant publications are for their area of work. Important new information needs to be on the front of everyone's mind as they chat around the water cooler.

Will they join the conversation? Similar online information portals, designed to feed off the social networking buzz and requiring user involvement to function well, have struggled to find an active user base. Abra Brynne of bitsandbytes.ca described their challenge to involve users; after designing an online portal that relied on members to post the latest research publications, the system lagged in currency when busy community members could not find time to post (A. Brynne, personal communication, May 31, 2010). Users want to feel that they are involved in a social information exchange, but the system must not depend entirely on user participation.

How can we make it work? The managers of similar online portals at the Resource Centre for Voluntary Organizations (now the Volunteer Alberta Resource Centre) and Imagine Canada (L. Baker, personal communication, May 27, 2010; M. Kwasnicki, personal communication, June 2010) advised that a successful information system should be managed by information professionals who understand information, technology, and information behavior—someone who can ask the right questions about user behavior and implement feedback into design. Looking at current social networking and communication trends, they echoed Brynne's reflections on user dependence and concluded that a successful system must invite conversation but not rely on user participation.

The Best Fit For Your Needs: Meet threeSOURCE

threeSOURCE was launched in October 2010 at www.threesource.ca; to create its title, we combined "resource" with the "three" of "third sector"—a term applied to nonprofit and social service organizations (following the "first sector" of government and the "second sector" of business).

As an information system, threeSOURCE is a hybrid between a library catalog and a bibliographic database. While some of the records in threeSOURCE are for traditional monographs on the shelves of the ESPC's physical library, a large proportion of the records describe print or electronic articles, conference proceedings, and other grey literature that is highly relevant to the user audience. Many of these records in threeSOURCE offer direct access to electronic full-text versions of these reports. A URL to the report on the publisher's website or a link to the file on our own server is available in the report's threeSOURCE record. As of this writing, the database contains 1411 records that either provide access to a PDF version of a report or a link to a report on the publishing organization's website. These records account for over 30% of all records in threeSOURCE. The electronic reports are being accessed far more often than books and other print resources in our physical library.

Because threeSOURCE was created with the existing shelf-bound ESPC Resource Library as its foundation, the preliminary collection was, with few exceptions, print-only. By contrast, current additions to threeSOURCE are almost entirely full-text electronic, apart from a few print-only monographs. Additionally, major efforts have been made to add full-text electronic editions to records previously created for print-only items. threeSOURCE was launched in October 2010 with approximately 3000 print-only items; two years later, with that print-only foundation still intact but with a heavy acquisition emphasis on electronic full-text, the portion of full-text items in threeSOURCE has risen to one third.

Underlying many initial design decisions, the structure of threeSOURCE was kept very basic in an attempt to move away from the complexity of library tools and towards the simplicity of the most-used Web search platforms. For a busy user community that loves Google, the front end of threeSOURCE provides a simple search box. Users should be able to find what they need by typing a few words into a single space. If the user is interested in running a more sophisticated, but not overly complex, search query to find the information they need, they can use threeSOURCE's advanced search interface. This allows users to search for reports with a particular title, subject focus, and publication date. Since it only has four fields and contains a detailed instruction guide, the search engine is a user-friendly tool that allows people to make the most of their experience using this database.

Innovation: Information Management in the Context of the Social Services Sector

The success of threeSOURCE as a tool that is relevant to users in the social services sector has depended on innovative librarians who can think outside the library. Creative solutions have been required from the early planning stages through the current implementation and promotion; if designed as a standard library tool, threeSOURCE would be less useful and less relevant to its target audience than it is now. A few pertinent examples highlight how threeSOURCE stands as a model for new ways of thinking about information management.

The Embedded Librarian: Being Aware of User Needs and Their Information-Seeking Behavior

The RC position at the ESPC is a unique type of information worker, a prime example of an "embedded librarian"—an information professional who is a part of the community that they serve. This position allows the information professional to understand the context they are operating within and deliver appropriate services that satisfy the unique information needs of the individuals and organizations they work with.

threeSOURCE is more than a website and more than an online library catalog—it is our new way of starting conversations with our community. The RC interacts with the database's user groups in physical (conferences and symposiums, social gatherings of sector professionals, business meetings involving the sector) and online (social media applications, ESPC website) spaces. Interviews with intended users revealed that members of this sector usually begin their search for information by asking their colleagues. Taking that into consideration, threeSOURCE has tried to become one of these colleagues. This means networking with users at community events and sector-specific functions. During these interactions, we learn more about user groups' information needs and demonstrate how threeSOURCE can connect them with research that they are looking for.

The RC represents the ESPC at meetings, conferences, community lectures, and social events that bring together individuals who work in Edmonton's social services sector. While attending these events, we encourage sector practitioners to use threeSOURCE to stay informed about new research on social issues affecting the community. In addition to talking about threeSOURCE with employees in this sector, the RC has the opportunity to set up displays at relevant conferences in Edmonton. These displays have included bookmarks that contain additional information about threeSOURCE; a laptop to show delegates the database's search functions and its research potential; and a paper form delegates could fill out to subscribe to threeSOURCE's acquisitions email list, which notifies subscribers about new publications added to the database.

Relationships with the user community have helped develop the collection hosted by threeSOURCE. We continually encourage nonprofit organizations in the Edmonton area to submit research reports that they produce. These organizations have become aware of the value of having a stable repository for their publications in a world where Web hosts cannot always be maintained by small organizations, and they are eager to see their publications shared more widely than their own publishing capacity would allow.

Knowledge Is Everything: Determining Information Authority

Information literacy in the social services sector relies on having an awareness of the sector in order to determine source authority. The minds behind threeSOURCE are involved in the community that is writing and publishing research materials for the third sector, and we are able to use this knowledge to select credible resources that can be added to the database.

Traditional information literacy principles surrounding source authority—credibility of author and publisher—are difficult to assess in a sector where much of the most pertinent information is published as grey literature. A research paper that appeared only on the website of a small institute may not look authoritative but may be the best source on its topic; conversely, a shiny PDF full of pristine charts and tables could seem to be a highly believable source but might be published by an organization known for presenting one-sided arguments based on incomplete research. In the social services sector, determining source authority comes not through traditional processes of looking at the type of publication or its origin but through interaction with the community of authors and publishers, and knowledge of which authors and publishers are producing the most relevant and reliable information (Hoyer, 2011).

The RC is employed by a research and advocacy organization that works with similar organizations in Alberta and other parts of Canada on projects related to social issues. As a result, we can draw upon our own and our coworkers' existing knowledge of authoritative social research institutions to select reliable publications for threeSOURCE. Moreover, we use our analytical skills to ensure that the reports that we add to this database are high-quality publications. We do this by reviewing them to ensure that they are well-researched, cite dependable sources of information, and are written by credible authors and researchers in their field.

Of course, our own values and those of the organization we have been working for shape our understanding of what a reliable source is. As a result, some reports that other researchers consider to be reliable may not meet our standards. As well, we may feel comfortable including some, but not all, of the reports that an organization publishes, even if all of their publications focus on subject areas that threeSOURCE covers. For example, we have chosen not to include reports on poverty written by a well-known think-tank in Alberta because we do not agree with their method of measuring poverty, which shapes their research on this issue. At the same time, we have added to threeSOURCE reports published by this organization that focus on other subjects that fall within our library's collection mandate.

While users may not have the experience or time to properly make these judgments regarding source authority, we can pass on our own expertise to threeSOURCE users by carefully selecting authoritative documents and declining potential acquisitions that don't make the cut.

Joining the Conversation

Realizing how much our users like to talk about information, we set up threeSOURCE as a means to create conversation. We start discussion around the break room with a series of lunchtime talks that profile important issues and organizations in the local third sector. The ESPC's highly successful Lunch and Learn Series is an opportunity for users to talk about what information they need and what information has helped them tackle the issues profiled at each of these events. Also, these lunches are an opportunity for the RC to share new publications and talk to social service workers about their information needs.

We begin electronic conversations by sending messages to those who have subscribed to the database's acquisitions email list. Subscribers receive an email that informs them about new research publications added to the database and provides them with a direct link to threeSOURCE records. Individuals can also learn about additions to threeSOURCE by subscribing to the database's acquisitions RSS feed, which is updated after a report is cataloged. Also, the ESPC's monthly email newsletter, *Research Update*, contains links to new and especially relevant publications, plus reviews of valuable and current research reports that have been recently added to threeSOURCE. Written by volunteers from various backgrounds, these reviews kick-start further discussions on timely publications. Below each review's abstract in the newsletter are links to threeSOURCE search queries that are related to the subject area of the particular review.

These days, social media is an ever-present tool for our conversation with current and potential threeSOURCE user groups. The RC uses the ESPC's social media applications to demonstrate how threeSOURCE is a valuable tool for retrieving publications on particular social issues in Alberta. During days, weeks, and months that recognize a particular social issue (International Day for the Eradication of Poverty, Housing Month, etc.), messages and tweets containing URLs to resources that focus on these issues are posted to the ESPC Facebook and Twitter pages.

Within the community of information professionals, we have started a dialogue about new types of information tools and information sources. A presentation at the Progressive Librarians Guild of Edmonton's 2012 Symposium brought threeSOURCE to the minds of forty progressive-minded information practitioners from the area, inviting our fellow librarians to realize the potential of non-traditional systems for information management. Although we do not have any proof that this poster presentation has increased discussion about threeSOURCE in the library community in Alberta, a link to threeSOURCE was added to a university library research guide by a symposium delegate once the conference concluded. Also during the symposium, Stephen MacDonald spoke to a librarian who expressed interest in adding a link to threeSOURCE to her library's website.

User Response

According to our Google Analytics page, visitors use threeSOURCE to access research on a variety of social issues affecting Albertans. threeSOURCE visitors tend to focus their research on a few major subjects that include poverty, income and income inequality, homelessness, affordable housing, food security, and topics related to family and children in Alberta (including family violence, child welfare, and child care). Other subject areas that visitors have explored on threeSOURCE are:

- immigration
- social inclusion and exclusion
- race and racism
- social enterprise
- sexual and labor exploitation
- education
- well-being of indigenous peoples
- social determinants of health
- health care
- nonprofit organizations
- women
- employment and unemployment

Our efforts have led to a steady increase in the number of individuals using threeSOURCE: From January 1 to December 31, 2012, threeSOURCE was accessed 1637 times by 1189 visitors. Users accessed 5520 pages in the database, viewing an average of 3.19 pages per visit. In 2012, threeSOURCE received 15% more visits, 27% more visitors, and 6% more page views than it did in 2011.

Starting a New Dialogue

Further ways for cultivating conversations about information in the social services sector have been identified. To start, we have created a compilation of email lists used by poverty and homelessness reduction advocates in Alberta, social services sector employees who work in the province, librarians both in the

Edmonton area and across North America, and other individuals interested in local social issues. Information about threeSOURCE will be distributed to these lists.

According to website statistics, threeSOURCE is being accessed by people who use computer networks operated by the City of Edmonton, other municipal governments in Alberta, the Government of Alberta, and the federal government. There is great potential for threeSOURCE to become a more regularly-used research tool among municipal, provincial, and federal public servants and politicians. We plan to promote threeSOURCE to public servants who are working on relevant social initiatives in order to help them access the latest and most pertinent information.

Librarians in public, academic, and special libraries need to become more involved in the conversation about resources related to social issues in their communities. Local librarians have shown that they are interested in and supportive of this research tool. In September 2012, academic librarians from universities across the province were contacted regarding adding threeSOURCE to their online subject guides. Because of this outreach, librarians at institutions such as the University of Alberta, the University of Calgary, and Grant MacEwan University have decided to add threeSOURCE to research guides that they manage. The ESPC will continue to promote threeSOURCE among academic librarians and demonstrate how university and college students in Alberta can use this database to collect research about social issues in this province.

The popular press is also providing space for threeSOURCE to demonstrate its value to the community as a research tool. The database will be featured in publications such as Peace Library System's monthly newsletter and the Edmonton Community Foundation's magazine, *Legacy in Action*.

Thinking Outside the Box

For information professionals, threeSOURCE has provided an opportunity to think outside the box, to focus more on a distinctive user community and its exceptional needs and less on the traditional service delivery mechanisms of online and physical libraries. Serving the needs of users who work in the field of social justice—whether as policy makers, researchers, or practitioners—requires information professionals to ask the right questions about information needs and use, and to listen carefully to the answers.

As mentioned in the introduction, the current shape of the Resource Coordinator position at the ESPC is also the result of a librarian thinking outside the box. More specifically, the fact that the RC is an information professional at all is because Jen Hoyer had decided to look for all jobs that required her skill set, not only jobs that explicitly advertised for her occupation.

In an increasingly information-based world, it is essential for information workers to look for new places to use their abilities, even where employers haven't realized that such a professional would be suitable for the job. Our expertise is becoming vital in a growing number of places, and it is up to us to educate the rest of society about where and how they need our skills. For a grant-funded position like the RC at the ESPC, convincing employers and funders of the value of having an information professional on staff is a continual process. In this context, the major investment that has been made into threeSOURCE and the role that the RC and threeSOURCE play as a locus for information produced by the ESPC form a strong leverage in favor of maintaining the RC position with an information worker on staff.

In the midst of worry over decreased hiring in traditional library settings, there are actually countless new opportunities waiting for information professionals who can look beyond the library job boards and convince employers that our training makes us the best fit for their positions. Associating with the status of a library institution or receiving the title of Librarian should ultimately be less important than working in an environment where we can do an excellent job of assisting in the use of information.

Reflecting on Librarianship: Back to Basics

threeSOURCE is a unique information project that works with and challenges the basic values of librarianship. The American Library Association's *Core Values of Librarianship* (2004)—including access, confidentiality/privacy, preservation, social responsibility, diversity, and intellection freedom—provide us with a framework for reflecting on how threeSOURCE embodies and challenges the way librarians regard their work. The design and implementation of three-SOURCE, as described above, required creativity and innovation; the questions posed by our values as information professionals take us a step back in thinking about why we make the decisions that we do.

Many of the issues that arise out of managing threeSOURCE are a direct result of the fact that this collection is primarily composed of grey literature. Reflections on the specific issues that grey literature raise for the values of information professionals are included where appropriate in the following discussion.

Access

Collection Access

threeSOURCE is a freely-accessible research database. Other similar tools, including most bibliographic databases, require a subscription to read content. Free access to threeSOURCE is a major benefit for nonprofit organizations that need current research but do not have the budget for database and periodical subscriptions.

Multiple online entry points to threeSOURCE provide access from the ESPC website: the front page of the website contains a permanent link to three-SOURCE and a brief description of the database, and the ESPC website's New Resources page provides URLs to records of recent acquisitions. This has proven to be a successful way of channeling users to threeSOURCE.

Beyond this, we have tried to imagine where our potential users might be looking for information and how we could guide them to the resources in three-SOURCE. Featuring threeSOURCE on academic library subject guides, as described above, resulted in several new external access points. threeSOURCE is also accessible from the Library and Archives Canada *Canadian Information by Subject* research guide.

Item Access

As mentioned above, the threeSOURCE collection contains a combination of traditional monographs as well as print or electronic articles, conference proceedings, and other grey literature that is highly relevant to the user audience. Decisions about higher levels of indexing (by chapter, paper, or article) are made entirely to enhance access.

threeSOURCE provides electronic full-text access to as many items in the collection as possible; if available, records in threeSOURCE link to a PDF version of the report housed on threeSOURCE's server, which can be downloaded directly from the database. threeSOURCE also contains records for digital reports that are stored on other websites. In these cases, our record contains a URL to the full-text report on the website of the organization that originally published it. In terms of these electronic resources, the collection is accessible to anyone with a computer and an Internet connection.

For print-only resources, visible online as only an item record, any member of the public can visit the ESPC library and access materials. However, not all threeSOURCE visitors live in the Edmonton area. A threeSOURCE user interested in a print-only resource who lives outside this region would be required to make special arrangements; off-site delivery of print formats is not generally possible. Also, only members of the ESPC are allowed to borrow publications from the library. Despite these limitations on access to the print materials themselves, the fact that threeSOURCE is a freely-accessible database allows any interested researcher to see what related publications exist.

Librarians are constantly challenged with interpreting rules of the profession—rules that might seem to recommend use of traditional subject classification schemes. Many libraries use standardized models that are created and updated by individuals who are unfamiliar with their library's collection. We believe that the basic tenets of librarianship should prioritize accessibility over tradition. When the answers to "does this classification scheme fit our collection" and "are our users so familiar with traditional classification schemes that they would have difficulty using new ones" are both a resounding "no," access is clearly improved with a collection-specific scheme. Is this true for every user? It is certainly not the case in every library, but it may be for more libraries than have implemented customized classification schemes.

threeSOURCE resources are indexed using a subject classification scheme developed specifically for the collection. As language becomes outdated, subject headings are replaced with more current terms to reflect vocabulary changes. In the case of threeSOURCE, this is most obviously demonstrated over the last many decades by an evolution of the subject term "Indians" to "Indigenous Peoples." The language of a classification scheme is always political, however. As an example, the possibility of adding a subject term to deal with publications related to bitumen extraction from oil sands would necessitate choosing between "oil sands" and "tar sands," a word choice that is part of a highly politicized debate.

Providing access points to grey literature raises another set of issues: an item may have several more authors than traditional publications do or may not list any author; or title, author, and other basic information may be represented differently throughout the document. Grey literature requires that the information manager make intentional choices regarding how to make the collection most accessible.

Confidentiality/Privacy

The RC uses Google Analytics to track the ISP networks of people accessing threeSOURCE, as well as their location, pages that they access, and other statistics related to the information-seeking behaviors of visitors to the website. Some of this information (including the ISP networks that accessed the database and location of users) is recorded in quarterly performance reports. These statistics are used to inform collection development and promotion of threeSOURCE, but confidentiality and privacy of visitors is ensured by not making this information publicly available. We track this data in order to better serve our users, while remaining conscious of the need to respect their privacy.

Preservation

By hosting full-text documents, threeSOURCE not only improves access to materials in the first place but also serves a second function as an archive. threeSOURCE operates in a sector where non-current information is often lost as organizations move offices, update computer systems, and change website hosts. This reflects a common issue when dealing with grey literature: grey literature can be less stable than traditional publications, with prime examples being electronic resources hosted on insecure servers or print documents produced on less-sturdy mediums (newsprint, for example). threeSOURCE acts as a secure repository for research publications that may be lost or poorly shared beyond their original publication and distribution.

In the digital realm, the argument that threeSOURCE adequately preserves electronic formats has limitations. All electronic versions of reports that are cataloged in threeSOURCE and stored on the ESPC's server are PDF files. Over time, these PDFs will need to be converted into newer formats. In addition, there are records in threeSOURCE that contain a URL to a full-text document hosted outside the threeSOURCE server. Websites change and disappear over time; it is possible that some of these links will become inaccessible if these external hosts go offline. Every library has a finite Web server capacity and a limited ability to host content. As a result, every librarian must make choices about the digital publications they are able to preserve.

Grey literature requires us to ask *what* we are preserving: in the case of a disintegrating newsprint pamphlet, is it necessary to find funds in a tight budget to stabilize the format, or is it only important to preserve the content of the item by scanning it and hosting the electronic version on a reliable server? threeSOURCE is designed to retain its contents in the public sphere for as long as possible. Some publications are publicly available, whether in print or digitally, only through threeSOURCE. In this situation, preserving content should take priority over preserving format.

Social Responsibility

threeSOURCE is a prime example of how information workers can use their skills to bring attention to deeply entrenched social problems that prevent certain groups in our society from reaching their full potential. By improving access to research on a variety of social issues in Alberta, threeSOURCE is part of the discussion around these issues and how they can be addressed.

The creation and maintenance of threeSOURCE also highlights a case in which someone convinced a hiring committee that the best fit for the role of RC—with the skills and background that could allow for the most socially responsible delivery of information—was a trained information professional.

Diversity

threeSOURCE strives to improve access to research publications around social problems that all Albertans face. It contains items that relate to issues involving Aboriginals, immigrants, refugees, and individuals from a variety of ethnic groups. However, the number of reports in threeSOURCE that focus on particular ethnic groups in Alberta is low in proportion to other subject areas. This may be linked to a lower publication rate on these issues, or it may be an indication that threeSOURCE must network more with diverse ethnic communities in order to discover more materials from a variety of cultural perspectives.

When conducting collection development, we have to ask ourselves if our traditional means of tracking new publications will really uncover every new item that is appropriate for the collection. In the context of grey literature, relying on publishers will be much less useful than networking with users who know what is going on in their sector and dialoguing with practitioners who produce relevant materials. Collection development that is truly diverse requires inventiveness and resourcefulness.

Intellectual Freedom

The RC adds publications to the collection based largely on an awareness of what will be useful to the user community. Because of the political leanings of current users, these publications tend to reflect a more progressive mindset. Research from conservative social policy think tanks is underrepresented in the collection. It can be argued that this contradicts our position of non-partisanship, and that the personal bias of the RC has too much influence over the selection process. However, it could also be argued that we are not intentionally selecting material with a left-leaning position but are instead selecting items that will be used rather than disregarded, based on user feedback and database statistics.

Many of the works in threeSOURCE are written by nonprofit organizations that also identify as being non-partisan; it is possible that social policy organizations that author these publications tend to look at social issues with a more critical and progressive stance.

Considering This...

A reflection on our core values as information professionals confirms the underlying thread of our discussion about the design and implementation of three-SOURCE: building an information system cannot always rely on doing what we've been taught to do, what everyone else is doing, or even what our users say that they want us to do. Every information system will be different because every community's needs are different. By taking ourselves back to the fundamental values of our field, we can ask ourselves the big questions that properly facilitate the way we think about information delivery in any given context. Finding the right information tool for the social services sector isn't impossible, and it isn't difficult either. Applying our skills as information professionals to a community in the best way possible, and asking the deep questions that will allow us to do this, is the best way for us to fulfill our role in the community.

In Conclusion

threeSOURCE is a new way to talk about and interact with information. With exciting new methods for delivery and interaction with users—arguably the best methods for the community it intends to serve—threeSOURCE can be viewed only as a successful information system.

And yet, the key goal behind every design and implementation decision has little to do with new techniques or new technology. Innovation without purpose is meaningless. threeSOURCE is all about looking at how the social services sector retrieves and uses information, how to meet needs based on user behavior, and ultimately how to deliver the information that will help practitioners and policy makers in the sector do the best job possible of dealing with current social issues. If users want stone tablets, we have to find a way to deliver them. Thankfully our users are keen on conversation and interaction, and threeSOURCE has found a way to join the dialogue and bring new information to the table.

References

American Library Association. (2004, June 29). Core values of librarianship. Retrieved from http://www.ala.org/offices/oif/statementspols/ corevaluesstatement/corevalues

Calgary Homeless Foundation. (2012). Preliminary report: The state of homelessness in Calgary in 2012. Retrieved from http://calgaryhomeless.com/ assets/research/The-State-of-Homelessnessonlineversion.pdf

City of Edmonton. (2012). Municipal census results. Retrieved from http:// www.edmonton.ca/city_government/facts_figures/municipal-census-results.aspx

Grey Literature Network Service. (2012). Home. Retrieved from http://www. greynet.org/

Hoyer, J. (2011). Information is social: Information literacy in context. *Reference Services Review*, 39(1), 10-23.

Krekoski, E. (2008). Community consultations on research needs: Final report. Edmonton, AB: Edmonton Social Planning Council. Retrieved from http://www.threesource.ca/documents/ESPCarchives/2000s/ 2008_communityconsultation.pdf

Homeward Trust Edmonton. (2012). Homeless count. Retrieved from http:// www.homewardtrust.ca/programs/homeless-count.php

Public Interest Alberta. (2012). Statistics of low-wage workers in Alberta. Retrieved from http://pialberta.org/sites/default/files/Documents/ Edmonton%20Low-Wage%20Fact%20Sheet-2012%20Statistics%20 Canada%20Data%20-2012-06-11.pdf

Statistics Canada. (2012). Table 202-0802: Persons in low income families, persons under 18 years, Alberta, annual. Retrieved from CANSIM database.

In the Seminar

Reading for a Better Future: Books For A Better Future (BFABF) and Sustainability Literacy in a UK Public Library

Dan Grace

Once a year, at the height of summer, the campaigning groups and concerned organizations in our city set out their stalls at the annual Green Fair. In the gardens of the venue, bands play on a small stage, cakes and vegan snacks are sold at tables to raise money for various causes, and kids dart about in the sunshine. Inside, stalls are piled high with petitions, letters to write, and leaflets informing on a wide variety of campaigns local, national, and international. Library colleagues and I set out our table and chatted with members of the public. The day passed like many other outreach events, until, that is, I had a conversation with one of our regular service users.

"What I'd really like is a book group where we could discuss some of these ideas," he said, indicating the range of books and magazines we'd brought along. "Do you think there'd be much call for it?"

"Well, I'm interested, so we could certainly give it a try," I replied.

Like many such projects, there was an element of serendipity to the beginnings of the Books For A Better Future (BFABF) reading group. As a library worker, I have always had a keen personal interest in the role of the public library in promoting sustainability literacy, as defined by Stibbe and Luna (2009) as "the skills, attitudes, competencies, dispositions and values that are necessary for surviving and thriving in the declining conditions of the world in ways which slow down that decline as far as possible" (p. 10).

It is possible to identify two methods of approaching this promotion, passive and active. Passive promotion primarily takes the form of infrastructural changes to the library service itself, e.g. considering recycling policies, energy use, or construction of new library buildings. Active promotion is the pursuit of specific sustainability outreach programs as part of the library's work, e.g. tours to highlight infrastructural changes; promotion of selected areas of the collection; or working with groups such as the Transition Towns, a movement to "inspire, encourage, connect, support and train communities as they self-organise around the transition model, creating initiatives that rebuild resilience and reduce CO2 emissions" (Grace, 2011, p. 15-17; Transition Network, 2012). Neither method is better than the other; in fact both are necessary if we accept the basic premise that the library, as a public institution, has a role to play in building more resilient communities.

The organization of the outreach session at the Green Fair represented my first attempt as a library worker to move towards a more active promotion of sustainability literacy, and from that chance conversation emerged the BFABF reading group, an attempt to further that activist agenda, now beginning its third year of existence.

Roles

"I think it is fantastic for the group to have a librarian involved... The main importance of the librarian is, I think, being a contact point for new members, as people looking to join a book club are most likely to start by asking at their local library."

~BFABF member

I had very specific aims in setting up the BFABF reading group. While establishing the group was answering a need expressed by a member of the community, I was also interested in finding ways to actively promote sustainability literacy in the community I serve. When I started the group, I had no clear idea how that might work in practice. I couldn't find evidence of any other library services doing what we were attempting. It was an experiment.

One of the hardest points to define when starting out with a new group such as this is the roles of members and of the librarian. Everyone arrives with different expectations and experiences. In order to better understand the views of those involved with the reading group, I put together a short and simple survey, asking questions on a range of topics including the role of the library worker, how individuals felt about their interactions with the group, and how they saw the group developing. I promoted the survey at our meetings and via our email list; however, there were only five responses from a possible 15 list members. While this is a lower response than I would have liked, it accurately represented the number of active group members at that current moment in time. Ideally I would have liked to get feedback from those who had attended and not returned. However, with the survey being voluntary, there was no way to ensure I got such feedback. All responses were anonymous. In addition to the survey, I have taken notes and reflected upon our meetings over the preceding two years, which has given me additional insight into how the group is functioning.

Responses from a mix of group members, both old and new, indicate that they view that the primary role of the library worker should be as a point of contact for those interested in joining the group, and to facilitate access to books and other material. Next in importance was the organization of meeting space for the group to use. One respondent favored a more direct role for the library worker in selecting texts for reading.

As the group went through its first few meetings, I began to view my role as a facilitator, and I hoped that over time I would be needed less and less in that capacity and would instead become just another member of the group. As a direct result of the cuts currently being imposed on library services in the UK, the extent to which I have been able to carry out group tasks during work time has varied. As an organization, the public library service I work for no longer has the depth of staffing to allow individual workers time to pursue any but the most essential tasks. Despite this, colleagues have been extremely supportive in allowing me to find time during the working day in which I can carry out some of the administrative tasks related to the group, such as maintaining the email list and updating listings on local websites. More recently, the group's engagement with a project run by the Reading Agency (a charity that encourages reading, often working in partnership with public libraries), where book groups were asked to read and review shortlisted titles for the Royal Society Winton Science Book Prize, has raised our profile among senior members of staff. This has led to time being freed up for me to carry out more functions related to the group during work time again.

It is a concern for me that the group be autonomous in its decisions and actions, that it be able to function without my input. The capacity for autonomous action is central to building resilient communities (Norris, Stevens, Pfefferbaum, Wyche, & Pfefferbaum, 2008). This, to me, would be the measure to which it has become sustainable, and group members have increased their sustainability literacy. I have my idea of why the group was set up, but once established, it should be free to explore ideas as it sees fit.

Ivan Illich encapsulates the dilemma in which I found myself, in his critique of the discourse surrounding needs. Needs, he argues, are not simply defined by general consent, a democratic process, but increasingly by professionals—that is, organized bodies of specialists, who create, adjudicate, and implement needs as commodities according to the logic of their own power (Illich, 2005, p. 16-17). To what extent was I attempting to define the needs of the group through my own ideological and professional lenses?

Professionalism is a major discourse in librarianship, and as such provides the ideological underpinnings of our understanding of our role in relation to library users. Yet it can be argued, following Illich (2005), that the logic by which this discourse operates is something that intrudes into the world of libraries from outside and above (Grace, 2011, p. 59). By behaving in a professional manner, I undermine the central premise of autonomy that is integral to educating for sustainability literacy. In order to try to avoid such a pitfall, a reflective approach must be adopted. This might be through journaling, or simply discussing these issues as they arise with a sympathetic fellow worker. An awareness of the power relationships involved is the beginning of avoiding the solidifying of such a dynamic and the undermining of the whole purpose of the endeavor.

One problem that has arisen is the question of dominant voices in the group. There are those who have more to say and are more confident than others in putting their views across. The survey specifically asked whether the role of the library worker should encompass chairing the discussions so as to mitigate this factor. There were no responses in favor of this approach. The desire seems to be that any such tendencies must be regulated by self-organization and not a single authoritative individual. Interestingly, despite my concerns, all survey respondents stated that they felt they had adequate capacity to express their views in the group sessions.

The group demographics, while reflecting a diversity of backgrounds, do not necessarily reflect the total diversity of the city in which we live. The group currently has an even split between male and female members (perhaps for the first time in its existence), ranges in age from mid-20s to mid-60s, and includes members from Belgium, New Zealand, Ireland, and Romania, as well as here in the UK. However, other minority and migrant communities of our city are not represented. There may be many reasons for this. The level of discussion can be quite high, with some technical language used that requires some effort to follow, even for native English speakers such as myself. This level is set by the members themselves, and as such acts as a self-imposed bar to entry. The group is interested in discussing these ideas in some detail, and that may not be easy or useful for a new arrival or someone just gaining confidence in English. Also, the barriers that might prevent someone new to our city from accessing public services also apply to their capacity to join our group, despite attempts to reach out into the community at events such as the Green Fair.

Purpose and Scale

"To be a model of sustainable group interaction."

~BFABF member

People come to projects such as this with very different ideas of how it might work and what it might achieve, as well as different levels of education and understanding of the issues likely to be discussed. In response to my survey, group members indicated that their primary reason for joining the group was intellectual—to encounter new ideas—shortly followed by social, and then, finally, practical. This progression is reinforced by responses to a question asking what the purpose of the group is. The most votes went to the options "discuss books" and "encounter new ideas." Only one respondent identified with the concept of "increasing sustainability literacy" as a primary purpose of the group.

This poses an important question: if the group is to encourage positive change, surely it needs to go beyond the simple discussion of books and new ideas? The extent to which action is encouraged and taken by members of the group is hard to gauge, although the majority of respondents to the survey indicated that being a member of BFABF had impacted their daily lives. Discussions at meetings do touch on local protests and meetings, as well as personal goals such as reduction of carbon emissions. Many of those in the group have links with local and national campaigning groups, e.g. Quakers, trade unions, UKUncut (a group concerned with tax evasion and avoidance by large corporations), Transition Towns, and the Green Party. As such, the group serves as a place to have discussions adjacent to these activities, to find a greater clarity in our involvement with these other activities, and to introduce new ideas that might influence them.

Over the last two years, we have had individuals come and go from the group, with a core membership of around four or five. Meetings have seen as many as seven or eight members present, or as few as one. Gaining new members has mainly come about through word of mouth, posters and bookmarks advertising the group, and posts to various websites and lists amenable to the material read and discussed. It would have been interesting to have more feedback from those who had left the group to set against the methods with which they were recruited to the project, to see which were the most successful.

Early on in the process, we established that there was an optimum number of individuals, approximately three to six, that would work for a constructive conversation in our once-monthly, one-and-a-half-hour-long meetings. Beyond that size, it is hard for all members to have their say and for a qualitatively beneficial discussion to take place. It is interesting to note that in his wide-ranging study of social organization, Sale (1980) identifies—albeit with regard to the slightly different situation of committees—five as the optimal group number being "good for decision-making, because of course it is odd and because it is large enough so that no one feels isolated when taking a stand (divisions are more often three-two) and small enough so that participants can shift roles and points of view without onus" (p. 343-351). While this may seem unrelated to a group whose primary decision-making function is simply what to read next, it reflects that we are working at a manageable, human scale in our attempt to engender long-term positive social change. Ideally, the BFABF reading group would form one of several nodes in a network of like-minded groups. As stated earlier, while we link in with campaigning groups across our city through individual actions, such a network is yet to take shape in any formal way. Our most recent meetings have included discussion of the idea of sometimes using a more workshop-like structure to try to address practical ideas related to the theories we discuss.

For the most part, survey respondents indicated that the group had met their expectations. One negative point that arose was the lack of enough copies in the library system of some titles chosen for discussion. This scarcity has led to experiments with what and how we read. The group has moved from title-based reading, where everyone reads the same book, to topic-based reading, where a topic is chosen and all members read around it, with a few suggested texts. This was a direct response to the lack of freely-available copies of the type of book our group wished to discuss. The success of this second approach has been limited, and ideally there would be enough of a single title to go around each month. Also, we have experimented with watching documentaries accessible free online, making library computers available for those who do not have Internet access at home. There has been very little progress in pressuring the library to obtain titles for the group, primarily due to the current state of funding for libraries in the UK. One reading set, of Richard Sennet's *The Craftsman*, was bought, but subsequent requests have not been successful.

Of the myriad topics covered by the group's reading, members felt that they had become most informed on ideas around alternative economics. The extent to which this represents a bias in the collection of the public library or is more a reflection of the current state of affairs is hard to discern. Other subjects covered have included sustainability, radical politics, psychology, and genetics. The books and topics chosen for reading were made by consensus at the end of each meeting. Working in a small group with similar interests makes such a process relatively easy. See the list at the end of this chapter for a sample of books read by the group.

Lessons and Hopes

"It has been a great experience to be involved. I particularly value meeting people that I wouldn't have met otherwise—probably the most important aspect for me is hearing other people's ideas, whilst understanding (something of) their background. This helps me form my own assessments of the books / passages / ideas we've come across, and I really value it."

~BFABF member

Four out of the five respondents to the survey said that involvement in the group had an impact on their day-to-day lives. Often this was in small and hard to describe ways, the causal relationship between being a member of the BFABF reading group and changes in lifestyle being hard to determine. Perhaps looking for large-scale differences in our lives and communities is to misunderstand the purpose of the project; instead it might be said that "the learning *is* the change" (Phillips, 2009, p. 210). The discussions we have at our meetings are impassioned, and attitudes towards each other have evolved as we have come to understand one another better. We are individuals already committed, to varying degrees, to changing the world for the better, halting ecological destruction, and creating a more positive future. In addition to serving as a place to discuss ideas and move our own practices forward, our aims include forming more significant links with like-minded organizations and hopefully establishing other, similar groups in our city, perhaps in conjunction with other community libraries and library workers.

Any attempt at educating for sustainability can positively influence the institution in which it takes place (Phillips, 2009). While support from the public library service has been limited, it still provides the space for the group, and it approved the initial outlay of my time to establish the group. It can only be hoped that the value of sustainability literacy programs will increase in the eyes of local authorities, as the incidence of high-profile climate-related incidents increases. To make this happen, the library worker involved with the program must attempt to raise the profile of the group within the local authority and encourage the group towards actions that will positively impact local resilience. However, should a library authority not be supportive of these efforts, a group like BFABF can still be established and maintained, provided there are a few dedicated individuals willing to ensure its success.

The hope for the future is what it has always been, that however small our achievements with the BFABF reading group, it might provide the seed for further actions and, ultimately, a better future for us all.

Examples of Books Read By the Group

Heat - George Monbiot
The Revenge of Gaia - James Lovelock
How to Be Free - Tom Hodgkinson
Sustainable Energy Without the Hot Air - David McKay
The Age of Absurdity - Michael Foley
The Craftsman - Richard Sennett
The Spirit Level - Richard Wilkinson and Kate Pickett
The Black Swan - Nassim Nicholas Taleb
Work - Crimethinc
True Wealth - Juliet Schor
Life Rules - Ellen LaConte
The Shock Doctrine - Naomi Klein
Whole Earth Discipline - Stewart Brand
My Beautiful Genome – Lone Frank

References

Grace, D. (2011). *The role of the public library in promoting community resilience: An autoethnographic study.* (Unpublished master's thesis). University of Sheffield, Sheffield, England. Retrieved from http://dagda.shef.ac.uk/dispub/dissertations/2010-11/External/DGrace_090125616.pdf

Illich, I. (2005). Disabling professions. In I. Illich et al, *Disabling professions* (pp. 11-41). London, England: Marion Boyars.

Norris, F. H., Stevens, S. P., Pfefferbaum, B., Wyche, K. F., & Pfefferbaum., R. L. (2008). Community resilience as a metaphor, theory, set of capacities, and strategy for disaster readiness. *American Journal of Community Psychology, 41*(1-2), 127-150. Retrieved from http://www.springerlink.com/content/1421626545438270/

Phillips, A. (2009). Institutional transformation. In A. Stibbe (Ed.), *The handbook of sustainability literacy: Skills for a changing world* (pp. 209-214). Totnes, England: Green Books.

Sale, K. (1980). *Human scale.* New York, NY: Coward, McCann and Geoghegan.

Stibbe, A. & Luna, H. (2009). Introduction. In A. Stibbe (Ed.), *The handbook of sustainability literacy: Skills for a changing world* (pp. 9-18). Totnes, England: Green Books.

Transition Network. (2012). About Transition Network. Retrieved from hhtp://www.transitionnetwork.org/about

Teaching in the Margins

Barbara A. Quarton

Research is a fundamental component of a university education. In the process of conducting research, college students develop a knowledge base for their future professions by exploring and critiquing the scholarship, ideas, and practices of their chosen field. Before they can engage in this kind of critical study, however, students of higher education in our information society should be enlightened about the political nature[1] of the information processes they will be interacting with (Andersen, 2006; Seale, 2010). It makes sense that students, who upon graduation will participate as educated citizens in civic discourse and action, should be aware of and able to negotiate the information hierarchies that shape our country's global influence. Academic librarians, because of our disciplinary knowledge, can give students this social framework for thinking about information and help them develop a degree of critical consciousness. "By developing critical consciousness," says James Elmborg, "students learn to take control of their lives and their own learning to become active agents, asking and answering questions that matter to them and the world around them" (2006, p. 193). Regrettably, in most traditional public universities, academic librarians do not have an opportunity to teach students about the social nature of information in an explicit, scaffolded way. Thus, students are not given a framework

---

1.   In this paper, I use Deborah Fink's definition of politics as "promoting a particular interest" (Fink, 1989, p. 21).

for how information flows, or how the evolution of ideas relates to their lives, or how information shapes and reshapes our society (Kapitzke, 2003). Instead, most students learn only mundane skills about how to use online resources to find information that is relevant to their university assignments. The reason for this startling educational vacuum about something as powerful and ubiquitous as the social nature of information is that administrators, faculty, and librarians in academia are wrestling with competing assumptions about information and struggling with their own and each other's roles in an era of technological and social change. In this essay, I describe an unusual program of information literacy instruction that could reform how and what university students learn about information and consequently could transform the way they think about and use information in their university courses and after they graduate.

In order for readers to understand the unconventional nature of this program, it is necessary first to explicate the complex environment in which most traditional academic librarians on university campuses work. Our colleagues—faculty, staff, and administrators—speak respectfully about the library as the titular heart of the university, but many of them act as if it is a thing apart, an entity disconnected from the academy and peripheral to student success in college. Librarians are often considered to be irrelevant because of the Internet. We labor under our campus colleagues' archaic notions about who we are, what we know, and what we do. Some of us who work on campuses where librarians have faculty status are recipients of, at best, personal gratitude from faculty for helping their students and, at worst, an undercurrent of professional disapproval because we are not obliged to have Ph.D.s and many of us do not teach academic courses. We are, therefore, isolated in the academy, and our disciplinary knowledge is invisible. Further, the academic librarian's teaching role is undermined by the fact that most faculty, like their students, are unclear about information's theoretical foundations and tend to minimize their importance to research practices. For some faculty—who are disciplinary experts and often take research for granted—information is a thing to be managed: they use common technologies and the Internet well enough to accomplish what they need to accomplish for their work. With some exceptions, they teach their students to do research in the ways they learned to do research in their own post-graduate programs. For example, most faculty insist that their students use credible information sources—typically, scholarly journal articles—yet they seldom explain the contextual purpose of this requirement or, even more rarely, the politics of peer review (Doherty, 2007) or how this influences the directions of scholarly conversations and, ultimately, social progress. Faculty, understandably, have no time in the semester or the quarter to teach students the conceptual foundations of information even when they are aware of them: their first allegiance is, necessarily, to their own disciplinary content. Unfortunately, most of their lectures and assignments consequently lack rhetorical context about information, and most required research is seen as a means (information retrieval) to an end (a paper) rather than a variable in the process of critical thought. In this scenario, librarians are needed only at the reference desk or in one-on-one research consultations scheduled as problems arise in students' search for information.

Professional library associations long ago recognized the threat of the Internet to the library profession (Tyner, 1998) and worked hard to reframe librarianship from the gatekeeper model—wherein the librarian, by virtue of having specialized knowledge, wisely chooses and stores and then accesses and evaluates information for those who seek it—to the instructional model—wherein the librarian uses that specialized knowledge to choose and store and then teach others how to find the "best" information. In reframing the librarian's professional role, however, library leaders preserved their professional control over information (Kapitzke, 2001; Pawley, 2003; Simmons, 2005). They embraced the business-born term "information literacy," and in 2000, the Association of College and Research Libraries (ACRL) adopted the strict standards[2] against which a student could be judged to be information literate or not. Academic librarians are expected to teach information literacy according to these standards, known officially as the Information Literacy Competency Standards for Higher Education (Association of College and Research Libraries, 2000), and to collaborate with faculty to integrate information literacy across the higher education curriculum (Rader, 1995). On the vast majority of traditional university campuses, this professional imperative is most often accomplished (Oakleaf, Hoover, Woodard, Corbin, Hensley, Wakimoto, & Iannuzzi, 2012) by librarians offering "one-shot" library sessions (Vance, Kirk, & Gardner, 2012), whereby a professor requests a one-time, one- or two-hour library session and a librarian uses the time to show the students how to search and find information for the assignment at hand. These one-shots, because of their brevity and their specificity to the professor's assignment, are primarily procedural rather than conceptual, and can provide students little framework for understanding why or

---

2. The information literacy standards are: (1.) The information literate student determines the nature and extent of the information needed; (2.) The information literate student accesses needed information effectively and efficiently; (3.) The information literate student evaluates information and its sources critically and incorporates selected information into his or her knowledge base and value system; (4.) The information literate student, individually or as a member of a group, uses information effectively to accomplish a specific purpose; and (5.) The information literate student understands many of the economic, legal, and social issues surrounding the use of information and accesses and uses information ethically and legally. (Association of College and Research Libraries, 2000, p. 8-14)

how the information they find impacts and is impacted by daily life and social forces. One-shot sessions have the side effect of reinforcing faculty's misconception of the academic librarian's work as skills-based rather than as a disciplinary practice based on theoretical foundations. Finally, the one-shot instructional model is contingent on the motivation of the individual faculty member to request the session, rather than on the developing research needs of the students. Even with these fatal flaws, as a result of the information literacy rhetoric crafted by library leaders in the last twenty-some years, information literacy has won the endorsement of accrediting bodies such as the Western Association of Schools and Colleges, which named it a "core learning ability" of a Baccalaureate program (WASC Accrediting Commission for Senior Colleges and Universities, 2008, p. 14). This is cause for celebration among academic librarians because it appears to legitimize our work, but the standards upon which students' information literacy are likely to be assessed are mechanistic, and the primary teaching model of information literacy instruction is a logistical nightmare for faculty and librarians alike. Faculty, because it takes one entire class session away from their time to teach their content, and librarians, because the number of specialized one-shots needed to teach 25,000 or more students across the curriculum is unsustainable.

Beyond the library, there is an ongoing struggle between faculty and administrators about power, money, and position that negatively impacts the integration of information literacy into the curriculum. Faculty, in many cases, must defend their academic principles to administrators who have espoused the business model of education that is anathema to faculty. Academic tenure and academic freedom, the institutions that safeguard freedom of inquiry and drive innovation, are problematic for many administrators who see themselves as trying to run a business, and some faculty are rightly suspicious of their motives. This mutual distrust between faculty and the administration feeds a climate of unease on most traditional university campuses that makes it difficult for those involved to adapt to any kind of change, either good or bad. Academic librarians with faculty status are part of this mix, representing a very small contingent of the faculty, with little authority on campus except in relation to the library itself. Library funding is approved (or not) by campus administrators who, like the faculty, have a blurred sense of the library's connection to learning and its importance to the academy. In this environment, most faculty understandably do not relish collaborating with librarians (whom they consider to be nice but irrelevant and who many do not consider to be professional equals) in order to integrate information literacy (which most of them do not understand, value, or have time to teach) into a curriculum that many believe is being watered down by administrative edicts.

Amidst this maelstrom, academic librarians fight for meaning. Our faculty status does not always give us the freedom to teach academic courses in our own discipline. We are expected (by academic library leaders and some library deans) to help faculty craft assignments that require their students to do research and use the library's resources. As noted above, however, there is an inherent problem with this directive: most faculty are unconvinced about the scholarly value of the library and information literacy instruction and naturally are wary about collaboration that could infringe on their academic freedom. Lacking a viable system by which to teach our disciplinary content, then, many academic librarians have become salespeople for the library and its resources. Instead of teaching students about the conceptual framework of information and how it influences what they know, the ideas they generate, and the world they live in, most of us teach students how to use specialized databases and the library space itself. Our disciplinary knowledge is hidden, and because of this, students learn only how to find information for a specific need rather than how to *think about* information. The endorsement of information literacy by the Western Association of Schools and Colleges (WASC), considered by some academic librarians to be a boon to the profession, is to others a threat. If assessment of information literacy is based on skills-based standards, librarians will be compelled to teach to them; we will be confined to teaching students an operational approach to information that is heavily library-centric. We will be unable to "…be explicit about the moral and political commitment to flattening rather than reinforcing current information and literacy hierarchies" (Pawley, 2003, p. 448). Our academic freedom (like that of our faculty colleagues) will be further eroded. And if the procedural one-shot continues to be the primary mode of information literacy instruction, not only will the conceptual foundations of information be lost to students, faculty will resent librarians for squandering their time teaching students database functionality and the "evils" of Wikipedia. Worse, as WASC requirements for teaching and assessing information literacy begin to be enforced, online assessments based on the old standards will be produced and sold to campuses desperate for a fast, simple solution to the information literacy conundrum. In the confusion, librarians' work will be further devalued and information's social roots, its political and historical context, will be left for others to champion. The content and structure of the traditional model of information literacy instruction is fraught with problems and must be reconsidered.

One Library's Approach

Our student population is roughly two-thirds Hispanic and African American. Eighty percent of our freshman class is comprised of first-generation college students. Most of our students have part- or full-time jobs, and 70% attend school on a scholarship. Our students are economically disadvantaged. They come to college with cell phones and social media accounts and the hope that a college degree will pave the way for a better life. Most of our students graduate with degrees in psychology and criminal justice and nursing, aiming for professions in which they can contribute to the social good and move up the socio-economic ladder. They will graduate into a global work force where competing for a good salary depends on their ability to interface with complex social issues deftly and diplomatically, most likely in bureaucratic settings. In order to be egalitarian problem solvers, they must have a mental model of the problem zone—the information field relative to the issues they face—and the understanding that "each stage in the cycle of information processing is susceptible to political influences" (Fink, 1989, p. 21). If our students are not fully cognizant of the social and political nature of information and its processes, they will be disadvantaged in the workplace and, more importantly, their ability to be agents of change in a competitive world will be compromised.

Given the challenges our students face in college and upon graduation, is it any wonder that we despair of simply teaching students how to use databases and how to evaluate information sources according to standards that "emphasize control rather than freedom" (Pawley, 2003, p. 426)? We should teach students about the economics of information, the politics of peer review and how that relates to social policy, and the historical and social value of attribution in an information society so that they understand the power of information in the world. A liberal education will make sense to our students (most of whom just want a good job) only if we are intentional about how and why these theoretical underpinnings of information practices matter to their daily lives. Instead of trying to control students' information habits, which the information literacy standards developed twenty years ago attempt to do, we should be helping them to think critically about the purposefulness and interconnectedness of all information. With an authentic framework for how information is socially constructed, students will know that different information sources exist and have different purposes, and they will know how to judge when and why various sources are useful in different life situations. Sometimes a scholarly journal article, for example, really is more relevant to an information need than, say, a blog post. This is valuable knowledge not only for thinking critically and writing papers in college, but also in our students' lives, especially when they graduate. Public policy, city planning, civil engineering, the law—the structures of our society—are founded on scholarly research and principles of peer review. Scholarship is a discreet part of society, and it should be made explicit so that people recognize that the world around them is not driven by chance, but by debate, consensus, power, and position. If students strive to be agents of change, to "make a difference," they must be able to recognize this dynamic about information so they can either work within it to succeed, or work within it to change it. If they are not motivated to be agents of change, if what they are looking for is a job with a salary that will afford them a comfortable life, it is even more important that they understand that politics is at work in information processes. Why? Because everything they do is affected by the social nature of information. When they watch different television shows that seek to influence how they think about the world; when they surf the Web and get their information from thousands of websites with competing "truths"; when they read or listen to various versions of the daily news or global events: if they do not recognize the underlying social influences on the way information is created and evolves, their personal power and their ability to think for themselves will be diluted.

"It is a fundamental responsibility for us as educators," according to Dane Ward, "to embrace a commitment to a more holistic information literacy that can make a difference in the world. The world cries for it. But how do we teach it?" (2006, p. 398). The new instructional model we use in our library is a direct result of our frustration with the de-contextualized information literacy standards that prevent students from learning about the social nature of information as well as the collegial but complicated campus climate that underestimates the significance of the social forces driving information. Our program is influenced by the literature of critical information literacy, which seeks to "highlight how information works" (Pawley, 2003, p. 448) and that "pushes students toward self-reflection, interpretation, understanding, and ultimately action" (Swanson, 2004, p. 264). Library scholars such as Elmborg (2006), Jacobs, (2008), Franks (2010), and Kapitzke (2001) write eloquently about the social nature of information and the broad potential of the critical information literacy paradigm to higher education. Swanson (2004) describes a series of librarian-led instruction sessions integrated into a first-year composition course that "reflect[s] how searchers actually search for information and mak[es] information literacy applicable to students' lives" (p. 259), and in recent years, academic librarians such as Sinkinson & Lingold (2010) and Torrell (2010) have begun infusing their seminars and library instruction sessions with social themes to animate discussions about the political nature of information. We have not found any evidence in the literature, however, of a comprehensive program that introduces students to foundational information concepts (such as social interpretations of the deep Web, the fluidity of the information cycle, the subjective nature of credibility, and the value of attribution) in a scaffolded, transparent way. Such a program, we believe, would prepare students to think about, search for, and critique information with a balanced perspective. Our library has developed a stand-alone program to fill this gap: it is specifically designed to help university students grasp the social nature of information and recognize its critical role in their coursework and in their lives.

What Our Program Looks Like

Our co-curricular instruction program consists of a beginning information literacy workshop series in the freshman year and an intermediate information literacy workshop series in the junior year. There are four workshops in each series, and the program's purpose is to teach our students how information works by presenting them with a blend of the theory and practice of information literacy as it applies to their information needs in college and beyond. We began our freshman series in the fall quarter of 2011. We introduced our junior series in the fall quarter of 2013. Our information literacy program is written to align with the current assessment-driven language espoused by WASC and professional library associations because we recognize the importance of working within the system. Thus, we have created student learning outcomes[3] fashioned after the ACRL standards but that are, we believe, more relevant to our students' lives and research needs. Our program helps students to

- distinguish search engines from proprietary databases, recognizing the economic and research implications of both;
- create and use effective search strategies in order to engage actively and confidently in recursive research processes;
- distinguish popular discourse from academic discourse, with the awareness that each has its own distinct purpose and audience;
- evaluate the credibility of information by its source and through investigation of its rhetorical and social context;
- use information ethically, recognizing the essential value of attribution in an information society.

Figure 1 shows the program's curriculum map. Note that outcome 2 spans all workshops and represents the practical application of each workshop.

3. According to the WASC handbook, student learning outcomes "set forth the antici-pated or achieved results of courses or programs" (WASC Accrediting Commission for Senior Colleges and Universities, 2008, p. 58).

Figure 1. The Library's Curriculum Map

The Library's Information Literacy Student Learning Outcome

1) Students will distinguish search engines from proprietary databases, recognizing the economic and research implications of both;
2) Students will create and use effective search strategies in order to engage actively and confidently in recursive research processes;
3) Students will distinguish popular discourse from academic discourse, with the awareness that each has its own distinct purpose and audience;
4) Students will evaluate the credibility of information by its source and through investigation of its rhetorical and social context;
5) Students will use information ethically, recognizing the essential value of attribution in an information society.

	Workshop 1	**Workshop 2**	**Workshop 3**	**Workshop 4**
Freshman Series	Concept: The Deep Web	Concept: The Information Cycle	Concept: Credibility	Concept: Attribution
	Skill: Keyword Searching in the Deep Web	Skill: Determining Purpose and Audience	Skill: Determining Purpose and Audience	Skill: Recognizing Parts of a Citation
	Workshop 1	**Workshop 2**	**Workshop 3**	**Workshop 4**
Junior Series	Concept: How the Deep Web Gets Its Content	Concept: What Is a Discipline and What Is the Literature	Concept: Different Ways that Disciplines Make Knowledge	Concept: Knowledge Is Continually Being Produced
	Skill: Identifying Scholar, Producer, Vendor	Skill: Subject Searching	Skill: Finding Genres in the Literature	Skill: Finding and Acknow- -ledging Alternative Voices

All of our workshops follow the same general design. Students are encouraged to adopt a meta-cognitive approach to information. The librarian facilitating the workshop introduces the concept under examination and creates situations in which students practice associated ways of working with and thinking about information. Students engage in activities and discussion rather than suffer through a "narrative" (Freire, 1970, p. 71) or observe drawn-out demonstrations of the use of sources. Our assumption is that students are comfortable with search technology and inclined toward discovering things on their own. Students work in pairs or in small groups to negotiate research scenarios and express their questions and ideas. Each session concludes with a free-write opportunity—our assessment piece based on content analysis—in which students reflect on the conceptual knowledge they addressed during the session. Most important: there is always a practical take-away.[4] Students leave our sessions having experimented with a new way of thinking about information that relates to the world as they know it and that helps them to do research for their classes. The following sections overview the student learning outcomes and rationales of each workshop in our program.

Workshop #1: The Web

Student Learning Outcome: "Students will distinguish search engines from proprietary databases, recognizing the economic and research implications of both."

Rationale: The overarching goal of the first workshop of both series is to introduce students to the deep Web, where much of the data that influences social progress lives and grows. In most cases, our students are unaware that there is information beyond that which they can access using public search engines. Freshmen are introduced to the free vs. fee paradigm and how it impacts their search for information in their college courses. Juniors will learn about the power dynamics of deep Web content and how these dynamics influence the information they find in college and in the professions.

Workshop #2: The Information Cycle

Student Learning Outcome: "Students will distinguish popular discourse from academic discourse, with the awareness that each has its own distinct purpose and audience."

---

4.   See our curriculum map on the previous page (Figure 1).

Rationale: The overarching goal of the second workshop in both series is to teach students about the different spheres of information—popular and scholarly—and how these two spheres are related to each other and to their lives. Freshmen experiment with the information cycle and make distinctions between the editorial practices and purposes of popular and scholarly information in order to distinguish the social value of both spheres. Juniors will delve into the scholarly realm and discover the differences among the various disciplines, finding that different professions approach issues in different ways. This lays the foundation for understanding credibility in the next workshop.

Workshop #3: Credibility

Student Learning Outcome: "Students will evaluate the credibility of information by its source and through investigation of its rhetorical and social context."

Rationale: The overarching goal of the third workshop of both series is to help students focus on context and make determinations about relevance. Having learned about purpose and audience in the previous workshop, freshmen are now prepared to make choices about where to find and how to analyze information for relevance to their particular assignments. Juniors will explore the scholarly literature in more depth, focusing on finding and analyzing the genres of the various fields, which will prepare them to work with these genres in their upper-division courses as well as in their future professions.

Workshop #4: Attribution

Student Learning Outcome: "Students will use information ethically, recognizing the essential value of attribution in an information society."

Rationale: The overarching goal of the fourth workshop of both series is to help students see that knowledge production is a continual process that involves many voices, and that every voice along the way is important. Information comes from people with ideas who build on others' ideas before them. Attribution maintains the lineage, preserving the integrity of information for future study both personally and professionally. Freshmen learn the purpose of citations, and juniors will use citation information to trace a scholarly conversation and consider the significance of gaps in the literature.

Reactions to Our Workshops

Our freshman workshops have gained a following among faculty teaching First Year Composition and Communication Studies as well as those teaching University Studies courses. Students register online and attend our workshops on their own time. The students who come to the workshops receive attendance confirmations to give to their professors, who often give extra credit for their participation. Feedback from professors has been very positive, for example: "I think the workshops have helped my students...for my freshmen comp class and probably throughout the rest of their undergraduate careers." They also report on students' excitement about their new knowledge and students' recommendations that other students attend the workshops. The post-workshop free-writes are encouraging; students describe their surprise and their curiosity about the new ideas they have encountered. For example, in the free-write, one student wrote, "I did not know that scholarly articles are usually written long after the event has happened. I guess it is common sense, but I don't think people usually think about it. Also it was nice to see the changes in diction as the sources went from popular to scholarly." They also point out the usefulness of the workshops to their course work: "This workshop...it really opened my mind to research." Finally, we are elated that students respond positively to the workshops. They participate in group discussions freely, they engage in the activities enthusiastically (we actually saw this comment in one of the free-writes: "I loved this workshop, it was really fun!"), and they ask probing questions and make cogent points. We are working with our Office of Institutional Research on a longitudinal study to assess participants' information literacy as a result of our program. We are committed to authentic assessment of learning in our program, however, and will avoid assessing library-centric skills that students will not need when they graduate.

For our part, because we have committed ourselves to being transparent about our knowledge and practices, explicit about the social structure of information and its relevance in our lives, and forthcoming about the shifting sands in the information landscape, we are hopeful about the future. We take our students' feedback seriously and rethink our workshop activities as needed. We know that as technology and social change move inexorably forward, our workshops must evolve to keep pace. It is exciting to ponder.

Conclusion

Social and technological change, our own professional angst, and the complexities of the higher education system collided and challenged us to reinvent ourselves and our teaching mission. We chose to create an information literacy program that is separate from but supportive of students' coursework at critical stages of their university career, that neither squanders faculty's time nor infringes on their academic freedom, and that affords us a measure of control over what and how we teach. More importantly, we chose to connect our disciplinary knowledge and practices to students' experience: our workshops are student-centered and focused on helping students develop their own informed way of thinking about and using information in their coursework and in life.

We have been approached about offering faculty workshops and establishing a faculty learning community on the topic of information literacy and/or the social nature of information. It may be that our work will lead to a culture shift about information literacy on our campus. Perhaps this will be the beginning of an authentic integration of information literacy: faculty, librarians, staff, and students working together to develop a shared language about what information literacy is and how it fits into their lives. I propose that the library's program could provide students a basic framework for how information works in our society, and that faculty could build on this foundation in their courses according to their disciplinary perspectives, making tacit information processes explicit in their lectures and assignments. The library's course-related instruction sessions would also play a strong role in this organic collaboration. Because students would have learned a basic information literacy framework in our program, librarian subject-specialists could offer students in specific courses not only skills-based guidance for particular assignments but also more advanced conceptual knowledge. We believe that our co-curricular information literacy program can "mak[e] a specific contribution to the learning process, one which complements other parts of the learning process occurring in classrooms, residence halls, and other parts of an academic institution" (Snavely & Cooper, 1997, p. 12). The drive to help students become information literate is an undertaking that must be shared across the university campus. As the five colleges in our university consider re-accreditation requirements for information literacy, the library's workshop program can serve as a foundation for and a natural complement to other university-wide efforts to enrich our students' information literacy.

References

Andersen, J. (2006). The public sphere and discursive activities: Information literacy as sociopolitical skills. *Journal of Documentation*, 62(2), 213-228. doi: 10.1108/00220410610653307

Association of College and Research Libraries. (2000). Information literacy competency standards for higher education. Chicago, IL: The Association of College and Research Libraries.

Doherty, J. J. (2007). No shhing: Giving voice to the silenced. *Library Philosophy and Practice*, June, 1-8.

Elmborg, J. (2006). Critical information literacy: Implications for instructional practice. *Journal of Academic Librarianship*, 32(2), 192-199.

Fink, D. (1989). Process and politics in library research. Chicago, IL: American Library Association.

Franks, S. (2010). Grand narratives and information cycle in the library instruction classroom. In M. T. Accardi, E. Drabinski, & A. Kumbier (Eds.), *Critical library instruction: Theories & methods (pp. 43-54)*. Duluth, MN: Library Juice Press.

Freire, P. (1970). *Pedagogy of the oppressed*. New York, NY: Continuum International.

Jacobs, H. M. (2008). Information literacy and reflective pedagogical praxis. *Journal of Academic Librarianship*, 34(3), 256-262.

Kapitzke, C. (2001). Information literacy: The changing library. *Journal of Adolescent & Adult Literacy*, 44(5), 450-456.

Kapitzke, C. (2003). Information literacy: A positivist epistemology and a politics of outformation. *Educational Theory*, 53(1), 37-53.

Oakleaf, M., Hoover, S., Woodard, B., Corbin, J., Hensley, R., Wakimoto, D., & Iannuzzi, P. (2012). Notes from the field. *Communications in Information Literacy*, 6(1), 5-23.

Pawley, C. (2003). Information literacy: A contradictory coupling. *Library Quarterly*, 73(4), 422-452.

Rader, H. B. (1995). Information literacy and the undergraduate curriculum. *Library Trends*, 44(2), 270-278.

Seale, M. (2010). Information literacy standards and the politics of knowledge production: Using user-generated content to incorporate critical pedagogy. In M. T. Accardi, E. Drabinski, & A. Kumbier (Eds.), *Critical library instruction: Theories & methods (pp. 221-235)*. Duluth, MN: Library Juice Press.

Sinkinson, C., & Lingold, M. C. (2010). Re-visioning the library seminar through a lens of critical pedagogy. In M. T. Accardi, E. Drabinski, & A. Kumbier (Eds.), *Critical library instruction: Theories & methods (pp. 81-88).* Duluth, MN: Library Juice Press.

Simmons, M. H. (2005). Librarians as discourse mediators: Using genre theory to move toward critical information literacy. *portal: Libraries and the Academy,* 5(3), 297-311.

Snavely, L., & Cooper, N. (1997). The information literacy debate. *Journal of Academic Librarianship,* 23(1), 9-14.

Swanson, T. A. (2004). A radical step: Implementing a critical information literacy model. *portal: Libraries and the Academy,* 4(2), 259-273.

Torrell, M. R. (2010). Negotiating virtual contact zones: Revolutions in the role of the research workshop. In M. T. Accardi, E. Drabinski, & A. Kumbier (Eds.), *Critical library instruction: Theories & methods (pp. 89-103).* Duluth, MN: Library Juice Press.

Tyner, K. (1998). *Literacy in a digital world: Teaching and learning in the age of information.* London, England: Lawrence Erlbaum Associates.

Vance, J. M., Kirk, R., & Gardner, J. G. (2012). Measuring the impact of library instruction on freshman success and persistence. *Communications in Information Literacy,* 6(1), 49-58.

Ward, D. (2006). Revisioning information literacy for lifelong meaning. *Journal of Academic Librarianship,* 32(4), 396-402.

WASC Accrediting Commission for Senior Colleges and Universities. (2008). *Handbook of accreditation.* Alameda, CA: Western Association of Schools and Colleges.

In the Struggle

Knowledge My Public Library Kept Secret: The Urgent Need for Culturally-Responsive Library Service

Taneya D. Gethers

"Until lions have their own historians, tales of the hunt shall always glorify the hunter"

~Igbo, Nigerian Proverb

In 1996, educator and sociologist James W. Loewen published his best-selling book *Lies My Teacher Told Me: Everything Your High School History Textbook Got Wrong*. The book, in the spirit of historians John Hope Franklin and Howard Zinn, challenges most of what we've learned about U.S. history, from the "Founding Fathers" to the Vietnam War. After examining 12 leading high school history textbooks, Loewen determines that the texts promote hero-making rather than delivering accuracy and truth. The accounts of American history that we've learned in school are predominantly historical myths, he discovers.

Why perpetuate untruths? Why omit important details about the past? While reasons are complex, Loewen (1996) answers that national identity is behind the fictitious hijacking of U.S. history. America's history books, he asserts, must reflect a discourse that matches the brave and powerful national persona presented to the rest of the world. As a result, a distorted national memory is what becomes the basis of our history textbooks, he says. Still, Loewen argues, our history textbooks with their flawed historical accounts are not solely to blame (p. 332). We—those who teach; who write books; who curate museum exhibits; who know better, but do not correct—are all complicit. "These cultural lies have been woven into the fabric of our entire society," says Loewen. "From the flat-earth advertisements on Columbus Day weekend to the racist distortion of Reconstruction in *Gone With the Wind*, our society lies to itself about its past" (p. 332).

Vividly, I still remember first encountering Loewen's analysis as a high school student. I was introduced to the text by my U.S. history teacher Don LaFraniere, an educator dedicated to teaching his students how to interact with and critically examine history rather than memorize and recite facts. Revisiting *Lies My Teacher Told Me* as an adult and a librarian—a community historian, of sorts—I began to question the multiple ways libraries aid in the great cover-up assessed by Loewen. Library institutions, public libraries in particular, are charged with preserving and providing equitable access to society's knowledge, history and culture. Concealing information is completely out of sync with the library's unique role in society. Yet, from my travels visiting public libraries across the country and engaging with librarian colleagues about their professional experiences, I have observed that our institutions, quite often, like the U.S. history textbooks examined by Loewen, perpetuate limited discourse and representation of our shared human experience.

Too often, the heroes, experts, innovators, and creators in the books and other materials that make up our collections typically look one way (white and male), and reflect the values of Eurocentric[1] culture. Even more damaging, some of our library collections, in small town America and major U.S. cities alike, leave you to believe that people of color—Asian, American Indian, Latino, people of African descent—do not exist, let alone have contributed any value to the world. Thousands of youth and adults that represent this *marginalized majority* enter neighborhood libraries that are void of their depictions, experiences, and contributions to society. Not nearly enough do children of color see characters whose faces mirror their own in library picture or chapter books. For adults of color, books displayed and housed on library shelves also exclude their existence by content and by author. And, for both, library programming predominantly celebrates mainstream society. Missing is the history, culture, and knowledge of self that public libraries purport to preserve for them. Entering and exiting their

---

1. Eurocentric/Eurocentrism is a consciousness or practice of placing greater emphasis and value on European, Western, and/or Anglo-American culture, ideals, and interests, and interacting with the world from this standard, generally at the expense of other cultures.

neighborhood libraries, youth and adults of color must silently wonder, *"Why is there knowledge my public library keeps secret?"*

For library professionals, there is an urgent need for us to right this deeply terrible wrong. We know firsthand that public libraries serve as educational and cultural centers and are far more than just storehouses for books. And, at a time when equitable access to education is growing increasingly limited, it is that much more imperative that we provide free resources, programs, and services in public libraries. Today's public library is essential to developing and sustaining progressive communities, and broadening the life opportunities of the people we serve (this a primary reason I decided to become a librarian). We have a social, moral, and professional responsibility to do this work with accuracy and care.

Culturally-Responsive Library Service

Exploring new public service models is not a radical concept for public libraries. Routinely re-examining the way we serve our communities has become crucial for maintaining our relevance and relationships with our patron base. Over the years, public libraries have introduced new service models to align with advancing technology and changes in staffing and funding; however, we have remained stagnant in our efforts to institutionalize and deliver culturally-responsive library service that holistically empowers the community members we serve.

Culturally-responsive library service, inspired by the culturally-responsive educational framework, supports the "intergenerational transmission of knowledge about our values, beliefs, traditions, customs, rituals and sensibilities" (Adelaide L. Sanford Institute [ASI], n.d.b, para. 1). The service model also emphasizes the importance of sustaining these traditions and values. A public library that is culturally responsive sees the "socio-cultural backgrounds, prior experiences, and worldviews" (ASI, n.d.b, para. 9) of their patrons as cultural capital. Paired with the patrons' "learning, behavioral and communication styles" (ASI, n.d.b, para. 9), these cultural riches are embraced to create a transformative library experience that is truly meaningful and impactful.

The Adelaide L. Sanford Institute,[2] a clearinghouse for best practices that explore the role of culture in education and the "social, economic, intellectual, artistic, scientific and historical development of America and the world" (n.d.a, para. 2), has developed a five-step process for using culture as a teaching tool.

---

2. The Adelaide L. Sanford Institute is named in honor of Dr. Adelaide Sanford, Vice Chancellor Emeritus of the New York State Board of Regents. For more than six decades, the nationally-recognized educator has dedicated her professional work to providing all students with access to high-quality education and increasing student academic success using culturally-responsive methodologies.

Originally formatted for the classroom learning environment, the steps are easily transferable to the culturally-responsive library service model. By replacing "students" with "library patrons," the Institute's five-step process[3] has been minutely adapted to form the foundational principles of culturally-responsive library service:

> **STEP 1. KNOWLEDGE**: Learn as much as possible about the values, beliefs, and behaviors of your *library patrons*.
> **STEP 2. OBSERVATION**: Watch carefully to see what your *library patrons* consider important.
> **STEP 3. QUESTIONING**: Ask about things that you do not understand.
> **STEP 4. AFFIRMATION**: Acknowledge *library patron* strengths as well as the things that are different from, and even contrary to, your values.
> **STEP 5. CELEBRATION**: Find opportunities to celebrate your *library patrons'* interests, history, and culture.

"Change From The Frontline": Applying The Culturally-Responsive Library Service Model

Now that we have outlined the *Five Foundational Principles* of culturally-responsive library service, the next step is transforming these principles into tangible policies and practices that can be implemented system-wide at library organizations. Frontline library staff, with day-to-day interaction with patrons, are uniquely positioned to lead this movement. We have firsthand insight ("Knowledge"/ "Observation") into the interests of our patrons, and, through one-on-one dialogue ("Questioning"), particularly with patrons who routinely visit our libraries, the ability to affirm those values more meaningfully than could high-level library decision-makers who do not share a special rapport. Through consistently infusing culturally-responsive practices into our delivery of frontline customer service and other related library routines ("Affirmation"/ "Celebration"), we can influence a system-wide shift in organizational culture and policies.

A grassroots approach to applying the culturally-responsive library service model requires frontline staff to be proactive. The three immediate areas of focus are *Collection Development and Merchandising, Community Programming,*

---

3.   The five-step process—*Knowledge, Observation, Questioning, Affirmation, Celebration*— comprises "Culture as a Teaching Tool," found in the Adelaide L. Sanford Institute's statement on Culturally Responsive Education (n.d.b, para. 13). Only Steps 1, 2, 4 and 5 have been modified for the Culturally-Responsive Library Service framework.

and *Library Environment*. Vital to maintain at the forefront of the roll-out of the culturally-responsive library service model is the belief that all patrons carry with them an inherent social and cultural value; non-Eurocentric cultural backgrounds are not deficient. Further, these individual and collective characteristics must be used to foster a library experience that celebrates and inspires our patrons.

Collection Development and Collection Merchandising

Books and media, like mainstream society, help to shape youth and adult perceptions of self. They have also been used to perpetuate stereotypes and myths about people of color, both overt (mammy, macho Chicano, savage Indian, slant-eyed oriental) and less blatant (omission of diverse perspectives in nonfiction; exclusion of multicultural characters in fiction altogether). Expressed repeatedly, these falsehoods begin to gradually distort self-perceptions and become accepted as reality (Project SEE, 1998).

The culturally-responsive library service model, on the other hand, requires creating a library collection that is inclusive and accurate in its preservation of society's knowledge, history, and culture.[4] Under the culturally-responsive framework, the selection of library materials must reflect diversity in both content and creator, including authors, illustrators, and publishers. Though material selection is conducted centrally at many of our library organizations, there are still a variety of methods to recommend new materials for purchase. One of the ways that I influence materials selection at my library is by contacting collection development staff directly, either by phone or by email, with print and non-print suggestions. I have also sought opportunities to indirectly influence collection development by getting involved within my organization. I have volunteered as a presenter at our New Children's Books Presentation, promoting multicultural titles and titles created by authors and illustrators of color. In addition, I presently serve as a member of my library's Children's Steering Committee, which is responsible for shaping children's services across the 60-agency system. My involvement enables me to simultaneously promote and model culturally-responsive library service.

---

4.   "Librarians have a professional responsibility to be inclusive, not exclusive, in collection development and in the provision of interlibrary loan. Access to all materials and resources legally obtainable should be assured to the user, and policies should not unjustly exclude materials and resources even if they are offensive to the librarian or the user" (ALA, 1990).

To aid in the development of a culturally-responsive library collection, there are several professional tools already in place. Below are a few examples:

- **Project SEE** (1998) provides a ten-step guide to detecting racism and sexism in children's books that can be applied to the selection of both juvenile and adult materials. The manual, originally developed by the Council on Interracial Books for Children in 1974, includes techniques on examining texts for tokenism, noting the heroes and whose interests the heroes are serving, and considering cultural and historical perspectives.
- *The MultiCultural Review*, a quarterly trade journal and book review published by the Goldman Group, reports news and trends in multiculturalism and maintains an electronic list of 3000 multicultural titles that is updated and sent out to subscribers monthly.
- **TeachingBook.net** provides a free comprehensive database of Coretta Scott King Book Award resources, including lesson plans, audio recordings, primary sources, and the opportunity to experience award-winning African American authors and illustrators through video as they discuss and read aloud from their books.
- In addition, several libraries and affiliate organizations maintain bibliographies on new and classic youth and adult books written about and by people of color, including:
- **Hedberg (WI) Public Library**, which has developed an audio book guide, "Read Around the World With Your Ears," allowing listeners to travel the globe and meet people through stories.
- The **Black Caucus of the National Council of Teachers of English**, sponsors of the annual National African American Read-in.
- The American Library Association (ALA) **Ethnic & Multicultural Information Exchange Round Table** (EMIERT), a portal for diversity news and resources.

Together, this small sample of resources provides access to hundreds of materials to help successfully develop a library collection using the culturally-responsive service model. There is a wide variety of high-quality books written about and by people of color to introduce to the community you serve, even if that community is not a diverse population. We entrap and suppress the intellectual and social development of our library patrons when we provide only a partial view of humanity. This censorship, or challenge to equitable access, upholds the idea that "whiteness" is the standard for normalcy and success. While the community you serve may be less than one percent people of color, the world looks a different way, and it would be unrecognizable without the existence and contributions of these citizens of the globe.

Disturbingly, there's often a misperception that there is a low demand for multicultural books and other materials; however, through proper promotion, a multicultural collection will circulate. During reference assistance, for example, I routinely incorporate books about and by people of color into my recommendations. If a patron is researching inventors, I will suggest scientists like Dr. George Washington Carver, the African American botanist and chemist who invented peanut butter and over 300 other inventions using peanuts, or pull from the stacks Dr. Ivan Van Sertima's *Blacks in Science: Ancient and Modern.* The community I serve has openly embraced my practice of introducing multicultural materials and non-Western/non-Anglo-American historical knowledge during reference help.

Merchandising multicultural titles in high-traffic areas of my library, such as near the computer reservation and self-check stations, is an additional way that I promote these resources. I also regularly create vibrant book displays that appeal to the cultural and socio-historical interests of my library community. These displays commemorate historical anniversaries, such as Juneteenth, and annual cultural celebrations like the West Indian American Day Carnival. As part of the display, I usually provide guides that further promote other multicultural print and digital resources related to the topic.

Community Programming

Community programming is another critical way that people of all ages experience their neighborhood libraries. Innovative and relevant programming strengthens the relationship with patrons who frequently use their libraries, and attracts new patrons not previously aware of their value. Applying the culturally-responsive library service model to the development of community programming begins with recalling the first and second steps of the *Five Foundational Principles*:

> **STEP 1. KNOWLEDGE**: Learn as much as possible about the values, beliefs, and behaviors of your library patrons.
> **STEP 2. OBSERVATION**: Watch carefully to see what your library patrons consider important.

Ultimately, your goal is to develop community programming that celebrates the cultural experiences of your patrons and encourages an exchange about other beliefs, customs, and rituals practiced around the globe.

Multicultural Celebrations and Holidays

Annually, multicultural celebrations and holidays such as **Chinese Lunar New Year** (January/February), **Black History Month** (February), **Asian Pacific American History Month** (May), **Hispanic Heritage Month** (September), and **National American Indian Heritage Month** (November) are observed across the country. Libraries can easily develop engaging community programming to join in on these celebrations. For instance, in observance of the Dr. Martin Luther King Jr. federal holiday, I invite youth and adult patrons to read an excerpt from one of Dr. King's speeches, and then I ask a community member to facilitate a discussion in which we analyze Dr. King's words in relation to current events. (Recently, a reading of Dr. King's 1967 "Beyond Vietnam" speech led to a lively intergenerational dialogue about U.S. wars and local violence today.) I also like to observe the King holiday by honoring youth who, in the spirit of Dr. King, are making a difference in their communities, either as student leaders or library volunteers.

ALA Celebration Weeks and Promotional Events

ALA's celebration weeks and promotional events lend another opportunity to apply the culturally-responsive library service model to community programming. While the celebrations are not cultural-based, they are still an occasion to ensure that a multicultural perspective is accurately reflected. A book discussion about a phenomenal work by an author of color, for example, is a wonderful way to note **Celebrate Teen Literature Day** (April). **Picture Book Month** (November) can be observed at your library by selecting a bilingual text with a fun, rhyming pattern to read during your regularly-scheduled storytime. (As part of my normal storytime practice, I also add multicultural songs and rhymes[5] to my reading of multicultural books to keep adults and little ones enthused about learning more about neighbors near and far.) **National Library Legislative Day** (May) is another platform to bring in your community by hosting a Friends Open House to recruit new library advocates and make them aware of the issues faced by libraries, including equity of access for people of color.

Partnering to Deliver Community Programming

Community programming can be further enriched at your library by partnering with local organizations that share your service-driven mission, especially educational, youth-based, and arts organizations with strong roots in communi-

5.   Children's music pioneer Ella Jenkins has a vast discography of fun, interactive songs and rhymes inspired by African, Asian, Latin American, and European cultures. An alphabetized catalog of her songs is available at www.ellajenkins.com.

ties of color. ALA's five ethnic affiliates—the **American Indian Library Association** (AILA), **Asian Pacific American Librarians Association** (APALA), **Black Caucus of the American Library Association** (BCALA), **Chinese American Librarians Association** (CALA), and **REFORMA**: The **National Association to Promote Library & Information Services to Latinos and the Spanish Speaking** (REFORMA)—are also allies. Local chapters would willingly support community programming with resources and professional recommendations, or by co-sponsoring special events. Over the past several years, I have partnered with the New York Black Librarians Caucus, a BCALA affiliate, to host community programs such as read-in events, Kwanzaa celebrations, and discussion panels involving contemporary topics such as Hurricane Katrina.

Library Environment— "Creating a Culture of Community"

Effectively implementing the culturally-responsive library service model also requires re-imagining your library environment. We are not overhauling the physical structure, but rather promoting a new culture that encourages a communal way of experiencing the library. Communalism, including group cultural investment and collective work and accountability, is part of the traditional belief system for many people of color. Embracing a communal philosophy can yield significant positive results for both your library and its patrons.

Previously, we outlined the importance of library patrons seeing themselves and their experiences reflected in the collections and programming offered at their neighborhood libraries. Equally, it is important that we create culturally welcoming library environments that empower those same patrons to take greater stake in their "home" libraries. In the late 1920s, Pura Belpré, the first Latina librarian hired at New York Public Library (NYPL), quickly became an advocate for Spanish-speaking children and adults in New York City's Spanish Harlem community by "instituting bilingual story hours, buying Spanish language books, and implementing programs based on traditional holidays such as the celebration of Three Kings Day" at the neighborhood's local library (REFORMA, n.d., para. 4). Belpré, herself an immigrant to New York City, was also well-known for her community outreach skills, which included involvement in the city's Puerto Rican civic organizations. Belpré skillfully facilitated that same civic and cultural engagement at her Spanish Harlem library. She created a culture of community where Spanish-speaking residents could find and share their homeland experience and take ownership in their neighborhood library. Through Belpré's efforts, NYPL's 115th Street Branch became an "important cultural center for the Latino residents of New York City" (REFORMA, n.d., para. 4).

How 21st Century Librarians Can Be More Like Culturally-Responsive Trailblazer Pura Belpré

Invite the community into your library. Libraries are places for communing, exchanging ideas, and creating together. Many library systems do this work effectively at their flagship locations but struggle to institute this same spirit at their neighborhood libraries. Librarians, however, can initiate change and foster these communal experiences by putting into action the tenets of culturally-responsive library service.

Welcome into your library the cultural capital that inherently exists within the community you serve. Recall that "Celebration"—*find opportunities to celebrate your library patrons' interests, history, and culture*—is the fifth foundational principle of the culturally-responsive library service model. Open your library's doors to local artists, writers, and scholars to exhibit and share their works (each month, I collaborate with my neighborhood artists' association to feature local visual artists; my library, as a community exhibition space, has become a popular site on our community's annual "Studio Strut"). Create a space for youth and elders to exchange cultural traditions and values (bi-monthly, my library hosts a quilting series in which young patrons learn quilting basics from community elders; we've also partnered with local genealogists in a monthly workshop to support oral history collection and help community members trace their family ancestry—this program is one of our most highly-attended). Additionally, invite community-based organizations to use your meeting room space and bring their energy, and audience, into your library.

Make your library visible in the community. Get out and meet local stakeholders. Attend community meetings, especially meetings of civic organizations that have a genuine, and proven, commitment to culturally empowering your patrons. Participate in key events. The community needs to know that your library is an invaluable partner and resource.

Twice a month, I attend a local meeting or event, such as a community board or police precinct community council meeting. (To increase visibility without overextending my commitments, I share attendance at community meetings with colleagues at nearby branches.) If scheduling or staffing conflicts don't permit me to attend, I send promotional materials on new resources and upcoming library events for distribution. I have also established a virtual presence in my community by using online platforms, including email, local blogs, and community lists, to stay in regular communication with stakeholders.

Call upon the community to lead and serve. Invite patrons to plan and facilitate community programs, such as a book discussion or an intergenerational conversation about a current event significant to the community. Employing community talents is a key component of culturally-responsive library service ("Affirmation"—*acknowledge library patron strengths…*) and a strategy in sustaining high-quality programming amidst the climate of the continually-shrinking public library workforce. One example of this type of community-driven programming is "Neighborhood Storytime," a story hour that I created in partnership with a local parent that is solely facilitated by the parents and caregivers in attendance. Neighborhood Storytime not only promotes early literacy but supports learning as a communal responsibility and experience.

Advancing the culturally-responsive ideal of creating a library culture of community, ALA (2007) has outlined six goals for building "Inclusive and Culturally Competent Library and Information Services":

1) To ensure equitable services to every community member or group, training and ongoing education that promote awareness of and sensitivity to diversity must be stressed for all library personnel.
2) Care must be taken to acquire and provide materials that meet the educational, informational, and recreational needs of diverse communities.
3) Efforts to identify and eliminate cultural, economic, literacy-related, linguistic, physical, technological, or perceptional barriers that limit access to library and information resources must be prioritized and ongoing.
4) The creation of library services and delivery operations, which will ensure rapid access to information in a manner reflective of the communities they serve.
5) A diverse workforce is essential to the provision of competent library services. A concerted effort must be undertaken to recruit and retain diverse personnel at every level of the library workforce. Opportunities for career advancement must also be available to these individuals.
6) To ensure the development and enhancement of library services to diverse populations, library personnel from diverse and underrepresented backgrounds must be encouraged to take active roles in the American Library Association and other professional library organizations.

Maintaining Relevance and Equity through Culture

The culturally-responsive library service model brings a refreshed purpose to library work. Out of this framework spring new and much more deeply impactful methods of engaging the public. This model also presents librarians with new opportunities for professional growth. We can either adapt, or become (…

or, for some librarians, remain) the "old-fashioned transmitters of knowledge" that Loewen (1996) warns against in the final pages of *Lies My Teacher Told Me* (p. 328).

Through the culturally-responsive library service model, we're given an opportunity to inject a much-needed dose of integrity back into the library profession. For too long, libraries have ignorantly, and in many instances willingly, participated in the cover-up of the true and complete human experience. This injustice cannot continue. When the voices of some are silenced, when their stories, struggles, and victories are erased from society's record, what value do we place on their existence? What space do we make for them—the *marginalized majority* introduced at the start of this essay—in the future? Undoubtedly, the culturally-responsive library service model provides a concrete framework to ensure that libraries are in fact safeguarding *all* of society's history, knowledge and culture. When we—librarians, information scientists, literacy educators, culture keepers—speak a true word, we can transform the world (Freire, 1996).

References

Adelaide L. Sanford Institute. (n.d.a). Mission. Retrieved from http://www.sanfordinstitute.org/

Adelaide L. Sanford Institute. (n.d.b). Culturally responsive education. Retrieved from http://www.sanfordinstitute.org/

American Library Association. (1990). Diversity in collection development: An interpretation of the Library Bill of Rights. Retrieved from http://www.ala.org/Template.cfm?Section=interpretations&Template=/ContentManagement/ContentDisplay.cfm&ContentID=8530

American Library Association. (2007). Diversity: Goals for inclusive and culturally competent library and information services. In *ALA policy manual* (section 60.4). Retrieved from http://www.ala.org/aboutala/governance/policymanual/updatedpolicymanual/section2/60diversity#60.4

Project SEE. (1998). 10 quick ways to analyze children's books for racism and sexism. Retrieved from http://www.chil-es.org/10ways.pdf

Freire, P. (1996). *Pedagogy of the oppressed* (2nd rev. ed.). London, England: Penguin.

Loewen, J. W. (1996). *Lies my teacher told me: Everything your high school history textbook got wrong.* New York, NY: Touchstone.

REFORMA: The National Association to Promote Library & Information Services to Latinos and the Spanish Speaking. (n.d.). Pura Belpré biographical notes. Retrieved from http://www.reforma.org/content.asp?pl=7&sl=43&contentid=43

Building a Culturally-Responsive Library: A Select Resource Guide

Cooperative Children's Book Center: Multicultural Literature Resources
http://www.education.wisc.edu/ccbc/links/links.asp?idLinksCategory=4

A comprehensive offering of multicultural titles, book reviews, book awards, and evaluation tools. In addition, the guide provides a listing of small presses owned and operated by people of color.

Project SEE/Council on Interracial Books for Children: 10 Quick Ways to Analyze Children's Books for Racism and Sexism
http://www.chil-es.org/10ways.pdf

A guide to detecting racism and sexism in children's books that can be applied to the selection of both juvenile and adult materials.

Teaching for Change: Anti-Bias Education Articles

http://www.teachingforchange.org/programs/anti-bias-education/articles

Over 100 free downloadable articles on anti-bias education, including curriculum and parent resources.

Teaching for Change: Recommended Teaching Resources

http://bbpbooks.teachingforchange.org/best-recommended/booklist

Book lists are organized into 30 themes by age group, including culture, identity, and sexual preference/sexual orientation. Each category is further organized into sub-groups, e.g. fiction, nonfiction, print titles, and media.

The Children's Peace Education & Anti-Bias Library

http://www.childpeacebooks.org/cpb/Protect/antiBias.php

Organized by category—*culture & language, racial identity, gender roles, economic class, abilities & disabilities, family structure, holidays, activism, infant/toddler books*—the list provides book recommendations for building an anti-bias children's library.

Library Programs and Information Access for Incarcerated Women: A Canadian Perspective

Moyra Lang and Gayle Sacuta

The authors wish to acknowledge the original members of the Women's Prison and Reintegration Committee (WPRC): Valla McLean, Kirsten Wurmann, Liz Dennett, Liz Fulton Lyne, Allison Sivak. We also recognize the numerous committee members (not named herein) who work tirelessly. This article reflects the experiences and opinions of the named authors only.

The Greater Edmonton Library Association's (GELA) Women's Prison and Reintegration Committee (WPRC) was established in 2006 after committee members attended a talk given by an ex-inmate about her time spent in a federal prison serving a life sentence. So moved by the woman's story and the lack of resources inside the prison, a group of GELA librarians approached the prison to help, and the WPRC subcommittee was formed. Our work provides programs, resources, and access to information for incarcerated individuals; raises awareness of the urgent and particular needs of prisoners; and encourages and assists in providing library services to individuals behind bars.

Librarianship and Social Justice

Librarians are caretakers of records and information. Acknowledging and addressing the role libraries and librarians have played and continue to play in perpetuating unequal distribution of information and library resources, librarians must bear our responsibility for systemic injustice in our society. Library workers' responsibilities increase substantively when library populations are grossly under-represented, lack legal recognition, or have restricted access to information. As Sergio Chaparro-Univazo (2007) suggests, "there is nothing more political than organizing and disseminating information" (p. 34). Providing books and information to those individuals, such as prisoners, who face severe restrictions not only creates opportunities for library workers to become acquainted with the corrections system and the inequities in that system, but through working with prisoners we experience a better understanding of our own situatedness and our inherent privileges. Prisoners lack the basic rights to resources and information that most of us generally take for granted. Library services for incarcerated women open doors and deliver opportunities for prisoners and volunteers alike to participate responsibly in democracy.

> Gayle: *The ability to work towards social change varies depending on social environment and communication skill. Even in regular society, freedom of expression can seem like an impossible mountain—the potential for social change inside the prison is almost easier to imagine than the prospect of being able to create societal change on the outside. When so much about our profession of librarianship, as with other social structures, is rigid and rule bound, I could not be a librarian without the hope of working towards change. When we're students, professors equip us with the tools to agitate for change by demanding rigor and reason, and demonstrate a framework on which to structure alternative library discourse. Within the position statements of the Canadian Library Association (2008; 1985) and the American Library Association (2004) regarding the core values of librarianship, especially diversity, democracy, access to information, and social responsibility, we find a pocket in the discourse that justifies and motivates work for change.*

Overview of Corrections Canada

In Canada, prisons are the responsibility of the federal or provincial governments. Federal prisons are for individuals sentenced to two years or more, and provincial prisons are for sentences of less than two years. The WPRC projects take place in a federal women's prison. The federal prisons are run by a government agency called Correctional Service of Canada (CSC). The CSC manages institutions (prisons), residential facilities, and parole offices across Canada (CSC, 2010).

The Canadian Association of Elizabeth Fry Societies (CAEFS) Fact Sheet on Criminalized and Imprisoned Women (2012a) provides a brief overview of women and corrections: "…common experiences of criminalized women: a high proportion of Aboriginal women; most are criminalized and/or in prison for the first time; most have experienced sexual and/or physical abuse; often as a result of unaddressed or unresolved trauma, many women anaesthetize themselves with legal and illegal substances; most are under the age of thirty-five; most are mothers and the sole supporters of their children before they go to jail." CAEFS argues that despite the increasing numbers of women in federal prisons—"In 2010, there were about 500 women in the federal prison system and in 2011 there are almost 600, an increase of 20% in one year"—crime rates in Canada reached a 25-year low during this same period. The escalating number of women in prison is clearly linked to the evisceration of health, education, and social services (CAEFS 2012a).

Other Canadian issues that contribute to the criminalization of women include: 1) poverty (80% of women in prison are imprisoned for economic related crimes, such as stealing food to feed their children); 2) under-employment (women in Canada account for 70% of all part-time employees); 3) lack of support (1,132,290 single mothers in Canada have the most unstable earnings and are among the most impoverished in Canada); 4) institutionalized racism (CSC routinely classifies First Nations, Metis, and Inuit women as higher security risks than non-Indigenous women in prison) (CAEFS, 2012c).

Incarcerated women in Canada face numerous other concerns. Prisoners are 30 times more likely to have been infected with Hepatitis C and seven to ten times more likely to be infected with HIV than the general Canadian population. Women in general represent an increasing proportion of reported HIV cases in Canada, with Aboriginal women three times more likely to be affected by HIV than non-Aboriginal women (CAEFS, 2012b). 71% of women in maximum security prisons have attempted suicide, compared to 21% of men (Sapers, 2007). Prison is expensive for society: the cost of incarcerating an average federal female prisoner in 2004/5 was $150,000-$250,000 (Prison Justice, 2008).

In 1982, under the leadership of Prime Minister Pierre Trudeau, Canadians established the Charter of Rights and Freedoms. Since the Charter has been adopted, Canadians expect a just society; however, since then justice has become increasingly understood as punishment in the form of time behind bars. The current Canadian political climate under the Conservative government of Prime Minister Stephen Harper is one of "getting tough on crime." The need to keep Canadians safe with "get tough on crime" policies are not supported by statistical information on crime rates, which have been declining over the past decade (Canada Human Resources and Skills Development Canada, 2009). The Police-Reported Crime Severity Index (PRCSI) reported that crime in Canada in 2007 was of a less serious nature overall than what was reported ten years earlier (Fournier-Ruggles, 2011). Harper has been pushing towards an American model of prisons with talk about privatizing prisons, a horrifying notion to most Canadians. Harper's agenda directs Canadians towards a system of punishment rather than one of crime prevention, justice (equity), crime control, and reintegration. However, media coverage of crime in Canada paints a different picture and although most Canadians have never been touched by crime, and never will be, there is an increasing fear provoked by the rhetoric of the Conservative government. Harper's plan creates longer sentences, fewer rights for prisoners, and reduced chances for early release or pardons. This is where GELA's WPRC work joins with the women in a local federal prison.

Access to Information

Prisoners have the same information needs as people outside the prison walls, with supplementary needs for legal rights and process. They also encounter increased levels of restrictions. According to one definition from Business-Dictionary.com (2012), information is:

Data that (1) has been verified to be accurate and timely, (2) is specific and organized for a purpose, (3) is presented within a context that gives it meaning and relevance, and (4) that can lead to an increase in understanding and decrease in uncertainty. The value of information lies solely in its ability to affect a behavior, decision, or outcome. A piece of information is considered valueless if, after receiving it, things remain unchanged.

Incarcerated women cannot get information when they seek it, or in the ways they want to use it. Access to all information is limited, especially technological information. Services are almost non-existent for non-English-speaking inmates. There is no Internet access in prison. Committee members have made arrangements to demonstrate new technologies such as digital readers, but these sessions cannot offer wireless capabilities. The lack of access to the Internet means that women who are incarcerated for a longer period will have a greater disadvantage when reintegrating back into their community, yet seeking and retrieving information is vital for women to reintegrate. Working with the local public library, Edmonton Public Library (EPL), we can connect reintegrating women with Community Librarians and put them in touch with libraries that run book clubs or hold computer-training courses. Working at the prison demonstrates how information goes beyond politics, media, or data—information behind bars is not taken for granted, although most prison situations remain unchanged even when a woman has successfully accessed some needed information.

The Women's Prison and Reintegration Committee (WPRC)

WPRC is not exclusively librarians, although the majority of volunteers are professional librarians or university students with diverse backgrounds including in academic, legal, and public librarianship.

Initially, when WPRC began meeting with prison staff and negotiating the corrections system, we surveyed the women in prison to find out what services and programs they wanted. Within the first year of WPRC's involvement, a storybook project and a book club in the general population were formed, the library was weeded, and a collection development policy was written. Five years later, numerous concurring programs run throughout the year. We hope our involvement helps incarcerated women access information, prepare for their return to their communities, and connect with their families during their time at the prison. We try to address and support the information needs of prisoners, and we work to expose, educate, and agitate for change.

Moyra: *The first time I went to the prison stands out—turning off a busy road that leads to the prison, I was surprised by how un-prison-like the buildings seemed from the far end of the parking lot. As I got closer, I saw the razor barbed-wire surrounding the top of the fence and the security cameras and reassessed my initial impression. I parked and walked to the gate, aware that several of the cameras followed me, watched me, and recorded me. The gate clicked as I reached for it, and I realized someone inside had monitored my approach. I entered the building and was instructed to sign in and place all of my items in a bin and place the bin on the x-ray scanner. The prison entrance set up was similar to airport security—at least it was until the guard asked for a personal item, my car key, and swabbed it with a tiny cloth to check for drug residual on an ion scanner. After I was cleared, I was instructed to walk through a metal detector towards another guard who waited with hand-held scanner in the event that I set off alarms; I did not, thankfully. I was given a PPD (Personal Protection Device) to wear in case I needed help from the guards (I never have needed this device; I feel completely safe with the women). This process involves registering the device with the Duty Guard so staff knows the location that I will be while inside. The PPD is a large black unit that attaches to your belt and has a large red button that is easily set off, as we have discovered since our first visit. Once I had been cleared, I gathered the book bags, entered the main building, and headed down a hallway towards the library. Each visit, the procedures can vary slightly. A few times we have had the drug dog go through our bags. Usually the guards are courteous and friendly, and the process becomes less intimating over time. However, there have been visits when we have encountered staff that were not very welcoming, and we felt intimidated.*

Fireweed Library

Located in the main prison building, a small room with a window is home for the Fireweed Library collection, along with a table, chairs, and a desk with a (very old) computer. Five years ago, when WPRC began work at the prison, committee members and the inmate librarian met in this room and began weeding the collection. Developing and following a collection policy that incorporates the limits of the federal corrections system present challenges, but today the collection is more suited to the needs of the women. Old textbooks and titles such as *The Champagne Diet* and *How to Plan a Wedding for Under $10,000* were removed and replaced with best-selling novels and non-fiction biographies. We keep a list of requested titles on our blog (gelaprison.wordpress.com) and put effort into finding these titles through donations. Since space is at a premium on the metal shelves, when we receive more books than we can house, we donate extra resources to other agencies or sell them during fundraising events. The dated computer equipment is unreliable and often crashes, losing the catalog; this is an on-going challenge for the committee and the inmate librarian. One highlight of the collection is a used set of the 2008 edition of the Oxford English Dictionary (OED) that we recently acquired. A rural Alberta library that was going digital offered their copy of the OED to any library that was interested. Several libraries responded, but the OED was given to the Fireweed Library due to its limited (non-digital) resources. The women were thrilled to receive the 22-volume dictionary, and the OED is well used in its new home. Although most WPRC programs take place in the library, hobby/craft room, chapel, or gym, the women are proud of the library space, and it has become more user-centered as well as a safe space for the women to meet and share.

> Laurie: *Without GELA WPRC programs, our library would be nothing. We have the best prison library and it's due to the programs offered by WPRC. Before our volunteers, the books were old, nothing current and mostly romance and classics. GELA WPRC has given us the opportunity to expand our experiences through books, art, music, and mostly through getting to know us. They have helped build a community with positive interactions between us.*

Storybook Project

Storybook Project, a very popular program started by WPRC, allows women to choose a book to read to their children, partners, or siblings. Volunteers bring in their laptops and record the women reading aloud (one favorite is Robert Munch's *Love You Forever*). During each Storybook session, ten to 12 women are recorded. Afterwards, the volunteers burn the recording onto a compact disc, and the book and disc are sent to the woman's family. Special security considerations have to be taken to bring electronics into the prison; the laptops are checked and all wireless capabilities are disabled. Storybook is popular but not cheap, and costs run at about $20 per package. We use some donated books, but usually new books are bought to send with the disc. Reports and feedback from family members indicate that this project is very well-received; many of the women have come to trust "the librarians," and Storybook sign-up is full every month. People outside the prison love hearing about Storybook. We have had local media run stories as a Mother's Day special news article. The Storybook Project is good for opening a dialogue with our colleagues, friends, family, and the general public about the women in prison, their information needs, and how the committee works within the corrections system.

Kristin: *My daughter listens to the book I sent her from the Storybook Project every night before she goes to sleep. She loves it. It made me cry when I heard that. We really miss each other.*

Book Club(s)

In the first year we had only one book club, General Population book club, and we met once a month to discuss the book we had read. A Young Adult (YA) book club was added in 2011 to accommodate the varied reading levels of the women; plus, copies of YA books were among the most popular in circulation. Book club volunteers borrow book kits from the local libraries or put out calls to friends and family for specific books. Library-borrowed book kits have only ten copies, so the women share or read aloud to each other. Book club has generated new communities amongst the women; in the yard, discussions of the books are shared between women who normally would not be talking with each other: "Hey, have you gotten to that part yet about…"; "Don't tell me that, I'm not there yet"; "What did you think about…?"; or "Oh my god, can you believe that X did that to Z?"

Helen: *I love book club!*

Moyra: *We had read* Kite Runner *a few months earlier, and the women loved it so we brought in Khaled Hosseini's new book,* A Thousand Splendid Suns. *After reading Hosseini's second book, one of the women shared a personal story – she referred to a line in the book that said something like "in one second my whole life changed." The woman told us that she could relate to this line because she too had made such a decision in so short a time, and that decision was what had led her here to a federal prison. This story motivated other women to share, and soon most of the women had shared their stories. For some of the women this was the first time they had spoken out loud about their crime, its effects, and their journey here, to a federal prison. That day when I left the prison I remember feeling humbled by the honesty and the suffering that I had witnessed.*

Amanda: *I've never been in a room with a bunch of people I don't know very well talking about anything other than what we have in common – crime. When I went to book club, we had the book in common and got to share about that instead of a bunch of negative crap.*

Lynn: *The last book we read in book club is the best book ever. I loved it and I'm reading it for the second time!*

Book Borrowing/Exchange

One committee member, with the support of the local public library, EPL, spearheaded a monthly book borrowing for the general population women. Initially, random titles were brought in to the prison, and the women were allowed to check them out. Eventually several other committee members began helping with the ordering, picking up, and delivery of the requested books, and we developed a system. Once a month, volunteers are responsible for picking up resources that have been specifically requested from the local library and dropping them off on scheduled visits. When book borrowing began, concerns were raised regarding resources going missing due to the changing population in the prison. So far there has been an excellent return rate, and it is now a permanent program. The institution has a secure unit where we now offer services including monthly book borrowing, similar to general population book borrowing. The secure unit has increased restrictions compared to other areas of the prison, but the women appreciate the chance to request and receive books.

Christina: *The book club and book exchange program make me feel excited. When I really want to read something it makes me happy. Sometimes it's hard to find happy. Storybook Project allows me to give my children something while I'm away. It lets me reach out to them in a way that makes us feel closer and more connected.*

Christina, Lynn, Laurie, Amanda, and more: *When are the librarians coming with the books we ordered?*

Arlene: *I didn't know libraries had music!*

Brandy: *I like that I can ask for books and music and they bring what I want. They listen.*

Art Show – "Hidden Truths"

Other projects have sprung from these on-going projects, such as an art show, which was held at a local gallery throughout April and into May 2012. A group of committee members organized local artists to visit and run art sessions with the women. Many women created art that was displayed at the gallery, and the group made a big collaborative piece that was central to the installation. Women worked together weekly, for five months, to produce their individual and joint pieces. The resulting art show, "Hidden Truths," was installed (by committee members and women who had been released) at a local gallery, Latitude 53, and was very well attended and hailed as a huge success by the women, the prison officials, and the committee members. The act of creating art, both independently and collaboratively, had a significant and unexpected effect on the women. As an example, two of the women with completely opposite backgrounds and experiences, who were at first wary of each other, worked on a shared space for the production of the collaborative art piece. These two women began to experience each other differently through their drawings and paintings. As the collaborative art evolved, so too did the relationship and friendship between these women. Not just these two, but all of the women bonded. Friendships were shaped alongside works of art.

> Thelma: *Sometimes I find it hard to believe that people out there care so much. I picture them picking up books, putting together art supplies, getting ready to come in on the weekends and it touches me. It's such a nice thing to do.*

Writing and Author Visits

Committee volunteers have introduced creative writing initiatives to support literacy, including a monthly group where women wrote poetry, stories, and songs. These activities increased interest in books about writing and writers and inspired the women to make two zines and put on their own poetry slam. The time commitment and the production and distribution costs for the zines exceed the capabilities of the committee, however, and unfortunately the creation of the zines has been discontinued.

Author visits, arranged by committee volunteers, have been well-received by the women and prison officials. Several Canadian authors, including local Aboriginal writers, have visited the women. The visitors included Richard Van Camp from the Dogrib Nation and author of *The Lesser Blessed* and *Angel Wing Splash Pattern*; Hiromi Goto, author of *Half World* and *Darkest Light*; Drew Hayden Taylor, author of *Motorcycles and Sweetgrass* and *Funny, You Don't Look*

Like One; and Gabor Maté, author of *Scattered Minds: A New Look at the Origins and Healing of Attention Deficit Disorder* and *In the Realm of Hungry Ghosts: Close Encounters with Addiction*. These visits have been very popular with the women, and in some cases the authors offer to return. Richard Van Camp has visited several times and holds writing workshops with any women who are interested.

Funding

Funding for our work is an ongoing concern. We operate on a budget of approximately $2500 - $3500 a year. So far, fundraising efforts have been productive, and they are supported and attended by the broader library community. Successful fundraising events have included a pub night (Beers for Books) and a yard sale of books that had been donated but did not fit into the prison collection. Another yard sale, held recently at a local community hall, saw committee members raise over $1300 for the projects. Committee members have also been invited to give guest presentations at conferences, which draw interest and awareness, as well as the occasional honorarium. Many of the volunteers also spend their own money on books and library supplies. WPRC members have bought or donated copies of books that the women have asked for, especially books that are the most popular and have the longest wait list at the local public library. We all understand the frustration of being caught in the midst of a trilogy or series only to find that the next book is unavailable for three months. We have also received donations from other library organizations and library supporters. Even so, fundraising is on every WPRC meeting agenda.

WPRC Meetings

We stay organized through regular meetings, held at the prison (when possible) so the inmate librarian can participate. The meetings last about one and a half hours, and we hear reports from committee members responsible for organizing each project: General Population Book Club, YA Book Club, Secure Unit, Book Borrowing, Storybook, and any others running at that time, such as author visits or the art show. A secretary and treasurer also report at meetings, which are scheduled through email with programming staff from the institution also in attendance. This helps clarify expectations among staff, residents, and committee volunteers and enables us to plan as far in advance as possible. At these meetings we discuss plans for fundraising events, ask for support for current or proposed projects, and brainstorm new ideas. Aside from meetings, we communicate largely by email. Issues that arise get attended to right away by whoever is on email at the time. Because we cannot communicate with the inmate librarian when outside the prison, we rely on other committee members to convey information regarding needs, interests, and possible programs or author visits when they go in, usually monthly, to participate in programs. Volunteers sign up from the local university library school, take part in volunteer training from the institution, and often begin involvement with Storybook. A WPRC volunteer coordinates security clearance forms and volunteer memos in order to streamline required paperwork.

GELA

WPRC operates under the umbrella of the Greater Edmonton Library Association (GELA), grounding our efforts in the prison within the regional association of librarians. This supports and benefits our efforts, and, in turn, our outreach efforts benefit GELA by demonstrating social responsibility and the professional dedication to ensuring access to information for everyone. Another impact of WPRC's work is in the forging of space for librarians who are motivated by information ethics and social justice.

The tenacity, professionalism, and crucial groundwork of committee members have opened doors for the innovative programming that goes on today. Layers of community support ensure the continued success of the WPRC. As librarians, we try to make a difference through promoting literacy and literature, and by establishing relationships. That's also what we do in the prison. By modeling alternatives to standardized practices to the women in prison, prison staff, and our library colleagues, we hope to work towards righting some of the structural wrongs. We will continue to fight for access to information for all people, especially incarcerated individuals.

Gayle: *The other women on the committee drew me to want to volunteer in the prison. They used diplomacy, skill, vision, and strength to make a difference. I wanted to be like them. Passionate about information ethics, they back up convictions with action and negotiate a challenging environment. The librarians who volunteer at the prison recognize the privilege of "having access" and take a stand against disparity of information access by raising awareness about the inequities and injustices of restrictive, little, or no access.*

Sometimes I have noticed that when members of WPRC speak about the work in the prison, they speak with humility, almost quietly. This requires the listener to work, focus, try to understand, and read between the lines. Speaking quietly is fitting if we think of the work in the prison happening in an area of liminal territory. The ability to do work is dependent on maintaining the trust of corrections, the women, and our colleagues.

Personal Challenges and Rewards

While volunteering at a federal prison enhances our lives and provides new experiences, we also face many challenges. Working with incarcerated women places us directly in an environment that calls into question many of our preconceptions about crime, prisoners, and the people who work with them. As volunteers inside a federal prison, we must see beyond the destructive tabloid headlines that offer easy solutions to complex problems. We ourselves are faced with emotional trauma just from witnessing life on the inside. Not everyone can handle the stress of prison work and coming face-to-face with institutional rigidity; mental health issues; addictions; and the ongoing suffering from past, present, and systemic abuse and violence. Our committee volunteers learn about prison life and the information needs of incarcerated women with effects that often change their own understandings of the justice system and crime in Canada. WPRC volunteers in turn educate their friends, families, and larger communities.

> Gayle: *Before going into the prison, I understood that the women in prison had lost the liberty to move around and be free in the world. I could not comprehend the limitations of their freedom to learn, know, and even think. A great number of the women have had limited access to education and experience difficulties articulating many of their information needs. Many have had negative experiences with literacy in the past while in school. In some cases their words have disappeared, been used against them, been manipulated, or been disregarded.*

Some of the things we learn quickly from the women include how complicated "justice" can be. Outside of prison, simplistic opinions of the justice system abound. Some opinions suggest prison is a deterrent for criminals, or that being incarcerated will provide people with the "help" they need. These opinions place the need for change firmly on the incarcerated person without considering the complexity of his or her life; societal stereotypes and prejudices; individual situations; or the intersections of poverty, abuse, addictions, and/or mental health problems. Through our work, we have learned that changes are necessary in the justice system and indeed throughout society in order to ensure that the system actually works for those it was designed to serve. When building relationships on the inside, we have learned that many women have been victimized throughout their lives by poverty, abuse, and crime, and that it is not just the prisoner who is being punished; it is their entire family and especially their children. Our intentions to supply books, information, and programs for women in prison has developed into working for change and finding our common and interlinked humanity with women behind bars.

> Gayle: *Undertaking such work can force a renegotiating of personal social supports. Relationships with friends and colleagues can become strained when conflicting values become illuminated, such as realizing that what some people understand as unjust and abusive behavior, others see as deserved punishment for "convicted criminals."*

Five years ago Fireweed Library was stark, and now it's brimming with books. Women come not only to find books, conversation, and information, but also to connect with each other. Together with the women in prison, we have built a community that is working for change. The library has become a central space for the women, and this is the most rewarding and tangible library work many WPRC volunteers have experienced.

> Moyra: *The inmate librarian supports our work in the prison by encouraging others to become involved and by organizing women on the inside – she has created community behind the prison walls as well as outside the walls with the committee volunteers. The library has become a hub of the prison community, and information is being shared within a group of women that have very circumscribed access. WPRC does not seek to speak on behalf of the women behind bars, but we do want to make sure that their voices are heard. The women who come to WPRC programs and share their experiences are the reason we do this. Their insights teach us, amaze us, and humble us deeply.*

Conclusion

Through the work of the WPRC with the incarcerated women, we are building an expanded version of community librarianship. New programs and projects are taking place in the prison library. The best result is that these initiatives are no longer just presented to the women; they are created by the women, as witnessed by the development of the art sessions and art show. The women request resources, express needs, and practice talking about their opinions of literature. Information ethics and issues of access, diversity, and intellectual freedom all motivate WPRC members, no matter how the prison system can constrict our work. The dichotomy of justice and injustice, responsibilities to vulnerable populations, and a dedication to access to information and resources underpin our commitment. We are learning from the women; they are our biggest teachers. For members of WPRC, this library work is a form of activism. Using our training in service of incarcerated women, working with women for reintegration, sharing books and information, and doing research for projects has heightened the women's skills as well as our own, and it has created new communities that work together for change. The Fireweed Library and the WPRC not only reflect this community, it *is* this community.

> Cathee: *I see so many changes in the women since our WPRC volunteers have been coming here. They come and tell me about their children's reactions when they get the books from the Storybook Project. The sign-up sheet is full every month for that activity. I see women crying out of gratefulness to be able to send their children their voices. The book clubs provide a place where people with "softer voices" can speak as well. This is not to say that the book clubs are filled with soft voices. I mean it's an opportunity to speak on something we all have in common — the books. Differences are set aside, opinions are exchanged, and we're able to just talk. It develops a sense of belonging, and I love it.*

> *The art classes and writing circles are amazing ways to express our creativity and individuality in an environment where conforming is rewarded by our keepers. We can be who we really are through our writing and art. This is such an important component in healing.*

> *The book exchange is my favorite. I have been incarcerated for 13.5 years and so much has changed in the world. With book exchange I can request books on subjects that interest me that I would otherwise have absolutely ZERO access to any other way. We have no internet here, so the exchange is an essential information line that is helping me to try and stay in touch with what is important to me. My cousin and I are reading the same book right now (*The Art of Happiness in a Troubled World*). We do this all the time and connect through the subject matter as we apply it to our lives inside and out. The women get very excited about the delivery of books and music the third week of every month.*

> *We had a library audit this month. National headquarters came down and were very impressed with how our library ran, the scope of people we could reach with our programs, and the degree of community involvement. We have no budget at all from the government, so to see a wonderfully-run library in the system was refreshing for them. I told National that all of our services are provided by volunteers who raise money from the community. We are extremely well supported. We are so fortunate and we owe all of GELA a huge THANK YOU!*

References

American Library Association. (2004, June 29). Core values of librarianship. Retrieved from http://www.ala.org/offices/oif/statementspols/corevaluesstatement/corevalues

Canadian Association of Elizabeth Fry Societies. (2012a). Criminalized and imprisoned women. Retrieved from http://www.elizabethfry.ca/eweek2011e/Criminalized_and_Imprisoned_Women.doc

Canadian Association of Elizabeth Fry Societies. (2012b). Health and mental health. Retrieved from http://elizabethfry.ca/wwdcms/uploads/Health%20and%20Mental%20Health.pdf

Canadian Association of Elizabeth Fry Societies. (2012c). Issues associated with increased criminalization of women. Retrieved from http://www.elizabethfry.ca/eweek2011e/Issues_Associated_with_Increased_Criminalization_of_Women.doc

Canadian Library Association. (2008, May 25). CLA position statement on diversity and inclusion. Retrieved from http://www.cla.ca/AM/Template.cfm?Section=Position_Statements &Template=/CM/ContentDisplay.cfm&ContentID=4713

Canadian Library Association. (1985, November 18). CLA position statement on intellectual freedom. Retrieved from http://www.cla.ca/AM/Template.cfm?Section=Position_Statements &Template=/CM/ContentDisplay.cfm&ContentID=3047

Chaparro-Univazo, S. (2007). Where social justice meets librarianship. *Information for Social Change, 25*, 33-38.

Correctional Service Canada. (2010). Women's corrections: Quick facts. Retrieved from http://www.csc-scc.gc.ca/text/pblct/qf/08-eng.shtml

Fournier-Ruggles, L. (2011). The cost of getting tough on crime: Isn't prevention the policy answer? *Journal of Public Policy, Administration and Law, 2*(1), 19-28.

Human Resources and Skills Development Canada. (2009). Departmental performance report - 2011–12 estimates. Retrieved from http://www.hrsdc.gc.ca/eng/publications_resources/dpr/dpr/dpr_2011_2012/page01.shtml

Information. (2012). In *Business Dictionary.com*. Retrieved from http://www.businessdictionary.com/definition/information.html

Prison Justice. (2008). Facts & statistics. Retrieved from: http://www.prisonjustice.ca/politics/facts_stats.html

Sapers, H. (2007). *Annual Report of the office of the correctional investigator, 2006-2007*. Ottawa: Minister of Public Works and Government Services Canada.

In the Archive

Let's Use What Works: The Radical Archives of Philadelphia and Traditional Archival Literature

Scott Ziegler

Introduction

When we lose the records of social movements, we lose the possibilities that they offer. We lose possible ways of living our own lives. Our world is poorer for the loss. Robert Helms (2006), explaining why we should care about the collection of anarchist histories he has struggled to compile and share, writes: "Often a young person will be told again and again that anarchist ideas are nonsense, by people who have an endless parade of generals and heads of state to use as examples for argument and role models for themselves." For anyone who wants a different way to live—a life free of the constraints of the state, in this example—the anarchists' stories are vital examples.

Andrew Cornell, writing about one particular organization—the Movement for a New Society (MNS)—makes much the same point:

> As such, it deserves to be not only remembered out of respect, but studied assiduously by contemporary anti-authoritarians so that we might take stock and introduce new variants into each and every one of our new efforts. As MNS makes clear, when we don't learn from our mistakes, we haven't fully learned from our great successes. (2011, p. 59)

Cornell, like Helms, wants to use political lessons from the past to directly influence political actions in the future. His history is meant to be "militant coresearch," by which he means, "research conducted by, with, and for radicals with the express purpose of gaining insights that concretely facilitate current and future movement activities" (p. 8).

Helms and Cornell both express desires to use history to engage with the future. Both recognize the importance of saving histories traditionally ignored by collecting repositories, and both focus on Philadelphia-centered movements. As such, each can be seen as issuing a challenge taken up by the Radical Archives of Philadelphia.

The Radical Archives of Philadelphia (RAP) is a repository dedicated to collecting, preserving, and promoting access to the material history of the progressive and radical left organizations and movements in Philadelphia, Pennsylvania. Founded in 2011, the RAP is an all-volunteer, collectively-run community archives with a growing collection of physical and digital collections from organizations, individuals, and protest movements that document the rich counterculture of the city.

This essay will use the RAP as a test case[1] to explore the relation between community collections and traditional archival literature. Like Helms and Cornell, I want to provide examples for others to use; in this case, the example is to help others when starting alternative archival collections in the future. To this end, I'll be offering advice based on the experience of the RAP. There is always more history than can be captured; there are always more examples to save. It is my hope that other people are motivated to seek out neglected material and work to save it for future generations.

This essay is concerned with two types of literature. The first is about community archives. I will argue that this literature offers no help for those of us interested in starting our own archives. I point this out to draw attention to the need for practical advice, not to claim the authors in question failed to do what they did not set out to do. The second type of literature is what I'll call traditional archival literature. This type comprises books and articles written by and for archivists. It represents the collected wisdom of the profession and is invaluable to those of us trained in archival science as well as those of us who are not. As we'll see, while there's plenty in traditional archival literature that is not applicable to those interested in starting their own community collection, there is

---

1. To do so, I'll be using the RAP as it exists at the time of this writing. As a relatively new organization, and as a collection that relies on free housing and volunteer labor, the Radical Archives of Philadelphia has gone through a number of significant changes in a short amount of time, and it is likely to experience more changes in the near future. However, many of these changes are secondary to the deeper concerns represented here; the central themes are expected to hold for the RAP, and continue to be relevant to other projects as well. To stay current with the changes, follow us at phillyradicalarchives.org.

much that is relevant. Out of concern that too much is lost when we ignore the literature completely, I argue that we should use what works from the tradition as we struggle to preserve the histories that enable new futures.

Community Collections

Before we move on to specific suggestions for starting and maintaining collections, some justifications are in order. First, some terminology. For the purposes of this essay, I'll be making a distinction between "community collections" and collections that exist in established institutions. By community collections, I mean collections created by grassroots efforts to save material that otherwise would be lost. Community collections are grassroots in that those doing the collecting tend to be involved in the organizations and movements being documented. Additionally, they are grassroots because they are formed in a "bottom-up" manner. Instead of being mandated by a governing body, they are formed by people who self-organize for the cause. Often the structure of the community collection matches the content of the collection. For example, the Radical Archives of Philadelphia is managed by a collective and relies on consensus decision-making. It is also important to note here that despite the use of the RAP as our example, community collections are not restricted to politically-oriented frameworks.[2]

The term "community collections" also has the benefit of not needing to draw a firm line between different types of collections. Many community collections have elements of both libraries and archives. Some material might be widely-distributed books and pamphlets that can be checked out by users. Other material might be committee notes and personal papers, which can be used only by researchers in-house. The term "community collections" cuts across these distinctions and allows us one term for the full spectrum.

Collections in established institutions, by contrast, exist in repositories such as institutional archives—within governments, schools, churches, etc.—as well as historical societies, manuscript repositories, and the like. They tend to rely on a "top-down" approach and are bureaucratically structured in a way that reflects this. To make this distinction is not to downplay the importance of established institutions. Rather, it is to draw attention to what falls outside of the established institutions and how these records can best be preserved in a manner befitting their creation and use.

---

2.   For a couple of Philadelphia-based community collections less overtly situated around political orientation, see the South Asian American Digital Archive (www.saadigitalarchive.org) and the Soapbox Zine Library (www.phillysoapbox.org).

Secondly, why should anyone care about starting a community collection? After all, there are many collecting repositories around the country. These repositories have buildings, climate control, staff, and budgets for basic supplies—elements, as we'll see below, that must be formed from scratch when one starts a new collection. There are many reasons some communities might prefer not to have their material housed in an established collection. One recent example is the efforts by various Occupy protesters to control the material created during the mass protests of 2011. Some protesters involved in Occupy Wall Street think of traditional archives as means for the powerful and rich to reinforce normative interpretations of society (Samtani, 2011; Schuessler, 2012). As such, they have attempted to maintain their own collections. Another recent example is the current dispute over the Protocols for Native American Archival Materials (PNAAM), which proposes the removal and/or restriction of some archival items wrongly appropriated from Native American communities (Mathiesen, 2012).

Philadelphia has a number of institutions that could, in principle, collect the material that the Radical Archives of Philadelphia exists to collect. However, many of the activists with whom the RAP works feel uneasy about giving material to these institutions. Reasons are numerous, but among the most cited are long-standing feelings of distrust toward university settings that continue to alter socio-economic landscapes of the neighborhoods in which many of the activists live and work. For example, two universities in the city are currently completing "master plans" that include buying land that is presently used for activist collective housing. The loss of long-standing activist centers to these organizations does little to ingratiate them to the community, and the archives of these universities are not seen as legitimate houses for the memory of the activists. There is the additional concern that the material would not be accessible to people without academic credentials or proper identification. These restrictions are seen as too exclusionary for many who resist submitting to standardized relationships to the state. Put bluntly, the universities (as well as many other collecting institutions) are often seen as power-hungry and elitist. A central impetus to the creation of the RAP was to provide a space to save activist material that escapes many of the criticisms of the institutional collections.

Community Archives Literature

Having made a distinction between community collections and collections in established institutions, and having explained why anyone would care to go through the trouble of creating community collections, we can now briefly explore the literature on community archives. The current article's emphasis on practical steps and considerations is meant to counteract a particular shortcoming in the literature on community archives. While it is the argument that there is much to learn from archives literature as a whole, there is much that can be improved in the literature on community archives.

Many articles on community archives fall into at least one of three categories. First, many highlight established institutions that have some subset of collections that document a community. These collections often trace themselves back to the original call by Howard Zinn and F. Gerald Ham to collect more broadly from underdocumented segments of society (Ham, 1975; Zinn, 1977; Henry, 1980). The Swarthmore Peace Archives is an example. The Peace Archives collects the records of movements and causes related to peace organizations (Brinton, 1951). The Peace Archives is a valuable resource to researchers—just as articles that highlight such collections are useful for a number of reasons—but the literature about it does little to help those of us who want to preserve neglected histories.

The second dominant trend in the literature on community archives is articles written from the outside. That is, community collections are described by those who do not work in the day-to-day function of the archives. There are, of course, reasons to appreciate these articles, not the least of which is the service they provide in arguing for the importance of community archives. Andrew Flinn, who publishes widely on the topic, argues that the material preserved in community archives "tell all our stories and that we all, professionals and non-professionals, need to find a way of ensuring that these community archives are preserved and not lost through our neglect" (Flinn, 2007). As important as these insights are, they provide little practical help for those interested in creating the collections that preserve these stories.

The third strand in the literature on community archives relies too heavily on theoretical discussions and philosophical debates to the detriment of offering positive advice on the creation of community collections. Many published accounts of community archives deal with issues of post-structural definitions of "identity" and "subjectivity." These issues are interesting, and some promote the cause of community collections to some extent. The problem, however, is that to focus on these issues when—and only when—dealing with community collections effectively separates these collections from the mainstream concern of established institutions. Christine N. Paschild (2012) critiques this practice. "The history," she writes, that community archives collect, "just like the community of its origin, is not inherently separate from, independent of, or marginal to the broader history of the United States. Nor is it any more or less subjective than the history documented by any other collection in any other archives" (p. 141).

Starting an Archive

Founding members of the Radical Archives of Philadelphia included professionally trained archivists who were familiar with the deep body of knowledge on archival practice and theory. An understanding of the literature also brings an understanding that our project represents a significant departure from the literature. But we did not need to start from scratch. Established archival literature includes numerous books on the subject of starting an archives. Of particular note are Elizabeth Yankel's *Starting an Archives* and Gregory Hunter's *Developing and Maintaining Practical Archives*. There is much to learn from these books, including practical advice on creating mission statements and collecting scopes. Indeed, the founding of the RAP benefited greatly from the advice and suggestions of these books. However, there are significant areas that are not applicable—or that need significant revision—for community collections.

For example, because these books assume the archive in question would be part of a larger organization, they stress the need to establish authority, often in the form of an official mandate, as well as funding and continued support (structurally and financially) from the larger institution (Yankel, 1994). Collections that seek to document a community do not have a clear body from whom to ask for authority. Often the authority to collect archives is tied to the fact that the members of the community to be documented have a central role in the archives.

For the RAP, like other community collections, there is no mandate to seek. Instead we met with members of the activist community. We attended meetings of local left-wing protest groups to explain the mission of the RAP. The authority that the Radical Archives of Philadelphia now has is based largely on our early efforts to explain our project and the intention of creating a space to preserve and share the work that these organizations are doing. Authority also rests on the political and ideological orientation of those of us who work with the RAP. To date, volunteers who have worked with the Radical Archives of Philadelphia have also been active in Books Through Bars, the Defenestrator, the Philadelphia Chapter of the National Lawyers Guild, the Radical Library of Philadelphia, and the Soapbox Zine Library,[3] as well as collective houses, which serve as long-standing centers for activism in Philadelphia.

---

3.   For more information about these organizations see, respectively: Books Through Bars: booksthroughbars.org; The Defenestrator: www.defenestrator.org; National Lawyers Guild of Philadelphia: nlgphiladelphia.org; Soapbox Zine Library: www.phillysoapbox. org; Life Center Association, for collective housing: www.vortexhouse.org/LCA/history. shtml.

Collection Development

The SAA Glossary defines collection development as the "policies and procedures used to select materials that the repository will acquire, typically identifying the scope of creators, subjects, formats, and other characteristics that influence the selection process" (Pearce-Moses). As such, collection development refers to the big-picture decisions of what an archives will collect. For example, institutional archives – archives that serve businesses, universities, etc. – determine the collecting scope based on the larger organization they serve (Cox, 1992). A university archives, say, collects material that documents the history and business of the university (Maher, 1992). Collection development also entails the means by which the collections grow within these scopes. For institutional archives, new material is acquired by working with the offices in the institution that make the records. This often includes working with the records managers and instituting record retention schedules (Maher, 1992).

For community collections, the collection scope is tailored to the community to be documented. To document a community, a community archives must understand what types of records are being created, and how best to acquire the records. Often, those involved in the community archives are also members of the community being documented. For the Radical Archives of Philadelphia, one of the central functions of many of our volunteers is to act as a liaison between the RAP and the various other organizations in which they participate. Many of our earliest collections have come from organizations that our volunteers are active in.

For community collections, the acquisition of new material can be as simple as picking it up off the street. An early effort by the RAP to document the current happenings in Philadelphia included collecting flyers "from the wild." RAP volunteers would remove flyers for events (meetings, protests, film screenings, etc.) from public places (coffee shops, telephone poles, etc.). This method of collecting has several significant advantages. First, it enables a type of snapshot of the activist community of Philadelphia. For all the benefit of new media, the majority of sizable gatherings still rely on flyers as a significant source of advertising. Second, it provides an easy way to get started. Interested in starting an archive, but not sure where to begin? Grab something that was made by the people you're interested in documenting and put it in a folder. Keep doing this until you have several thick folders, and name your new collection "miscellaneous flyer collection." A third benefit is that this encouraged the RAP members to stay up-to-date on the happenings in the community. If something big happened and we didn't see it coming, we knew we weren't doing as well as we could.

Archival Housing

How best to store archival material is, understandably, a central concern in archival literature. Archives are, in many ways, defined by their holdings, so the manner in which the holdings are housed is of central importance. For the purposes of this essay, housing has both a micro and a macro level. The micro level refers to what we use to store the individual records in, namely boxes and folders; the macro level refers to the building we use to house the collection. Archival literature has plenty to say about both. Early archival practice moved from the use of boxes to the practice of binding together manuscripts and other records, only to move back to boxes again (Schellenberg, 1965). Contemporary practices, collectively known as holding maintenance, emphasize the use of acid-free folders and boxes, and the storage of material in easy-to-use storage containers that offer sturdy physical support to the material (Garlick, 1992). The use of acid-free folders and boxes is now an industry standard.

Community collections have a lot to learn from the archives tradition in terms of housing. The use of boxes and folders to support, separate, and protect material is a basic step in the arrangement and description of archives, and one of the central means by which to prepare material for researcher use and long-term storage. However, acknowledging the benefits of holding maintenance is only the first step. Because many community collections lack the resources to purchase acid-free folders and boxes, understanding how to work around financial obstacles is an important second step.

The Radical Archives of Philadelphia balances the need for proper holding maintenance against the reality of operating on the budget of a small, independent community archive. We have found that when larger archives in the area perform large-scale re-housing projects on their collections, they are often willing to donate used material to us. This is a good way to receive inexpensive boxes and folders, although there is a risk that used housing will acquire acidity from the material it housed, a process known as acid migration (Roberts & Etherington, 1982). Such acidity can be detected, and the risk mitigated, with the use of a Ph testing pen—a simple and cost-effective tool.

For new community collections, seeking housing material can be tied together with efforts to reach out to established archives and make valuable connections. Local and regional archives associations exist across the country and can be used as a front door to the archives community in the area. Seek out the communication channels of the association (email lists, blogs, social media sites), and announce the formation of your new collection. Let the wider archival world know that you exist, and that you are looking for donations of used material. There's a good chance that a nearby repository is doing a re-housing project, so catch them before they throw all of those folders away. If you don't hear anything back from the group as a whole, seek out individual repositories that you think might be interested in hearing more about your project. Be friendly and open, but also know your audience. If you are preserving the records of abortion-rights proponents, say, don't expect a lot of enthusiasm from archives attached to Catholic churches.

The macro level of archival housing refers to the location of the archives. Concerning the location of the building, it is important to be near the community that you are serving. The placement of an archives says a lot about it. The archives literature provides community collections with a lot to think about in this regard. Where should we be? Who should we be near? In his discussion of the formation of archives for colleges and universities, William Maher (1992) points out that the placement of the collection—in the library, in the basement, in the alumni office—sets the tone for how the collection is treated within the larger institution.

Because community collections are often not associated with larger institutions, location presents both a special challenge and a unique opportunity. How best to situate a community collection? First, consider where a substantial portion of the records are created. Does the community in question have a space that acts as a central location for decisions or activities? Second, consider where the people in the community are likely to be. When the archives are in a recognizable location, the importance of the collection to the community is more easily understood.

The Radical Archives of Philadelphia takes a semi-centered approach to the issue of macro housing. To house the majority of our physical collection, we sought out a location of central importance to the activist community in the city: an anarchist, collectively-run bookstore that has long served Philadelphia as a central meeting place for the individuals and organizations we are documenting. The benefits to this location are many. First, we are easily visible to a large portion of the people that we are likely to approach when we are seeking out new records. Second, this visibility legitimizes the collection as part of the community. And third, it is convenient to have the collection where we already spend time; as members of the activist community, many RAP members are likely to frequent the location.

Any location also has its downsides. Ours has a few. Environmental controls are few and far between (more on this below). The crowd that frequents the bookstore tends toward a homogenous demographic. This restricted user base can give the impression of an unwelcome environment to other people—a particularly unfortunate side effect for those of us trying to capture a wide variety of protest movements. The location also tends to scare off potential researchers and donors who might not feel they are appropriately committed to an activist lifestyle to feel comfortable spending time in the bookstore. This type of unconscious exclusion is a constant struggle for the RAP, just as it is for many of the organizations with whom we work. Writing about this same problem in activist circles, Cornell (2011) points out, "what we need to realize is that people who want to change the world come from many places, have different visions of what that new world will be like, do their political work in different ways," and pursue the change in a variety of different ways (p. 182).

Several of these concerns led the Radical Archives to adopt our current semi-centered approach. While we house much of our material together, there are collections that are housed in other locations around the city. At the time of this writing, as we negotiate with new organizations and individuals, we ask about housing. As part of our initial survey, we inquire as to any possible space the organization has that they can use to store the material. Under this model, the material will be fully processed by the RAP and kept with the organization. When researchers wish to view it, we will either treat it as off-site storage and bring the material to the central location for use, or coordinate with the organization to have the researcher use the material there. In either case, a member of the RAP will be on hand. As the RAP continues to acquire material, we foresee the semi-centered model becoming increasingly important.

Environmental Controls

Discussions of archival housing often include issues of environmental control as well as the placement of an archival collection (Balloffet, 2005). Environmental controls refer to the ability to mitigate the damage to material that happens as a result of temperature fluctuation, humidity, and light. These considerations are important, and implementing them is often very expensive. Usually, community collections have no choice but to focus on the more manageable tasks of properly housing material on the box and folder level. Though it would be ideal to also offer comprehensive environmental controls, many community collections can rightfully take comfort in the fact that material is in much better care than it would be if never collected at all. In the world of community collections, it is important to strive for the best; it is also important to not let the perfect become the enemy of the good.

That being said, there are some basic steps that any community collection can take to help alleviate some environmental concerns. First, consider the macro housing. When deciding where to keep your archives, consider—along with the behavior and meeting places of the community—the safety of the building.

Are there any environmental controls—air conditioning in the summer, heat in the winter? An environment with stable temperature and humidity is best. Are there water pipes near the collection? These could leak or burst, causing irreparable damage to the collection. Is it feasible to move the collection away from pipes, or cover the collection with tarp? Can you keep the material at least three inches off the ground in case there is a flood?

Second, consider multiple locations for material. While it's important to have a location that clearly associates the archives with the community, it's also important to have a backup plan in case of an emergency. The RAP works with a network of other community collections in the Philadelphia area to ensure mutual emergency housing if any collection needs it. Should the RAP need to evacuate our central location, we feel confident that there will be a temporary location for us to continue our work.

Conclusion

The Radical Archives of Philadelphia—like all community collections—represents an important effort to save and preserve examples that would otherwise be left out of the historical record.

Community collections, often started and maintained by volunteers with small or nonexistent budgets, have much to gain from paying attention to the established archival tradition. They also have much to gain from understanding how to change the aspects of that tradition that do not apply to them. The above considerations serve as a starting point to understand how community collections can strike this balance. The topics that were chosen barely scratch the surface of the literature created for and by archivists. There is much more to learn for those interested in using what works from the tradition as we strike out on a new path, including fundraising, volunteer relations, and researcher access. It is the hope of the author that the practical advice gained from the formation and continued evolution of the Radical Archives of Philadelphia points the way for future projects.

References

Balloffet, N. (2005). *Preservation and conservation for libraries and archives*. Chicago, IL: American Library Association.

Brinton, E. S. (1951). Archives of causes and movements: Difficulties and some solutions as illustrated by the Swarthmore College peace collection. *American Archivist, 14*(2). Retrieved from http://archivists.metapress.com/content/q658728853172774/fulltext.pdf

Cornell, A. (2011). *Oppose and propose!* Oakland, CA: AK Press.

Cox, R. (1992). *Managing institutional archives: Foundational principles and practices*. Westport, CT: Greenwood Press.

Flinn, A. (2007). Community histories, community archives: Some opportunities and challenges. *Journal of the Society of Archivists, 28*(2), 151-176. doi: 10.1080/00379810701611936

Garlick, K. (1992). Archives preservation update holdings: Maintenance. *The Book and Paper Group Annual, 11*. Retrieved from http://cool.conservation-us.org/coolaic/sg/bpg/annual/v11/bp11-36.html

Ham, F. G. (1975). The archival edge. *American Archivist, 38*(1), 5-13. Retrieved from http://archivists.metapress.com/content/7400r86481128424

Helms, R. (2006). *Dead anarchists*. Retrieved from http://www.deadanarchists.org/

Henry, L. (1980). Collecting policies of special collections subject repositories. *American Archivist, 43*(1), 57-63.

Hunter, G. (2003). *Developing and maintaining practical archives* (2nd ed.). Chicago, IL: Neal-Schuman.

Maher, W. (1992). *The management of college and university archives*. Metuchen, NJ: Scarecrow Press.

Mathiesen, K. (2012). A defense of Native Americans' rights over their traditional cultural expressions. *American Archivist, 75*(2), 456-481.

Paschild, C. N. (2012). Community archives and the limitations of identity: Considering discursive impact on material needs. *American Archivist, 75*(1), 125-142.

Pearce-Moses, R. *A glossary of archival and records terminology*. Retrieved from http://www2.archivists.org/glossary

Roberts, M., & Etherington, D. (1982). *Bookbinding and the conservation of books: A dictionary of descriptive terminology*. Washington, DC: Government Printing Office.

Samtani, H. (2011, December 26). The anarchivists: Who owns the Occupy Wall Street narrative? Retrieved from http://thebrooklynink.com/2011/12/26/39230-the-anarchivists-who-owns-the-occupy-wall-street-narrative

Schellenberg , T. R. (1965). *The management of archives*. New York, NY: Columbia University Press.

Schuessler, J. (2012, May 2). Occupy Wall Street: From the streets to the archives. Retrieved from http://artsbeat.blogs.nytimes.com/2012/05/02/occupy-wall-street-from-the-streets-to-the-archives

Yankel, E. (1994). *Starting an archives*. Metuchen, NJ: Scarecrow Press.

Zinn, H. (1977). Secrecy, archives, and the public interest. *Midwestern Archivist, 2*(2), 20-21.

"Less Rent, More Control!": Creating an Accessible Archive for New York City's Oldest Tenants Union

Maggie Schreiner

Introduction

For over half a century, the Metropolitan Council on Housing (MCH) has been at the forefront of the most important struggles for tenant justice in New York City. Founded in 1959, MCH originally brought together liberals and radicals working to oppose urban renewal projects in communities across the city. Since then, the organization has employed a diverse array of strategies in pursuit of decent, integrated, and affordable housing for tenants in New York City. These tactics have included rent strikes, rallies, annual lobbying trips to the state capital in Albany, occupations or pickets of government agencies and homes of abusive landlords, and support for squatters. Branch offices have offered tenant-staffed rent clinics, hotlines, and educational seminars, and the organization publishes a monthly newsletter, *Tenant/Inquilino*, as well as hosting the weekly radio show "Housing Notebook." Throughout its history, MCH has rejected formal paths to political power, instead relying on grassroots organizing and tenant mutual aid.

Over the course of decades of grassroots organizing, direct action, lobbying, and public education, the organization has assembled a large collection of unique historical materials, including documents, ephemera, newspapers, and photographs. Many of these items were donated to the Tamiment Library and Robert F. Wagner Labor Archives at New York University in 1995. Drawing my inspiration from the community archives movement and collaborative history production, my aim has been to make the archival materials accessible particularly to the organization's tenant membership. The first phase of this project, completed as the final requirement for the Archives and Public History Masters program at New York University, resulted in the creation of an online digital exhibition and archive that can be viewed at www.metcouncilonhousing.org/our_history. The site was designed to display the rich depth of materials in the MCH archives, provide contextualizing information, and inform the current political work of the organization.

[Banner for the online exhibition
and archive, May 2012]

A community-university partnership formed the basis of the first phase of the project: MCH provided direction and the overall framework of the project, while New York University supplied the technical and academic resources to develop a publicly accessible archive. This project phase encompassed the following components:

- Research: Primary and secondary source research to identify key political campaigns and organizers
- Digitization: Preservation-quality digitization of over 300 photographs and manuscript materials
- Exhibition: Development of an online exhibit highlighting archival materials within a contextualizing narrative, and an online display of additional archival materials with associated metadata

MCH staff identified the type of project that would be the most useful to the organization; the Tamiment Library and Robert F. Wagner Labor Archives housed, preserved, and provided access to the archival materials; and NYU's Digital Library Technology Services provided advice and equipment for the digitization process. Finally, historical scholarship informed the framework and content of the project, and current authorities in the field provided feedback on the online exhibit.

Overall, this project was intended to be a case study of a community-university partnership that aimed to document an important activist organization.

After a brief discussion of the academic literature informing this project—including calls for political engagement in the archival profession and recommendations gleaned from case studies of the community archives movement—I will discuss the process of developing a collaborative project design with several stakeholders, as well as building institutional partnerships. Discussion of the project implementation forms the bulk of this essay, and this section includes research and digitization, metadata standards and Web development, exhibition planning and review. I conclude with a summary of the challenges, outcomes, and future plans for this project. Through the project itself and its description herein, I hope to demonstrate the role that archives and collaborative history production can have in supporting grassroots organizing, community building, and daily struggles for justice.

Background Literature

Over the past decade, there has been a growing scholarly debate challenging the long-assumed impartiality of the archive. The profession has increasingly engaged with the idea of the archivist as an active constructor of the historical record, prompting in turn a growing imperative to deliberately democratize the archive through revisiting traditional assumptions about archival professionalism and pursuing community and political engagement. This debate began with Howard Zinn's challenge to the archival profession, issued at the 1970 Society of American Archivists Annual Meeting:

> [T]he rebellion of the archivist against his normal role is not, as so many scholars fear, the politicizing of a neutral craft, but the humanizing of an inevitably political craft.[...] Our choice is not between being political or not. Our choice is to follow the politics of the going order, that is, do our job within the priorities and directions set by the dominant forces of society, or else to promote those human values of peace, equality, and justice, which our present society denies. (Zinn, 1977)

Zinn concluded his presentation with two proposals: that archivists actively campaign for open access to government documents, and that they intentionally include materials related to ordinary people in the archival record.

The issues that Zinn brought to the 1970 meeting of the Society of American Archivists have emerged as central themes in the current discussion about political engagement in the archive. A diverse body of scholarship acknowledging the power of the archive has emerged from South Africa, Europe, Canada, and the United States. Verne Harris (2005) states that "the archives *is* politics—not that it is political, but that it is politics" (p. 173). Specifically, Harris has explored concepts of justice in the archive through the South African experience of the destruction of records in the last years of Apartheid and through the Truth and Reconciliation Commission. Not only did the Apartheid government's destruction of records conceal human rights violations during that era, but their theft of records from anti-Apartheid activists resulted in the loss of a rich archive documenting struggle against the Apartheid state (Harris, 2002, p. 223).

Randall C. Jimerson has also written extensively, from a North American perspective, on the professional responsibility of archivists with regard to social justice (2007, 2009). He suggests that if we, as archivists, shift our professional understanding from archives as serving the nation-state to archives as serving the public and democratic accountability, we must assume a high degree of political responsibility. Jimerson (2009) rejects the notion of the archivist as an impartial custodian of the historical record and instead champions that of the archivist as politically engaged and in a position to "address social issues without abandoning standards of fairness, honesty, detachment and transparency" (p. 237). He unites traditional values of archival professionalism with contemporary calls for political engagement and outreach.

During the decades in which archivists began to grapple with the implications of archival silences, many communities excluded from the formal archive began to develop their own independent archival collections. The community archives movement directly addresses several political concerns surrounding the formal archive: diversity and inclusion, cultural contextualization and control. Through their investigation of the community archives movement in the United Kingdom, Andrew Flinn, Mary Stevens, and Elizabeth Shepherd have developed a comprehensive exploration of the theory and practice of community archives, which centralizes these concerns. Flinn defines community archives as "the grassroots activities of documenting, recording, and exploring community heritage in which community participation, control and ownership of the project is essential" (2007, p. 153).

While communities are often wary of involvement with the traditional archival sector, archivists' pursuit of political engagement necessitates that they develop community partnerships and outreach programs as central elements of the profession. Stevens, Flinn, and Shepherd identify five key areas of mainstream involvement with the community archives sector: custody of archival materials, targeted records collecting to rectify silences in the archival record, curation and exhibition of materials, advice and training in archival skills, and consulting communities as sources of specialized knowledge. Successful partnerships require professional flexibility and an understanding and recognition of community expertise and challenges (Stevens, Flinn, & Shepherd, 2010, p. 63–72).

A common thread that can be found throughout the literature on community archives is the intersection of community history projects and political struggles for recognition and self-determination. Flinn, Stevens, and Shepherd (2009) argue that "most community archives offer an important and empowering assertion of community resistance to otherwise exclusionary and (often) marginalizing dominant narratives" (p. 83). Across communities fighting for recognition and self-determination, the archive serves a critical political function: facilitating the development of historical knowledge and narratives of community resistance, which can be used as collective tools for social justice. In developing a collaborative digital history project with the Metropolitan Council on Housing, I approached my work as a politically-engaged and professional archivist, employing the lessons and recommendations of the community archives movement and archival best practices. Through this project, I aimed not only to increase historical knowledge of the political contributions of the MCH, but also to build the power of current organizers working for tenant justice in New York City.

Collaborative Project Design

I undertook this project not only as an archivist but as a community organizer interested in exploring techniques for building historical knowledge within social justice organizations. Having worked with activist organizations with high rates of burnout, rapid turnover, and, thus, short historical memories, I wanted to create a project that would allow organizers to learn from the successes and failures of previous political campaigns. Therefore, creating a project design that foregrounded the needs of the organization was critical. I began the process by meeting with Mario Mazzoni, the principal MCH organizer. We discussed MCH's goals for this project and the outcome that would be most useful for its current members, tenants from across New York City. Before the meeting, I had brainstormed a list of potential projects that could be used to communicate the organization's history to its membership. These ideas included a physical exhibition of materials, an online exhibition, a history zine, a small oral history project with an accompanying radio podcast, and a calendar highlighting one historical document per month. After discussing the various strengths and limitations of these potential projects with Mario, he and I settled relatively quickly on an online exhibition and archive.

There were numerous reasons why this was the most appropriate type of project for MCH at that particular juncture in its history. Two overarching limitations determined the form of this project: a lack of funding and a lack of physical space. There was no budget for a project such as this, and the small size of the MCH office eliminated the possibility of a physical exhibition. MCH wanted a project that would highlight the wealth of archival documents and photographs that had been accumulated over its 50-year history, and an online exhibition and archive would make these materials accessible not only to MCH members, but also to people interested in tenant organizing worldwide. Moreover, an online project would integrate easily into a major website redesign that was already underway. Digitization of archival documents and photographs was also seen as protection against the potential loss of materials, should anything ever happen to the approximately 4000 photographs stored in MCH's East Village office.

Having decided on the broad contours of the project with MCH, I began to reach out to the other institutional partners whose cooperation would be necessary to complete this project. Since MCH had donated the bulk of their archival collection to New York University's Tamiment Library and Robert F. Wagner Labor Archives, I met with Acting Director Chela Scott Weber to discuss the project. My priority in this partnership was to gain permission to digitize a small portion of the 70-linear-foot collection using the equipment at NYU's Digital Library Technology Services. For the Tamiment Library and Wagner Labor Archives, it was important to conduct digitization in such a way that the digital images could be related back to the physical objects, and therefore made accessible through the Tamiment Library database. For this purpose, we decided to use a standardized strategy for file name identifiers, which were linked to the Tamiment Library database. Finally, I involved NYU's Digital Library Technology Services[1] and developed a schedule to complete my digitization work using the equipment and resources made available for student and faculty digitization projects.

Project Implementation

Implementing this project involved three phases of work—research and inventory, digitization, and exhibition development—which took place over the course of approximately eight months. Throughout these three phases, and as the project design was further reified, I continually returned to lessons gleaned from case studies of the community archives movement: the necessity of professional flexibility, the acknowledgement of and adjustment to community limitations, and the prioritization of the needs and perspectives of the organization.

---

1. I was employed at Digital Library Technology Services during the period that I was working on this project.

Research

The first phase of the MCH project implementation was primary and secondary source research about the history of the organization. Broadly, I was interested in identifying the key political campaigns in which MCH had participated, and the activists who had kept the organization relevant and vibrant for the past fifty years. MCH staff had identified specific research questions, including the organization's historical engagement with radicalism and the evolution of its membership and financial structures. Through these questions, the staff sought to further an understanding of the organization's past in an attempt to rearticulate MCH's position in the modern tenant-organizing environment of New York City. In addition, MCH's current financial instability encouraged its members to explore the organization's varying structures and financial arrangements in earlier decades.

Rapidly, I discovered that while there has been a significant body of historical literature written about urban renewal and tenant organizing in New York City, there was little that directly discussed MCH in depth. A comprehensive summary of the organization's history would have to be stitched together from primary source research, information gleaned from secondary sources, and the organization's own dated historical overviews. I combined primary source research with inventory and selection of materials for digitization. I examined all the historical photographs stored at MCH's office and 25 boxes of materials at the Tamiment Library and Wagner Labor Archives. As I examined materials for research purposes, I kept notes of the locations of items I was considering for digitization. At this point I also began to make a rough outline for the structure of the online exhibition.

Digitization

During the inventory and research process I selected approximately 200 photographs and 100 documents for digitization. Photographs were prioritized for digitization, due to their unique historical value and the fact that their storage in MCH's office made them significantly less accessible to researchers and at higher risk for damage than materials at the Tamiment Library and Wagner Labor Archives. When selecting items for digitization, I attempted to represent the wide range of activities that MCH had engaged in, to reflect the gender and racial diversity of the organization and also to portray the historical timeframe of its organizational activities. I also attempted to select items that had enough accompanying metadata (such as date, location and other identifying information) to be historically valuable. Finally, I took aesthetic concerns into consideration, selecting items that would be visually interesting when displayed in an online exhibition and archive.

Before beginning the physical process of digitization, I had to determine standards for image quality, metadata, and file name identifiers. Given the unique nature of the materials contained in MCH's archive, digitization was undertaken for long-term preservation of the materials as well as current use. I followed professional standards for preservation digitization: all material was scanned or photographed at 400ppi or 600ppi (depending on dimensions), with a color target included in each file and saved as uncompressed TIFF 6.0 files in CIE RGB color space. These standards were developed based on the recommendations of NYU's Digital Library Technology Services and will help to ensure that these digital "master" files remain useable as computer technologies evolve and change. I also created "derivative" files for online display, in which

["Master" file, saved as a TIFF 6.0 in CIE RGB color space, with color target included.]

I cropped out the color target but maintained the original ppi, file format, and color space. The derivative files were used in the creation of the online exhibition and archive and were also given to MCH for future use by the organization.

As I digitized items, I created a spreadsheet of metadata associated with each image. The information collected included the creator, date, dimensions, original format, subject, file name identifier, and other elements. My decision to collect these categories was based on the Dublin Core metadata standard, but ultimately I included much less information in the final online archive. Although additional metadata might have increased the range of possible uses of any given image, I wanted to prioritize accessibility of the images. I worried that including 15 to 20 lines of technical information below each image might alienate potential users of the website. The information included with each image on the final website was description, date, creator, original format, and citation. This level of information aims to meet the needs of academic researchers while remaining accessible to more casual users of the site.

Exhibition Development

The next phase of work for this project involved developing an online interface for presenting digitized items and writing a contextualizing narrative. I researched and experimented with a variety of platforms for the online exhibition and archive, including Omeka, Wordpress, and Drupal. Omeka, an open source Web-publishing platform developed for cultural heritage institutions, was my original preference for the online archive and exhibition. It is easy to work with, has a variety of display options for both archival and exhibition presentation, and is widely used for similar projects. However, incorporating an Omeka site with the existing MCH Drupal-based site would have required a substantial time investment on the part of MCH's Web developer. Since MCH did not have the resources to support the time-intensive development of an integrated Omeka site, we decided it would be best to use the existing functionality of MCH's Drupal-based website. Although this required more time on my part to format and write the code for the archive and exhibition, it was a necessary decision based on the needs and limited resources of the organization.

The narrative text of the exhibition was developed through archival and secondary source research. During the research process, I wrote down key words and themes, and I gradually reduced my list to six thematic topics, through which I sought to highlight significant aspects of MCH's history:

- "Organizer Biographies" aimed to humanize the work of the organization and to highlight the central role of women and people of color.

- "Early Grassroots Political Action" communicated the main political campaigns of the organization during its early years, including contesting urban renewal and demanding increased public housing.
- "Grassroots Political Action of the 1970s and 1980s" examined MCH's support of the citywide squatters movement, collaborations with radical organizations such as the Black Panther Party and the Young Lords, and the campaign against vacant apartments.
- "Legislative Campaigns" gave a brief overview of MCH's work to defend and expand rent control in New York City, including the Flynn-Dearie Bill for statewide rent control during the 1980s.
- "Collective Action and Mutual Aid" discussed the main political tactics employed by MCH (such as rent strikes, rallies, and occupations) as well as the evolving organizational structure.
- "Solidarity" outlined MCH's engagement with other political campaigns, particularly the civil rights movement.

In creating these themes, I was also attempting to incorporate the historical questions that MCH had identified during the project's development: the organization's past engagement with radicalism, and previous organizational and financial structures. I also included an introduction, to discuss the founding of the organization, provide a chronological timeline, and offer a brief thematic overview for readers.

Through the exhibition text, I aimed to provide a balanced history of the organization, including both successes and failures. In a project attempting to inform MCH's political work and educate current organizers, it was important to write an unglorified history. Learning about past successes can be inspirational, but past difficulties and failures can often be more informative. MCH supported the inclusion of campaigns that were ultimately unsuccessful, and my contacts in the organization also encouraged coverage of internal disagreements about political strategies, even asking me to expand the discussion of one that I had referenced only casually in the text. I had feared that including negative aspects of the history would be a source of tension between myself and the organization, and I was pleased that these issues were easily discussed and negotiated.

Over the course of my research, I discovered that the history of tenant organizing in New York City, and of MCH specifically, is very complex. Over the past fifty years, the movement has involved thousands of individuals, hundreds of buildings, and dozens of organizations working on a variety of issues, in ever-changing coalitions. To ensure that I was representing this history accurately, I reached out to two professors to act as historical advisors on this project; their advice was invaluable. Professor Marci Reaven encouraged me to refine my description of urban renewal and challenged my interpretation of the work of a key scholar in the field. Fordham University professor Roberta Gold corrected many nuances and provided clarification on a variety of historical campaigns and coalitions. Finally, to guarantee that MCH members felt accurately represented as an organization and were comfortable with the exhibition text that would appear on their website, staff member Mario Mazzoni reviewed the text and offered feedback before the website went live. All of these suggestions and corrections strengthened the exhibition and allowed me to feel more confident that the narrative I was presenting was both accurate and representative, though the review process had required me to balance the concerns of reviewers with a variety of perspectives. Although time-consuming, this process was necessary to develop an exhibition text that met the rigorous requirements of academia but remained grounded in the needs of the organization.

Finally, I developed the display pages for the digitized images. Each thematic section of the exhibition has thumbnail images embedded in the text,

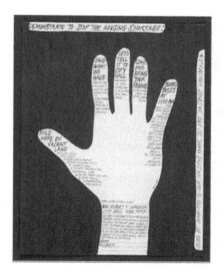 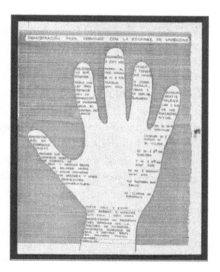

Description: English and Spanish language posters for a demonstration at City Hall to demand an end to the housing shortage in New York City by building public housing on vacant land and imposing a mortorium on the demolition of habitable buildings. The demonstration was organized by the Committee to Save Our City's Homes.

Date: January 1962

Creator: Save Our City's Homes

Original Format: Black and White publication, 8.5 x 11 inches

Citation: Metropolitan Council on Housing Records, TAM 173, Box 2, Folder 28, Tamiment Library and Wagner Labor Archive. Digital ID = tam173_ref36_000001d (English) and tam173_ref36_000002d (Spanish)

[Online display of archival materials, May 2012]

with a gallery of ten to 20 additional images at the bottom of the page. Each image links to a larger format image, which is accompanied by associated metadata. Approximately one hundred photographs and documents are displayed on the site in this fashion. With the digital project, I have aimed to provide an accessible and engaging exploration of MCH's history through the exhibition narrative and image archive and to display the abundant archive of photographs and documents associated with MCH's decades of organizing for tenant justice in New York City.

Outcomes and Future Steps

A few months after completing the online exhibition and archive, I met again with Mario Mazzoni, MCH organizer, to discuss the outcomes of the project. I was curious how Mario thought this type of project could be used to improve political organizing by MCH. Mario observed that many longtime members had recently left the organization, and that this turnover in membership meant that the organization's historical memory was very short. Current organizers knew little about previous campaigns and past organizational structures. The exhibition and archive project allowed MCH organizers to gain a better understanding of how the organization had evolved and what distinguished MCH's work from that of other groups in the past. Additionally, Mario felt that this type of knowledge was essential for both funders and new members; it allowed them to develop an understanding of the broader goals of the organization, beyond the specific objectives of current campaigns. The collaborative project documented and made accessible the history of MCH, allowing organizer tenants to gain a broad understanding of the successes and failures of past campaigns, and to use this knowledge to build organizational capacity within the tenant movement in New York City and beyond.

The project was also fortunate in that my collaboration with MCH was easy and effective, largely because MCH had already articulated the need for a historical documentation project. Current MCH organizers were aware of the value of this type of project to the organization. They had, furthermore, identified the significance of their archival collections and donated a portion of these materials to New York University's Tamiment Library and Wagner Labor Archives. They had also articulated the central goal of making these historical materials more accessible for the purposes of informing their current political work. MCH's awareness of the value of archival records, documentation, and historical education for the organization was the key to the success of this collaboration.

Unfortunately, the general membership of the organization was not as involved in the project as Mario and I would have wished; this was the main challenge identified during our conversation. This project began during a period of financial crisis for MCH, which meant that political work had been de-prioritized in favor of fundraising and providing basic services. One result of this shift in resources was a less dynamic office environment, and therefore fewer volunteers to engage in the MCH history project. Future phases of this project aim to reach out more actively to MCH members, for example by encouraging people to provide information about unidentified photographs, obscure documents, and unrecognized past organizers. Additionally, as founding and long-term members of the organization enter their 80s and 90s, recording oral histories will be vital to collecting and preserving the history of the organization. Although such an initiative was beyond the scope of the current project, we hope to conduct these interviews in the near future. Finally, we hope to continue to expand the website until all digitized items are displayed.

Conclusion

This project benefited from numerous personal and institutional connections. My association with New York University, both as a student and an employee, gave me access to knowledge and resources that MCH could not afford or access independently. Creating these institutional partnerships to support my work with MCH allowed me to channel the resources and privilege of academia towards concrete action for social justice. These partnerships had to be thoughtfully constructed and negotiated to ensure that the needs and goals of the organization were prioritized.

To inform my understanding of this process, I referred to the strategies identified by Stevens, Flinn, and Shepherd (2010) from their study of the community archives movement in the United Kingdom. The most central of these were the need for professional flexibility and an understanding of community expertise and challenges. From the conceptual foundations of this project to determining work timelines and metadata requirements, I attempted to always remain accountable to and cognizant of the perspectives and needs of MCH. This approach required creativity and adaptability to work with and around the limitations that are often inherent to grassroots community organizing: limited budgets, insufficient physical space, and overworked organizers and volunteers. While institutional partnerships can provide financial support and resources for these types of projects, they are by no means necessary to undertake this work—community-based and DIY solutions can also be used to fulfill knowledge and resource needs. Here in New York City we can look to the Lesbian Herstory Archive and the Interference Archive as examples of independent, community-based projects.

Finally, throughout my work with MCH, I strived to model archival and historical best practices, adapting Dublin Core metadata requirements, applying professional standards for digitization, and incorporating feedback from current scholars in the field. Through this case study, I hope to have concretely demonstrated the possibilities and challenges for integrating these practices with the priorities and needs of community organizations, with the aim of supporting grassroots organizing, community building, and the struggle for social justice.

References

Flinn, A. (2007). Community histories, community archives: Some opportunities and challenges. *Journal of the Society of Archivists, 28*(2), 151-176. doi: 10.1080/00379810701611936

Flinn, A., Stevens, M., & Shepherd, E. (2009). Whose memories? Whose archives? Independent community archives, autonomy and the mainstream. *Archival Science 9*, 71-86.

Gold, R. (forthcoming). *City of tenants: The struggle for citizenship in New York City housing.* Champaign, IL: University of Illinois Press.

Harris, V. (2002). 'They should have destroyed more': The destruction of public records by the South African state in the final years of Apartheid, 1990-1994. In R.J. Cox and D.A. Wallace (Eds.), *Archives and the public good* (pp. 205-228). London: Quorum Books.

Harris, V. (2005). Archives, politics and justice. In M. Proctor, M. Cook, & C. Williams (Eds.), *Political pressure and the archival record* (pp. 173-184). Chicago, IL: Society of American Archivists.

Jimerson, R.C. (2007). Archives for all: Professional responsibility and social justice. *American Archivist 70*, 252-281.

Jimerson, R.C. (2009). *Archives power: Memory, accountability and social justice.* Chicago, IL: American Library Association.

Reaven, M. (2009). *Citizen participation in city planning: New York City, 1945-1975.* (Unpublished doctoral dissertation). New York University, New York.

Stevens, M., Flinn, A., & Shepherd, E. (2010). New frameworks for community engagement in the archive sector. *International Journal of Heritage Studies, 16*(1-2), 59-76.

Zinn, H. (1977). Secrecy, archives and the public interest. *Midwestern Archivist 2*(2). Retrieved from http://www.libr.org/progarchs/documents/Zinn_Speech_MwA_1977.htm

In Real Life

From Haiti to Miami: Security, Serendipity, and Social Justice

Béatrice Colastin Skokan

A life of migration stretches and breaks open one's view of the world. Concepts of identity and belonging are challenged and often redefined, and they present opportunities to find a centered self in an ever-changing world. These moments of insecurity in the immigrant experience can be mitigated by serendipity that leads to new paths of growth and service. My encounter with the South Florida Social Justice movement is such a story.

The 1980s saw the tail end of a brutal 30-year dictatorship in Haiti, my parents' homeland. Part of the story that is seldom told is that organized grassroots movements throughout the country challenged the dictatorial regime, and that one of the strengths of these new activists lay in diffusion of information in ways unforeseen by power holders. The radio is a popular and cherished means of communication in Haiti and with the diaspora. As portable radios became widely available in all corners of the country, people were able to access news bulletins outside of the territory, without any filters, in the privacy of their own homes. But the "information revolution" really took flight when select radio stations, such as "Radio Haiti" and "Radio Soleil" (or "Radio Sun," the national Catholic radio station), started to diffuse information in Haitian Creole (Haitian Creole and French are the two national languages, but only Creole is spoken by all inhabitants of the country). The radio created a safe space for the articulation of ideas, commentary, and critical analysis of the nation's power structure. Average citizens could be educated in matters of democracy and freedom of speech, both explosive concepts that turned journalists, artists, and commentators into role models and targets to be tracked down, arrested, exiled, or killed.

Rural and agricultural cooperatives were foremost featured in the news broadcasts. The local reporting revealed articulate and self-empowered communities in the "forgotten" rural areas of the country. Under leaders such as Chavannes Jean-Baptist, who organized Mouvman Peyisan Papay (Movement of the Papay Peasantry), agricultural populations fought for the right to own and keep land, criticized foreign dumping of goods into the local market, and demanded to be paid fair prices for their produce. What came to be known as the "peasant rural movements" was no longer hidden by the logistics of being cut off from the handful of metropolitan areas such as Port-au-Prince and Cap Haitien. The radio, in addition to a source of information, also became a sheltered space of performance for folk singers such as Manno Charlemagne, whose lyrics echoed the trials of grassroots movements and the many forms of social and economic oppressions inherited from a stratified colonial period that value a person based on ancestry and the class into which they are born, regardless of their personal accomplishments.

While we learned about the French Enlightenment and the Haitian revolution from high school textbooks, outside of class I listened avidly to late 20th century applications of these concepts. These were formative years that elicited a strong desire to be proactive and supportive of progressive voices. The uncensored news broadcasts imparted knowledge about so many of these local and proactive groups that refused to be victimized. These values and viewpoints continued to be fostered even when our family immigrated to Miami and we struggled to find our place among the diverse population of South Florida. Ironically, while I had welcomed media as an empowering tool for the censored citizenry of Haiti, I also experienced its ability here, in the U.S., to shape a dour image of black masses landing on the shores of South Florida as "Haitian boat people." These snapshots of information created a narrative of black economic refugees, not political exiles, come to burden South Florida and the U.S. This image led to both official and unofficial discriminatory treatment, and so the Haitian diaspora began to organize. Activists established their own local radio stations and advocacy groups, beginning with the now defunct Haitian Refugee Center and later with others such as the Haitian Women of Miami and Take Back the Land. Little did I know that it would be through the path of information science that I would encounter the social justice movements of the Haitian exile community.

Library work as a paraprofessional, and ultimately manuscripts librarian, has stimulated and nourished a life of the mind and an insatiable curiosity. I initially worked at the University of Miami Richter Library in order to have an on-campus full-time job while completing my graduate degree in International

Studies. I worked in various capacities as a library assistant in bookbinding, acquisitions, serials, rare book cataloging, and finally, archives. I was particularly drawn to archival materials because of the immediacy of the experience of primary source documents. I love the personal, uncensored, and creative potential in diaries, letters, photographs, and oral histories. I realized that by getting an MLS I could combine my experience of intellectual stimulation and nourishment with professional and economic security. I was pleasantly surprised that my MLS classes would provide an opportunity to intellectually explore the issues of social justice that meant so much to me. For one class on assessing the information needs of different groups, I interviewed Fr. Jean-Pierre, a trilingual Haitian Roman Catholic priest serving Hispanic and Haitian communities and helping them interact with the Anglo world they had immigrated into. His experiences testified to the enormous disempowerment of many immigrants due to barriers of language, literacy, and legality, and caused me to realize how important effective information outreach can be. He also suggested I interview Marleine Bastien, leader of the Haitian Women of Miami, a grassroots organization that advocated for the social and economic well-being of an exiled community with a particular focus on the empowerment of women and children. I didn't interview her at the time but would later have an opportunity to work with her. In another class on information policy, we discussed the potential risks to privacy associated with the information technologies developed to counter global information security risks. This topic had a reality for me that it may not have had for some of my classmates, as I had come from a country with secret police where people were arrested and tortured for expressing their opinions. For me it also punctuated the rights and rule of law we enjoy in the U.S., how fragile they are, and how we citizens must remain vigilant and continue to work to preserve them.

I experienced the federal government's important role in information preservation when, as part of my transition from a paraprofessional to a professional archives position, I attended the Modern Archives Institute in Washington D.C., thanks in part to the Modern Archives Colonial Dames scholarship and the encouragement of my then-supervisor and future mentor, Maria Estorino. Learning about curating historical documents, the Freedom of Information Act, public programming, and ethical records management in the nation's capital only reinforced my growing conviction of the links between free access to information and a free civil society. Washington, D.C. is structured as a perpetual reminder of the highest human endeavors, with all its museums, its historical landmarks, and a faithful stream of people exercising their right to dissent. One moment stands out amongst all the lectures and site visits that are integral to the training at the Modern Archives Institute. The morning our group got a private viewing of the U.S. Constitution and the Declaration of Independence was both stimulating and stilling as we walked in the silence of the church-like space before the morning crowds. The experience could only be described as reverential. Nevertheless, my need from earlier years to contribute to my communities and be civically engaged remained unmet. My immigrant experience had highlighted the need for economic stability and for the material survival and emotional security my children derived from my presence, and I saw these as necessarily my first priorities. Although my chosen profession continued to meet my financial needs, it seemed that I could not contribute to social justice within the structure of a private university's archives. The career choice of librarian remained a curiosity in the familial culture accustomed to the success stories of new immigrant accountants, doctors, or lawyers; special collections seemed to me an elitist specialty far removed from the information needs of the majority of the population.

The apparent disconnect between civic engagement and special collections began to end in 2006. An interesting chain of events began one afternoon with a conversation about Howard Zinn's viewpoint on the historical contribution of the common people with the new interim department head of Special Collections, Maria Estorino, a second generation Cuban-American who understood the lack of representation of non-majority communities in history in general and in archival collections specifically. I was an archives assistant and about to arrange the papers of Seymour Samet, a Jewish civil rights leader living in Miami in the 1960s. Along with a group of religious leaders from the area's various denominations, Mr. Samet was pivotal in the creation of what came to be known as the Miami Dade Community Relations Board (CRB). The CRB's leadership sought to mitigate tenuous religious, ethnic, and race relations in South Florida from the 1960s to the 1980s and beyond.

In the next couple of years, Special Collections became actively involved in outreach, seeking to add absent African American civil rights collections to the repository begun with the Samet Papers and the CRB. Miami has a rich history in civil rights advocacy, and some university members had been involved in the desegregation movement of the 1960s. A current African American trustee at the time, Bob Simms, was a living testimony of this history. Raised by parents who were teachers at George Washington Carver's Tuskegee Institute in Alabama, he had moved with his young family to Miami in 1953 to take a faculty position at the segregated George Washington Carver School in Coconut Grove, Florida. Simms was also enamored of photography and had taken numerous pictures of students, athletes, staff, and events from the school before desegregation. These images, which are now part of the Bob Simms Collection at the University of Miami Special Collections, are widely sought after as unique instances of documentation of Miami's era of a segregated community. Interestingly, the collection also includes records of Mr. Simms' 20-year tenure as executive director of the Miami-Dade Community Relations Board, the aforementioned CRB. In the past couple of years, I have used the content of these materials to curate exhibits, instructed students in the use and importance of primary sources of history, and provided them as supporting documentation of local oral history projects that educate the public about South Florida's history of race relations. We are glad to use and promote this material but are conscious of the work involved in their inclusion in the archives. The decisions to process Samet and to focus on neglected Miami civil rights struggles and their connections to Simms expanded our reach into the community and brought additional papers of other known civil rights leaders from the African American community.

Our new library deputy director, Yolanda Cooper, provided crucial support and institutional leadership for this opening of our archives onto the Miami civil rights movement (located online at scholar.library.miami.edu/miamiCivil-Rights). She envisioned this work as a collaborative process with the surrounding community, which resided outside of the academic environment and was segregated until 1962. The lack of "black" historical documents was addressed on two fronts. We engaged in outreach efforts that brought people into the archives with public events that focused on new collections and exhibits from known church and civil rights leaders. Mr. Simms was a respected figure in the Miami civil rights community and facilitated these openings and trust-building endeavors. Celebratory moments provided an opportunity not only to speak of the importance of preserving historical evidence from a multiplicity of points of view but also to educate the general public about the role of the archives in the preservation of communities' memories. The crossing of these physical locations and the ensuing dialogues helped to dismantle internalized relics of segregation that were still vivid in the memories of African Americans that had not been allowed to visit "white" university campuses and never did so even after Florida officially desegregated its schools in the 1960s.

We were establishing a seed collection of civil rights activism that focused on historically black and segregated schools; locally-based community relations organizations; and political campaign materials from the first black female judge in the state of Florida, Leah Simms, Bob Simms' daughter. This focus on our immediate local environment led to the acquisition of the papers of Rev. Theodore Gibson, President of the Miami chapter of the NAACP in the 1960s and a descendent of the original Bahamian immigrants who settled in South Florida at the beginning of the 20th century. The new civil rights focus also included the papers of Dr. John O. Brown, president of the Miami Congress on Racial Equality (C.O.R.E) chapter in the 1960s. Under the initiative and leadership of

Deputy Director Yolanda Cooper, we have now formalized this work under the Collaborative Archives of the African Diaspora (CAAD):

> CAAD is a shared archive of manuscripts, posters, and other ephemera documenting African American and Black history, culture and experiences in South Florida and other Florida destinations and the Caribbean. The CAAD Partnership is made of institutions and agencies dedicated to the preservation and access of these materials and the development of educational resources broadly accessible to the global community. (University of Miami Libraries, n.d.)

The primary function of the CAAD project rests in the ability to reach out to other institutional partners for the pulling of resources that reside with various agencies but are made available to the general public on the Web.

It was intellectually stimulating to learn about this history and emotionally grounding to bring these stories to a larger public. Surprisingly, the concepts of "profession" and "meaningful work" seemed to have found a common ground. In 2006, Maria Estorino had an inclusive vision of the repository that she successfully conveyed to me. I was being mentored into an established tradition of community archives where the professional immerses herself into a living, local history and incorporates this recorded experience into the cultural institution. I cherished our visits to community leaders to explain the purpose, necessity, and value of this archiving activity. Trust had to be established with patience, honesty, and many conversations, facilitated by introductions from people like Bob Simms who are respected leaders within their communities. Potential donors were invited to visit the library to see how we stored, cared for, and preserved the materials. We gave examples of how their donations contributed to students' learning about and researchers' investigation of hidden histories that never make it into textbooks. We explained the open access policies of the Special Collections and that our materials were open to anyone in the general public, not just to our faculty and students, welcoming all to use the physical materials on-site and the digitized collections online. We publicized the new acquisitions in press releases, public lectures, and exhibitions for the university and local communities, especially the donating communities. People cannot feel that their gifts are being stored away, hidden, and forgotten. Finally, we were unequivocally honest and upfront about past institutional biases and discriminations and the resulting lack of diversity in our collections. We explained that our current documentation efforts were started to remedy and enrich the repository in order to present a more balanced view of history, and that we could accomplish this only in collaboration with communities whose histories are still hidden. Just as we had stepped outside of the confines of our library, we thus brought our local community history in.

When I became a full-time faculty librarian, I continued this civically engaged documentation activity through conversation with student activists and community leaders. I have primary responsibility for the hiring and training of the students who work in the archives and enjoy exchanging ideas with them. The very nature of handling historical documents leads to the most interesting conversations. I still remember speaking to Rudo Kemper, a graduate student in International Administration, about the apparent erasure of current social activism in South Florida. We were both convinced that this neglect could and should be remedied. He was very interested in the work of Haitian-American Max Rameau with Take Back the Land (TBL). This local activist group was concerned with issues of affordable housing, gentrification, and overall land ownership, all very pertinent to the recent South Florida history of rapid urban sprawl and construction:

> Take Back the Land (TBL) is a land and housing rights movement that seeks to elevate housing to the level of a human right and struggles for the control over land on behalf of disempowered and poor communities which are threatened by gentrification, privatization of land, fluctuating home prices, and diminishing public housing. TBL originated in 2006 in Miami, Florida, as a response to the incipient housing crisis. Its first action was the erection of a shantytown on an unused piece of land in Liberty City that became known as Umoja Village. Five years later, TBL has moved to the national level and provides support to organizations that fight for housing rights. TBL also directs its own "positive action" campaigns consisting of eviction defenses and liberations of foreclosed homes. (Kemper, 2011, p. iv)

I wrote to Mr. Rameau regarding Special Collections' civically engaged documentation activity and invited his group to our archives. We subsequently visited their small office. I still regret not taking along a camera to photograph the Take Back the Land headquarters with shelves of books for inmates, handmade banners made by activists for the Umoja Village shanty town, and posters from Michael Moore's 2010 movie "Capitalism: A Love Story" in which TBL's work is featured in the section "The Banks Kick Them Out, Max Kicks Them Back In." After establishing the TBL Archives, Special Collections successfully hosted one of our most well-attended events, "Archiving the Fringe: Documenting Countercultural Activism in Miami" (Lyle & Rameau, 2011). Large groups of students, local activists, and faculty attended the talk featuring Max Rameau and Erick Lyle, a zine artist, former South Florida squatter, and activist in his own right. Both Max and Erick were articulate and well-informed about the many social issues that plague the region. It was my first experience with the University of Miami's student organization known as S.T.A.N.D, Students for a New Democracy. This group of students had led a successful campaign to secure better wages and health benefits for the University's service workers. They subsequently approached the archives and agreed to start a collection documenting their work. S.T.A.N.D is now actively leading a new campaign for securing better working conditions for the campus's food service employees. It is also thanks to Max Rameau that I was introduced to Marleine Bastien, the founder and executive director of Haitian Women of Miami (FANM), whom he describes as "the most prominent Haitian activist in Florida" (Rameau, 2008, p. 41). The organization recently celebrated twenty years of advocacy for children, women, and immigration rights. Over the next year, I frequently visited the Haitian Women of Miami office in the Little Haiti neighborhood and, with Marleine's guidance, was able to identify records from their storage area that would become part of the new archives. In a very kind note, she later thanked me for my patience and understanding. There is a hierarchy of needs in working with socially- and civically-engaged organizations. Very often she had no choice but to cancel our meetings to keep people from being deported, attend various hearings, or advocate for working families. A curator wishing to be involved with advocacy groups must remain flexible and open to the demands of a grassroots organization whose primary purpose is the betterment of people's lives, even when its staff understands the benefits of historical documentation for teaching and research.

We sought the early 21st century "invisible" activist communities of South Florida working to end gentrification, fighting for immigration rights and more recently for migrant farmworkers. These "new" areas of civil rights were ironically the result of the same political turmoil that had prompted the forced migration of many Caribbean and Central and South American residents in the 1980s. Documenting Miami in the 21st century meant revisiting human rights issues from Haiti in the 1980s. Haitian radio stations in the U.S. remain as pivotal a source of information as they were in the homeland. They provide a forum for the exiled community and a continued source of information about happenings both locally and in Haiti, especially for those who do not speak English and often lack literacy even in their native tongue. The radio stations provided yet another secure space for illegal or marginalized immigrants to voice their concerns directly or through local activism. While individuals challenged by their status may have had to function outside of the confines of official institutions, their experiences have been documented by human rights advocates.

The latest phase of the documenting activity revealed emerging networks of activists and overlapping missions. Connections between advocacy and social services for Haitian immigrants in the FANM archives, issues of affordable housing in all African diaspora communities through the Max Rameau Papers (a Haitian American with a Pan-African ideological focus), and points of contact with all immigrant communities with the Florida Immigrant Coalition (FLIC) illustrate their overlapping missions. My serendipitous path of introduction led from one activist to another, all supporting each other in particular missions, demonstrating an unplanned but vibrant network. Further immersion into local human rights issues recently brought me to the Coalition of Immokalee Workers of Florida (CIW) and their food justice movement. The often-exploited agricultural workers primarily include people who migrated from Central America and the Caribbean. CIW's advocacy for and provision of social services to these invisible agricultural immigrants to Florida once again highlight these many organizations' overlapping missions. Their central office is a warm and welcoming place, with murals inspired by those rural grassroots leaders I listened to on the small radio stations in the 1980s in Haiti. Interestingly, one of the organizers had gone to Haiti to train with Chavannes Jean-Baptist, the organizer of Mouvman Paysan Papay who had first inspired me in adolescence and was featured in the CIW murals. I also found out they were well acquainted with Max Rameau and Marleine Bastien. These networks seemed to expand even further while taking on the shape of a circle closing, with significant personal importance.

It seems that the path of my professional life is like a circle, going around, returning to points previously visited while remaining open to new experiences that serve to reinforce what is most important. I could not have predicted all the ways that serendipity has served to integrate my efforts to meet my needs for security with my other needs to contribute to my communities and their struggles for social justice. I remain grateful and ready to serve in whatever way I can.

References

Lyle, E., & Rameau, M. (2011). Archiving the fringe: Documenting countercultural activism in Miami [Presentation]. Otto G. Richter Library,
University of Miami, Coral Gables, FL. Retrieved from http://vimeo.
com/23267802

Kemper, R. (2011). *Taking back the land: Social mobilization and radical politics in Liberty City, Florida.* (Master's thesis). University of Miami, Miami,
FL.

Rameau, M. (2008). *Take back the land: Land gentrification and the Umoja Village Shantytown.* Miami, FL: Nia Interactive Press.

University of Miami Libraries. (n.d.). Collaborative archive from the African
diaspora. Retrieved from http://scholar.library.miami.edu/caad/

Inside and Outside of the Library: On Removing Barriers and Connecting People with Health Care Resources and Zines

Jude Vachon

Introduction

In writing this chapter, I spent time thinking about where I see a connection between social change efforts and my library and information work, and also why I believe that my intention to affect social change is a legitimate way to perform it. I work within an institution and field that I think primarily sees our role as being neutral providers of information services that can and should be provided equally to every patron (or "customer," as they're referred to in some libraries, including in our library system).

I see my role in the library as well as in my volunteer healthcare project as that, but more important for me is attempting to act as an ally to oppressed people. I want to talk here about my process of learning how I might do that, including the ways in which I know that I've failed at it.

I am grateful to keep struggling for all of us to find and share the information, stories, and resources that we need to live well and with meaning and joy.

Seeing My Role as Closer to Ally than Customer Service Provider

Public libraries are inherently radical in that they're non-commercial spaces that offer free resources and services. People can sit in our building the entire day, without having to buy anything. This type of space is a complete rarity. As long as we resist attempts to make people unwelcome, resist tiered services or unaffordable fees, and resist commercialization, we can empower people without even trying hard.

We're a nonprofit, public institution. I like the distinction that Mark Rosenzweig (2001) makes between corporate globalization, "which, despite its claims, reinforces existing social, economic, cultural inequalities" and democratic globalism, which "acknowledges the obligations of society to the individual and communities, and which prioritizes human values and needs over profits" (p. 71). This is the framework within which I see public library and information work happening. The quality of our service and its relevance to people are what really matters. Our commitment to serving human needs must be the starting point for what we do and how we evaluate it.

Public libraries are nonprofits, but I do see a similarity between for-profits' pushing to exploit new markets and our moving too quickly to do new things without a real understanding of whether there is a need for them, e.g. new construction when operations are suffering, adopting new technology without much discussion or training, adopting new e-resources very quickly...new can but doesn't necessarily mean improved, and it may not serve our community best.

Jessamyn West (2012) said recently: "If our digital public library is truly public, it is for everyone, even those who are hardest to serve." I think this is completely applicable to all types of libraries and information services. Who are the people that we serve? Are we reaching out to and including everyone we can, and most importantly those who need us most? We can't just offer the same thing to everyone and call it good service, since the starting point for people is not the same. Some people haven't been given the tools, whether it be technology skills to use the library's online catalog, databases, website, or e-resources; or the self-esteem to feel that they even belong in the library in the first place, to access any of our resources. Others have. And different people need different content to serve their particular needs. "Ensuring a standard level of service" is okay and is useful for maximizing profits, but it is "disastrous for libraries if they want to root themselves in their local communities" (Durrani and Smallwood, 2006, p. 120).

Everyday choices that we make at our library have an impact on the accessibility of our space and its materials, whether those choices are conscious or not. Examples here are: the displays that we create (our displayed books circulate like crazy); the books we choose to face out when shelving; "staff picks" selections; whether we order for collections from multiple sources or use one ordering tool; whether we wake up sleeping people (homeless people may not sleep well at night and end up falling asleep in our library); what programs we offer; how much we focus on e-resources that only our users who own a computer, smart-phone or e-reader can use; how easy our catalog is to use; whether we shelve items based on library conventions or normal human user needs; whether we keep giving the transgender homeless person a guest pass to use the computer against policy (she could not provide proof of address because she has been harassed at shelters and feels unsafe staying in them, so she lives on the street); whether we do Black History Month or Women's History Month program-ming at all and, if we do, whether we put real effort into it by reaching out to African American or women coworkers and related community organizations to collaborate—and whether we have relationships with those people in the first place; and whether we have separate genre collections for marginalized cultures and what we call them. It makes a difference, for example, whether we call a col-lection for lesbian and gay literature "LGBT" or "LGBTQ" instead of "GLBT." Here's one person's take on putting the L in front:

> [F]or some, moving the 'L' to the front of the line constitutes an important political statement. "I always understood it as a nod to feminism," says [Deb] Greenspan. "For a long time, the gay community was not inclusive of women, and lesbians had to forge out on their own in a lot of ways. The balance still isn't perfect, but I think the L in front is a recognition of that." (Hess, 2010)

I could go on and on. Yes, our work is inherently political, because we make choices every day in large and small ways that show who it is that we are truly serving. If we don't consciously make our choices, we'll end up serving those who are easiest to serve, with the resources and services that are easiest to provide.

We can and should do more by focusing on seeing and hearing our com-munity (including people that we don't yet work with) and proactively includ-ing, welcoming, and serving them in the particular ways that they need. By "proactively including," I mean reaching out to and building relationships with all members of the community, so that we can listen to them about their needs and interests and let them know what content and services we have that might be of use to them.

If I make choices to serve everyone well, but to pay particular attention to those who I think most need my support, I would say that I then define my role more as someone trying to become an ally to oppressed people. I say "trying to become" deliberately here. As Anne Bishop (2002) says:

> No matter how much work you have done on that area of yourself, there is more to be done. All members of this society grow up surrounded by op-pressive attitudes; we are marinated in it. It runs in our veins; it is as invis-

ible to us as the air we breathe. I do not believe anyone raised in Western society can ever claim to have finished ridding themselves completely of their oppressive attitudes.[...]

The other thing that makes members of an oppressor group always oppressors, no matter what kind of education process we have been through, is that, until we change the politics and economics of oppression, we are still "living off the avails." We would not be where we are, doing what we are doing, with the skills and access we have, if we did not have the color, gender, sexual orientation, appearance, age, class, or physical abilities we have. Resources and power continue to come to us because we are members of the dominant group in relation to the particular form of oppression where we seek to be allies. So, until we succeed in making a more humane world, yes, we are racist (or ageist, or classist, or heterosexist, and so forth). (p. 114)

I have the privileges of a white, lower middle class person, and the power in my position as librarian to share information with users that makes it easier for them to use the catalog, find materials in the building, use the public computers, and more. I can make exceptions to policies, or I can refer people to others, for example to pursue a payment arrangement for fines. My being welcoming and willing—or not—can affect people's experiences and their ability to locate what they need. I can order materials that are relevant to them, or not. That's power, and I need to stay aware that I have it. I choose to keep trying to share it by doing as much as I can to make our systems and operations transparent and finding and making available resources that may be helpful to people. This is an endless process.

Be Well! History

I started Be Well! Healthcare Options for the Uninsured at the end of 2005. I was uninsured, had a problem with my shoulder, and needed an MRI. The sliding-scale community health clinic that I was going to referred me to get one. When I asked how much it would cost, the clinic people said that the MRI facility would work something out with me. What the facility offered was to pay $500 up front, and put another $500 on a payment plan. This wasn't at all doable for me. I ended up spending a few months trying to get care for my shoulder, a period when I experienced pain that at times kept me up at night and caused a loss of mobility and full use of my arm.

I had been aware of the horrible state of our health care system before this situation, and I had been uninsured at other times in my life. But my experience specifically with my shoulder, and the experiences of the many people who commiserated when I was going through it (e.g. a coworker's grandmother who was in serious credit card debt from cancer drugs), made me realize more than ever how completely unacceptable the situation was (and still is).

When people shared their stories about not having access to care, I sometimes had a resource to give them from my own research. If not, I did more research to try to find something for them. I started to gather this information. I had computer access and am computer-literate, have research skills, and can advocate for myself fairly well. I am also a white person who is low-income but not poor, and who I think could be middle or upper middle class if I wanted to be. I eventually got care through some serious persistence on my part and advocacy on my behalf from a consumer health organization and a social worker, and still it took months. I realized that if I had the difficulties that I did in getting affordable care, many other less privileged people and/or people with less access were having a much worse time.

Knowing that so many people were really suffering emotionally, physically, and financially due to lack of health care while I was finding more and more free or low-income resources that weren't at all well-publicized was really upsetting to me. It was an intense experience of an information gap that I lived personally. I believed and still do believe that we need a radical redo of our healthcare system, but in the meantime I want for people to be as well as they can now. That's the intention of sharing resources through Be Well!.

In 2006, I applied for and got a grant from a local community organization. I printed 6,000 *Be Well! Healthcare Options for the Uninsured* booklets and left them all over the city. I continue to distribute them to health clinics, social service providers, corner stores, braiding salons, laundromats, and other sites where low-income people might find them. At times I've had help from volunteers doing service hours for their nursing degree, other times I have friends drive me to distro spots, and sometimes I distribute them myself by bike. I try to update listings and print a new set of booklets every year, and I usually do. I started a blog with the booklet information and more in January 2008. The blog got an average of 3500 hits per month in 2012.

The real challenges for me with this project closely parallel those of my library work. It's a matter of trying to keep identifying my blind spots in terms of who I am not helping, or not helping well enough, to access what they need. It's been a meaningful, humbling process, which I'll talk about more below.

Library History: Zines

I came to library work from a history of community education jobs. I taught mainly outside of schools—in literacy programs, after school programs, tutoring sessions—before I got my library degree in 2007 at the age of 42. Shortly after I started working in January 2008 as a part-time librarian at the main branch of a public library in a large city, I decided that I wanted to try to start a zine collection there. I submitted a proposal for the collection in October 2008, helped tremendously by the proposal template that Jenna Freedman posted on the Barnard Zine Library website, and also by the fact that a coworker in another department had once created and managed a zine collection for a few years. (Some other library school students and I had invited Jenna to present about Radical Reference and zines at a Progressive Library Skillshare that we organized in 2007, and her talk at that time energized and inspired me.)

The proposal was approved, and I started cataloging and displaying the collection in December 2008. We now have over 1200 zines in our browsing collection, with a few hundred waiting to be cataloged. I order, catalog, and maintain the zines; work with zine volunteers; do zine programming inside and outside of the library; and, along with zine volunteers, write for and maintain a zine collection blog. The scope of the collection is mainly contemporary zines with a broad coverage of subjects and cultures but also with a focus on local needs and interests. We basically accept all zines produced locally.

I came to zine librarianship more out of love for what zines generally are and can do, and for their function inside and outside of libraries and archives, than out of lots of subject knowledge or from a place of zine fandom. I was clear to myself and tried to make explicit to collection users that I wanted to act as a facilitator and was in no way an expert on zines, although I intended to work hard to learn as much as I could about them over time.

I love zines' accessibility to readers and writers. They're the most accessible way to publish thoughts and feelings that I know of, in terms of their language, design, physical format, and cost. I love that they're a way to allow users to become part of our collections. It's particularly exciting for me to have people in the community see their work become part of the body of knowledge accessible to our patrons. I love the way that zines broaden our coverage of topics and include cultures often excluded from a general discourse. I love all this and more. Notice that I have come to love zines, and that my interest isn't abstract anymore. (Zinesters have also inspired me and given me the courage to start making zines myself now. This is a big deal for me.)

Like Kate Angell (2012) says in *My Feminist Friends*:

> [Z]ines give people a voice. You don't have to have access to any kind of privilege to make a zine, nor do you have to be an academic or intellectual. Anyone can make a zine on her/his own terms, and that really appeals to me as a vehicle for allowing people to express themselves. By allowing those people who might not normally be a part of the power structure to be heard, it allows us to deconstruct old ideas and notions about gender and any other topic. (Introduction)

Zines are the perfect materials to make available in order to include marginalized people and their experiences in the library. They also often explicitly critique our society and call for social change. Both the content of zines and the process of working with them relate to social justice work for me.

Advocating for My Own Needs at Times

Anne Bishop (2002) talks about fighting one's own oppression as being an important component of ally work, and I agree. It seems to touch on charity or a self-destructive, guilt-laden model of social work to operate with no regard for my own needs as a worker or as a feminist. Oppressions intersect in the public library. It can be very tricky to untangle them, but even though my primary focus is to serve our patrons' needs, I find it crucial at times to advocate for myself. I do this in order to respect myself and also because it's all part of social change work.

Examples of challenges include being treated badly by patrons like any service worker can be, and dealing with sexist behavior. Like many service workers, librarians at my library are often expected to perform emotional labor as well as other parts of the service. I do a lot of this emotional labor willingly. I see it as trust- and community-building work that makes people feel more welcome in the space and willing to ask for the help that they need. It's sometimes necessary and difficult to set boundaries on this work, though. We often play the role of listener, being drawn into people's personal lives and interests, and I am often expected to continue to do emotional support work outside of the library—at the bus stop, on the bus.

I do feel like this is partly a gender issue and partly a labor issue. Service employees are often expected to give emotional attention and support as part of their job. Also, women have traditionally been expected to do more emotional labor at home, in public settings, and at work, and librarianship is a feminized profession.

My male coworkers are sometimes expected to provide emotional labor as well. I do notice, however, that the women working the reference desks get remarks from male patrons that the men don't get, asking us to smile, or "joking" about our not being available, or commenting on our not being in a good mood. I do think that we're sometimes expected to provide certain types of attention to male patrons that male library workers are not.

I consider grappling with my own oppression at my library as social change work as well. I find myself having more difficulty setting boundaries with people whom I perceive as being marginalized, for example, the homeless people who use the library. Reading Bishop, I see myself when she talks about letting ourselves be manipulated because of our guilt. There is one African American homeless man in particular who can be dominant and rude, and I have been strangely friendly to him. I think that my guilt-driven behavior is actually patronizing. I think it belittles my needs but also belittles him. I am in a sense not seeing him and his behavior and, possibly, his power.

Lessons Learned/Learning: Better Service with Zines

In my library work, I have done things that, for me, relate to social change, such as maintaining the Homelessness and GLBTQ Resources pages on the library website; researching and distributing referrals to food, showers, and shelter for homeless people to our security staff; and creating a job search resource guide specifically for ex-inmates, but the zine collection is my biggest work responsibility outside of desk coverage, and I focus there.

Where do I start in terms of talking about my learning? I have really fumbled and failed at times. Probably the biggest and most important piece of learning has to do with the subject categories that I originally created for shelving the zines. The list was too basic and combined subjects to the point of being insulting to zine creators and the communities being discussed. I also wanted to make our subject category definitions and decision-making process more transparent for collection users and volunteer catalogers. The new list with definitions is available on the bulletin board in the zine collection space, and I show the list to all volunteer catalogers when they are trained.

I don't want this to function as a disclaimer, but I do want to acknowledge that my job structure does at times make it difficult to make thoughtful decisions. I work half-time and have willingly taken on a number of responsibilities. I have an average of four hours per week off the reference desk to work on projects, but, like most librarians and support staff, we have a group office with seven desks and no walls or dividers. Time to work without interruption is virtually non-existent. These limitations, combined with the fact that I personally can have focus issues, make it extremely important that I consciously find a way to slow down and consider what I'm doing and its possible effects on others. I often take this time at home and off the clock.

It's very hard for me to admit this, but I actually had a GLBTQ/Gender category for the zines. I moved too fast when creating these categories and lumped people and issues together. I realized about a year ago that they were awful and that we needed to change them. I spoke with Amanda Stevens at the Anchor Archive Zine Library in Halifax, Nova Scotia, and got permission to borrow from their Box Categories list of subject headings with definitions, and they helped me be much more thoughtful about our subject list. First, there is the issue of order—GLBTQ versus LGBTQ, which I discussed above. Next, I realized that we don't really have Gay or Lesbian zines at this point. We may get some, but right now we really don't have any, although we do have zines about queer or transgender experience. Also, there is a difference between gender issues approached from a feminist critique of traditional male and female roles, and stories of completely new conceptions and experiences of gender. I decided that transgender zines needed their own space. So now we have Queer and Transgender subject categories, and the subject definitions remind catalogers to use Feminism as the subject if gender issues are discussed from a feminist perspective. We do have one zine on asexuality, which is shelved in the Sex subject category. If I come across more zines about asexuality, we may create a new category. I haven't seen any intersex zines yet, but I would possibly create a new category if we acquired some.

When I was working through the Personal section, it became clear to me how many of the zines really belonged in another category because they were actually depictions of personal experiences through the lens of political issues. Those zines were personalized, but they were trivialized by being defined as "perzines." This is not to say that perzines are trivial, but we were overlooking other, important facets of the miscategorized zines.

There are many ways that the collection development process can challenge the status quo and be more inclusive. I am only recently able to order from more than one source, and from a distro other than Microcosm Publishing, which my colleague who had created the zine collection in another location had ordered from. I do not want to, in a sense, automate my ordering by using Microcosm, which only distributes zines that are popular, meaning that they sell at least 40 copies per issue per year. As Jenna Brager and Jami Sailor (2011) write in their intro to *Archiving the Underground* #1:

> The collective's 2011 financial statement reads: "Microcosm strives to add credibility to zine writers and their ethics." The idea of credibility attached

to increased market visibility is both in direct opposition to the idea of "cred" and makes us wonder why an ethic that disavows expertise, celebrity, and capital gain needs added credibility and from who?

I am now able to order from multiple sources, and I do. Although I think that some zines and zine authors become popular because they resonate with readers, I don't want to prioritize the popular ones. I don't want to work against the best thing about zines—the way that they affirm the significance of all people's experience and their right to share it.

I think that outreach is powerful. Marginalized people may not expect to find what they need or feel comfortable in the library, but they may feel more hopeful after a positive experience outside of the library. This is what I mean when I talk about being proactively inclusive. I'm now bringing part of the collection into relevant spaces in the community for "zine reading hangouts." I brought the Queer and Transgender zines to a queer- and transgender-supportive coffeehouse and had a great turnout of engaged readers. I've scheduled a bike zines reading hangout at a bike-friendly bar. I recently talked at a homeless men's shelter about zines and the call for submissions from the People of Color Zine Project for a compilation zine about surviving and thriving when living at or below the poverty level. We had an amazing conversation and brainstormed a list of knowledge and skills that they think are important, and some of the men wanted to submit to the zine. The intern from that shelter is going to see if veterans that she works with want to write about their experience for a zine, and I'm supporting her on that project.

Iverson in *Questioning Neutrality* (2006) says "while librarians have been avidly anti-censorship, they have not been avidly anti-racist" (p. 27). More fumbling: I hadn't become conscious of the current representation of people of color in the zine collection until about a year ago. What I have been doing to work on that is to actively seek out zines authored by people of color, and to build into our cataloging procedures that all zines authored by people of color receive a "people of color" tag, along with a tag for the author's specific culture or cultures, so that they're more accessible in the catalog. I did a display of zines by people of color, including speakers who came for the People of Color Zine Project reading tour, to promote that tour. I need to build more relationships with people of color in the community.

Other ways that I've tried to be responsive are involving the community more in purchasing decisions, for example via an email list discussion about ordering from Microcosm; including users in decisions about how to use the zine collection budget both generally and specifically in terms of titles they want me to order; and creating a way for people to leave feedback on the bulletin board in the zine collection.

I know I have more to learn for as long as I do this.

Lessons Learned/Learning: Be Well!

I've had similar struggles with the Be Well! project. It's been important for me to find my blind spots in terms of people's needs for healthcare resources. I've discovered a number of them over the years. I thought that older people basically had what they needed, until a clinic manager let me know that they can't get care if they can't get to their providers, and that dental, vision care, and prescriptions are tough for many seniors to access. I've needed to think about where I distribute the booklets and how I get them to spaces where low-income, uninsured people of various cultures are—braiding salons, immigrant community locations, African American churches (which often have a health minister), and LGBTQ-safe spaces. Over time I added resources for homeless people, who tend to get healthcare on the street or from shelters or food pantries. I also added LGBTQ-friendly providers, as well as alternative and preventive resources such as information on growing your own food, accessing farmers' markets with a public assistance card, free or low-cost yoga, bike repair and ownership programs, and more.

I realized at one point that I was paying no attention to the physical accessibility of sites. I had an excruciatingly embarrassing conversation with a disabilities advocate who let me know that it's not just about being able to get in the front door, but about being able to use the restroom at a space. If people in wheelchairs can't use the restroom at a healthcare facility, they don't want to risk going there. I called up all of the clinics in Be Well! and asked them about accessibility in terms of getting in the front door, and whether their restroom is wheelchair-accessible and has handrails, and I now list that information. I also learned about gynecological exam tables that can be safely lowered for women in wheelchairs, and I include sites that have them.

This learning is about me seeing past my privilege and really trying to understand what people need and then connect them with it.

What Now

I don't want the zine collection at my library to take on the role of the place where we have "edgy" viewpoints and cultures represented, as though we have it covered because we have some zines. It's our responsibility to represent the community more fully in all of our collections and programming. I also want the information in the collection to be taken more seriously than being seen as cute or edgy. I want people to actually engage with the work and the ideas in it.

In *Zine Librarian Zine* #3 (2009), an anonymous author talks about the dangers and annoyances of being the "zine queen" in their library, and that resonated with me very much (p. 10-13). For me there is a legacy issue with the zine collection, and also with Be Well!. It's partly about me being less controlling, and, in the case of the zine collection, about further expanding the commitment to the collection—further outside of myself, and further outside of the institution. In each of these cases, I need to not be the focus. I need to be a facilitator of something that should be relevant enough to and grounded enough in the community for it to function without me. I don't want to act like an expert and take sole ownership of these projects. (As you've read here, I'm not an expert anyway). I need to keep finding ways to involve and rely on others—whether they be coworkers, volunteers, or interns. This is really, really hard for me. I am intensely attached to both projects and very picky about the work.

The zine collection work isn't shared, unlike for other collections. With those, a few people might do the ordering, catalogers and others process the items, and multiple staff shelve and check out/in items. I do all of that myself with the zine collection, with some volunteer help. When someone who has been in charge of a collection leaves their position, their collection gets assigned to someone else. I'm not sure that would happen with the zine collection, and I've been afraid to ask. I think that I reinforce the otherness and even the disparaging perceptions of zines when I assume a defensive posture about them. I think that I need to directly address these issues—ask to involve a coworker in the collection management, and explicitly ask what the plans are for the collection if I should leave.

I feel so strongly about Be Well! that I have been very hands-on, not wanting to spend my time on bureaucracy—I'm not interested in becoming a 501(c)(3) organization with a traditional advisory board, and I've been hesitant to apply for some grants because I don't want to be beholden. I think those decisions have allowed me to make very effective use of my time, truly focusing on the core of the work, but at some point I do need to connect with others more if I want to pass on the project.

What I'd Like to See – the Future of Our Field

I'd like to see an awareness of the political nature of our work, and I'd like to see people in the field take responsibility for that—in the general discourse in the field, in library school programs, and in our workplaces. I'd like to experience a safer and more vital atmosphere for these types of conversations, not a fear- or apathy-filled work culture when it comes to the basic questions of what we're doing and who we're doing it for. All of the denial and resistance to political conversations dissipate energy and rob us of opportunities to genuinely serve everyone, and to serve them in a way that helps create joy and crucial change.

Epilogue

In May 2013, I decided to end the Be Well! Pittsburgh project after eight years. It's as yet unclear what health care coverage will look like and what health care needs and financial struggles for low-income people may emerge when the Affordable Care Act individual coverage mandate takes effect in January 2014, but that's a different and new set of challenges. I am committed to universal health care now more than ever, in particular after witnessing resistance to Medicaid expansion and to increased employer responsibility to cover employees. Health care is a human right. Let's finally ensure that all of our community members have it.

References

Angell, K. (2012). Introduction. In K. Angell (Ed.), *My feminist friends* [Zine] #3.

Bishop, A. (2002). *Becoming an ally: Breaking the cycle of oppression in people.* Halifax, NS: Fernwood Publishing.

Brager, K., & Sailor, J. (2011). Introduction. In K. Brager & J. Sailor (Eds.), *Archiving the underground* [Zine] #1.

Durrani, S., & Smallwood, E. (2006). The professional is political: Redefining the social role of public libraries. In A. Lewis (Ed.), *Questioning library neutrality: Essays from* Progressive Librarian (pp. 119-140). Duluth, MN: Library Juice Press.

Hess, A. (2010, May 19). Ladies first: Does D.C. have a GLBT community or an LGBT one? *Washington City Paper.* Retrieved from http://www.washingtoncitypaper.com/blogs/sexist/2010/05/19/ladies-first-does-dc-have-a-glbt-community-or-an-lgbt-one/

Iverson, S. (2006). Librarianship and resistance. In A. Lewis (Ed.), *Questioning library neutrality: Essays from* Progressive Librarian (pp. 25-31). Duluth, MN: Library Juice Press.

Name Withheld. (2009). When bad things happen to good zine librarians. In R.E. Murphy, J. Freedman, & A. Sellie (Eds.), *Zine Librarian Zine* [Zine] #3.

Rosenzweig, M. C. (2001). A program for international progressive librarianship. *Progressive Librarian, 18,* 71.

West, J. (2012, October 31). In re books, wrap-up [Blog post]. Retrieved from http://www.librarian.net/stax/3947/in-re-books-wrap-up/

In the Movement

Whatcha Doin' after the Demo?: The Importance of Archiving Political Posters

Vince Teetaert

There are political posters everywhere in Quebec Public Interest Research Group (QPIRG) Concordia's offices: posters covering the walls marking Montreal social justice campaigns past and present, and current campaign posters set out on a table waiting to be put up across the city. QPIRG Concordia is a resource center and meeting place for activists engaged in grassroots social justice. Posters of past campaigns and events are displayed to inspire, and to instill a connection to the past. Underneath the table is a three-drawer cabinet into which staff members deposit copies of new posters that will be cataloged, digitized, and filed by volunteers, to become part of QPIRG Concordia's Political Poster Archive. This is an attempt by the social justice group to preserve its history through archiving posters produced both by the group itself and by its working groups and allies.

To activists involved in the social justice and community groups that create political posters, there is value in preserving them long past the event or campaign they were produced for. The 2007 publication of *Picture This!: Posters of Social Movements in Quebec (1966-2007)* is a compilation of political posters used in Quebec over four decades that highlights the archival work being done by the Centre de recherche en imagerie populaire (CRIP). In its forward, Dave Widgington (2007) writes,

> The ephemeral aspect of posters—torn down, weather worn, and generally lost soon after an event is over—makes their collection, archiving and

accessibility that much more important; particularly the ones that portray the more marginal, obscure and less accessible perspectives of society not presented anywhere else. They too have an influence and play a role in a society evolving toward social justice. (p. 12-13)

Picture This! not only speaks to the importance of preserving the images and slogans of political posters so that others may be inspired and the collective memory of social justice movements can be maintained, it also gives out the call to social justice groups in Quebec to actively archive their own posters.

Inspired by the work by CRIP and by *Picture This!*, QPIRG Concordia started a Political Poster Archive in 2008. The purpose of the archive was two-fold: to preserve the posters, and to make them accessible for research. PIRGs in Canada have operated differently from the consumer advocacy groups set up in the United States in the 1970s. QPIRG Concordia was started in 1981 and, like other PIRGs in Canada, is a campus-based social justice group that receives the majority of its funding through a student fee levy. However, the organization is completely independent from Concordia University and the students' union; it serves as a resource center for student and community organizing and for community-based social justice research. One way QPIRG Concordia promotes activism and organizing is through its Working Group program, which supports small grassroots groups that organize around specific issues, projects, or events (QPIRG Concordia, 2012).

Photocopying and printing services in the offices of QPIRG Concordia for the Working Groups means that posters are printed in the office on a variety of issues, including indigenous solidarity, prisoner solidarity, and migrant justice. With Working Group posters being printed in-office and those by their community allies being displayed on QPIRG bulletin boards, it was easy for QPIRG Concordia to start collecting posters for their archive.

It was through my membership with one of the Working Groups of QPIRG Concordia that I got involved with the poster archive. Radical Reference (RR) Montreal is a collective made up of professional librarians, library technicians, and library students who provide reference and information support and education to activists, independent journalists, and social justice groups. RR was asked to help out with the poster archive. The archive's progress had been limited; posters were being collected but were not organized or cataloged. It was easy to collect the posters; the hard part was for QPIRG Concordia, a small organization with limited staff, to find time to deal with the boxes of posters being collected.

The archive falls under the coordination responsibilities of the Resource Library Coordinator at QPIRG Concordia. The coordinator position is a temporary contract and a part-time one, relying on two sets of funding grants that come at different times of the year. In practice, QPIRG Concordia must go through two hiring processes each year in order to have a Library Coordinator. The coordinator is supported by the Library committee, a group of volunteers interested in libraries and radical resources. Committee members have varying amounts of experience with institutionalized libraries and may not be formally trained in cataloging, classification, or archival practices. When I met with the Library Coordinator in the summer of 2011, the biggest issues were figuring out how to process the posters, and finding the time to do it. Through circumstance I was looking for an internship placement to fulfill a course requirement for the library technician program I was in. I would be able to dedicate three days a week for seven weeks to processing the political posters.

The recognition of the archival value of political posters is a fairly recent one—there is no universal standard of how to archive them. Researchers for *Picture This!* found that the political posters collections they looked at had varying preservation and cataloging practices (Widgington, 2007). In the book *Agitate! Educate! Organize!: American Labor Posters*, archivist Lincoln Cushing and political art historian Timothy Drescher (2009) surveyed public and private collections of American labor posters in a continuation of the work Cushing had done previously, including building a database on the subject. Their discoveries were similar to those of *Picture This!*: collections were rarely fully cataloged or digitized, and often the documents were scattered, existing as parts of larger collections. Although their research brought them into contact with dedicated collectors and library and archival staff, in general more resources were needed to ensure that collections were adequately preserved and cataloged, and to make the posters accessible to researchers (p.1-3).

After a quick survey of the posters QPIRG Concordia had collected, I soon realized how much work would need to be done. Thousands of posters had been amassed, but there was no policy on how they were to be collected, so I would find 30 copies of one poster, while others had only one or two. Tape, staples, and sticky tack had not been removed from the posters, causing them to stick to each other and rip. Pamphlets and flyers had also been collected along with the posters. These would have to be sorted out and boxed for another archival project. Through a process involving the Library Committee, QPIRG Concordia staff, and the QPIRG Concordia Board of Directors (who had voted to start the archive), collection guidelines were developed on how many copies of each poster would be collected, and priorities for poster collection were set.

When starting my internship with QPIRG Concordia, I was very sensitive to how I should work with staff and Library Committee members, volunteers, and the board. I was the one with the training and I had some fairly fixed ideas of how I wanted things to go. But I believe in a non-hierarchical approach to work and wanted to adhere to the collective, consensus-based structure of the group. This would mean complete transparency in each step I was taking, and constant consultation with the staff and library committee members. I did not want to come up with a system that would die the day my internship was over. In the article "Disciplining Dissent: NGOs and Community Organizations," Aziz Choudry and Eric Shragge (2012) tackle the issue of the professionalization of community organizations and the consolidation of power that comes with it. They argue that participation in community organizations creates opportunities for learning and knowledge sharing in informal settings. These opportunities occur less frequently when spaces have been professionalized (p.113-18).

Luckily, the work was such that I had to rely on the staff and volunteers as references to the parts of the QPIRG Concordia's collective history that I did not know. I would often walk to the staff offices with posters find out what year the event took place, or whether QPIRG Concordia had organized the event or just sponsored it. As well, the library committees served as a valuable resource ensuring that consensus-based decisions were made rather than by me unilaterally. I was not on an island by myself but rather part of a group.

The next task was organizing and cataloging the posters. Political posters present certain challenges to archivists. There is no standard practice as to how they should be treated. Susan Tschabrun's (2003) article "Off the Wall and into a Drawer: Managing a Research Collection of Political Posters" discusses the many challenges political posters present for archivists wanting to make their collections accessible to researchers. For the most part, large archives have tended to overlook the importance of political posters. Museums have traditionally deemed them "too popular a medium," and archives have scattered posters through their collections, including them as parts of larger collections in adherence to archival practices (p. 304-305). One of the reasons for lack of attention to archiving political posters by large repositories has been the posters' subject matter. The struggles of the socially-marginalized and the politically-excluded have been absent from mainstream library and archival collections, and archivists and researchers have undervalued their historical relevance (p. 323). Political posters, however, are incredibly important historical records, as the political events and campaigns for which the posters were created may not be documented in any other way. Their use by socially marginalized groups in campaigns for social justice provides researchers with primary sources not found anywhere else. Research of political posters has grown over recent years, making political posters important sources for multiple disciplines of study (p. 305-306).

As stated above, having an archive with material that was accessible to researchers was one of the goals QPIRG Concordia had set when the poster archive was established. Community-based social justice research has evolved over time to be an important part of QPIRG Concordia's mandate. Projects like the Community-University Research Exchange (CURE), Study in Action, and the *Convergence Research Journal* have been created to develop community-based research and publication. Establishing links between researchers and activists and promoting research by social justice groups has become a major aspect in the movement for social change. In "Activist Research: Mapping Power Relations, Information Struggles," activist researchers Aziz Choudry and Devlin Kuyek (2012) argue that developing relationships between social justice movements and researchers allows for community input in the research being done and establishes networks that freely share the researchers' findings. The hope is that an accessible political poster archive could serve as another connection between researchers and groups engaged in social justice.

Making QPIRG Concordia's Political Poster Archive an important resource for researchers meant cataloging in such a way as to make the information in the posters easily accessible. If we wanted to bring out the information in the posters for researchers to see, each poster had to be cataloged at the item level, like a book. This presented a number of challenges. Posters are not like books, which have long-established cataloging practices. The political posters we were dealing with were created for the purpose of promoting an event or campaign, with little regard for the preservation that may occur later. This meant that posters rarely included such information as the year of their creation, or the creator or artist of the work. Usually, but not always, the group sponsoring the event was noted. We decided that the more information about the poster included in the documentation, the less physical handling of the actual poster would occur. The posters were cataloged keeping in mind that the information would be displayed digitally with a digitized image of the poster.

As someone interested in cataloging and its powers, I would be remiss to not talk a bit about the technical aspects of how the posters were cataloged. At the time of my internship I was a student in a technician program, looking to put into practice the training I had received in archival practices. In Canada, the archival standards are the Rules for Archival Description (RAD), so with my RAD and my *respect des fonds* I went into the physical processing of the posters well-trained. Then my bubble popped. The idealistic world of my training did not match the conditions I was working under. The offices did not have room to house the boxes containing the *sous-fonds* I was going to create. I had a poster management problem. Luckily I received some advice from a records manager who told me not to think of my problem as an archival problem, but as a filing problem. We needed to create a filing system that would be easily understood.

Chris Dodge (2008), in his essay "Useful Cataloging," passed along some sage advice: "Catalog users are best served by catalogers less concerned with correctness than *usefulness*, Sanford Berman has long asserted. I agree" (p.165). We designed a system that broke the posters up into three series, based on who produced the posters: QPIRG Concordia, Working Groups of QPIRG Concordia, and Community Groups. From there, posters were filed by the year the poster was created, ensuring that the top file would always be the current year and making it easy for the volunteers to find and file new posters.

A work flow of poster processing was also developed. Each poster would be given a unique item number displaying its series and year of creation. The poster would then be scanned and filed digitally, using its unique item number as a file name. The poster was now ready to be cataloged.

The information taken from the posters has been organized in fields that will be searchable in the archive's online platform. Guidelines have been set up to ensure control and uniformity of documented information. The fields displayed in the cataloging record are pretty straightforward, including the item number and poster series, as well as the tag line or prominent slogan used as the title, the date (month/year), the group that created it, any allies who sponsored the event (other groups), the language and size of the poster, whether it is color or black and white, and the artist, if noted. Tags and subject headings can be added by the cataloger, in order to display more information about the poster for keyword searches. The subject headings come from a controlled vocabulary used to classify books in the QPIRG Concordia's lending library. This was developed to represent the language used by activists and members of working groups to describe the work they are engaged in. It is also not as complex as other controlled vocabularies, to allow for ease of use.

There are still incredible amounts of work to be done on the poster archive. New posters are created every day and need to be cataloged, scanned, and filed. While many posters are scanned, cataloged, and ready for display online, the uploading of files and tweaking of the online platform takes time and resources. There is still more information to be taken from the posters and displayed for researchers. Subject headings describe only the political nature of the posters, and descriptions of the images on the posters have not been documented. Without this additional work, the catalog does not express the artistic value the posters have.

When thinking of the posters as artistic objects, copyright becomes an important issue that needs to be addressed as the collection is digitized and put online. While some of the posters in the collection are produced by QPIRG Concordia, the vast majority are created by Working Groups and community groups outside the QPIRG Concordia umbrella. For the time being, because of copyright concerns and the capacity of the archive, political posters from community groups will not be displayed online. Mechanisms are in place with Working Groups to help ensure their cooperation with the archive. Once the images are online, there are steps the archive can take to define how the images are used. Using Creative Commons designations allows the creators of the posters to define how others can use them, and a watermark could be used on the images to discourage its non-sanctioned use. Copyright is a complicated issue that faces the archive and our wish to put the poster collection online. It is an example of the ongoing discussions we have and of the work that the poster archive still needs to do.

In "Archives for All: Professional Responsibility and Social Justice," Randall Jimerson (2007) explains that the power of archives has been used by society's elites to solidify their control, and that as archivists we must disrupt this status quo (p. 254). He reminds us of the late historian Howard Zinn's challenge to archivists to compile documentation of "the lives, desires, and needs of ordinary people" (p. 269). Disenfranchised groups that are excluded or under-reported by existing archives have formed their own archives, understanding the power these repositories have (p. 267-268). Archives like the Political Poster Archive at QPIRG Concordia are part of the movement building the capacity for research and knowledge-sharing in order to inspire social change. As radical librarians and activist archivists with a commitment to non-hierarchical approaches, we are part of this movement.

"510 Missing & Murdered Native Women Since 1980"
March 2009 • 11" x 17" • color
Group: QPIRG Concordia
Allies: 2110 Centre, Simone de Beauvoir Institute
Tag: Programming

References

Choudry, A., & Kuyek, D. (2012). Activist research: Mapping power relations, information struggles. In A. Choudry, J. Hanley, & E. Shragge (Eds.), *Organize! Building from the local for global justice* (pp. 23-35). Montréal, QC: PM Press.

Choudry, A., & Shragge, E. (2012). Disciplining dissent: NGOs and community organizations. In L. Montesinos Coleman & K. Tucker (Eds.), *Situating global resistance: Between discipline and dissent* (pp. 109-123). New York, NY: Routledge.

Cushing, L., & Drescher, T. W. (2009). *Agitate! Educate! Organize!: American labor posters.* Ithaca, NY: ILR Press.

Dodge, C. (2008). Useful cataloging. In K.R. Roberto (Ed.), *Radical cataloging: Essays at the front* (pp. 165-169). Jefferson, NC: McFarland.

Jimerson, R. C. (2007). Archives for all: Professional responsibility and social justice. *The American Archivist, 70,* 252-281.

QPIRG Concordia. (n.d.). History. Retrieved from http://www.qpirgconcordia.org/?page_id=2522

Tschabrun, S. (2003). Off the wall and into a drawer: Managing a research collection of political posters. *The American Archivist, 66,* 303-324.

Widgington, D. (2007). Wheat paste, powdered milk and other means of social adhesion. In J.P. Boyer, J. Desjardins, & D. Widgington (Eds.), *Picture this! 650 posters of social movements in Québec (1966-2007)* (pp. 9-12). Montréal, QC: Cumulus Press.

To Spread the Revolution: Anarchist Archives and Libraries

Jessica Moran

For anarchists—those defined in the most general terms as believing in a political and social theory of society without government and through voluntary relationships—the written and published word has been central to their movement. From early on, anarchists in the United States and Europe published their ideas and collected their written work. This published literature was one of the main sources of anarchist propaganda and a means to communicate and spread ideas. Newspapers, pamphlets, and books were instrumental in sharing and documenting the philosophies and actions of the anarchist movement; anarchist libraries were a natural continuation and followed shortly thereafter.

Many early English language anarchist periodicals produced pamphlet series, often with some sort of anarchist library subtitle. For example, early American journals such as *Liberty, Free Society,* and *Mother Earth* had pamphlet series called the "Liberty Library," "Free Society Library," and the "Mother Earth Library." The long-running English anarchist paper *Freedom* also maintained a pamphlet series called the "Freedom Library." The collecting of anarchist ideas in this format became a regular feature of anarchist periodicals and publishers and developed a body of knowledge—or library—usually not available elsewhere, that anarchists and those curious about anarchist ideas could draw from, discuss, and share.

But anarchists were not only interested in publishing and distributing their ideas in pamphlet and, later, book series; they were also interested in libraries in the more traditional sense. In Philadelphia, a Radical Library was established as early as 1895 by the Ladies Liberal League of Philadelphia, a group that included anarchists Voltairine de Cleyre and Natasha Notkin and whose mission was to "repair a deficit in the public libraries by furnishing radical works upon subjects at convenient hours for working men and accessible to all at only a slight expense" (Falk, Pateman, & Moran, 2003, p. 459). This library would continue in various forms for at least the next 20 years. It became a social and political center for anarchists in the Philadelphia area, with anarchist Joseph Cohen taking an active role in their activities throughout the 1910s (Avrich, 2006, p. 60-61). Anarchists formed similar libraries and social centers in other major cities, such as the Progressive Library in New York City, where in 1906 a group of anarchists was arrested while holding a meeting to discuss Leon Czolgosz's assassination of President William McKinley five years earlier (Falk et al., 2003, p. 200).

In Europe, a similar interest in anarchist libraries was present in the Spanish Modern Schools. The Modern Schools were a rational educational project begun by Spanish anarchist Francisco Ferrer, and as part of this initiative, a publishing program and library were created (Avrich, 2006, p. 19-23). These Modern Schools spread to the United States after Ferrer's death, and when a Ferrer Modern School was founded in New York City in 1910, it included not only a school and meeting rooms, but also a library. A Francisco Ferrer Club in Chicago contained a "free library and reading room" (Avrich, 2006, p.78, 62). Later, in 1921, following Russian anarchist Peter Kropotkin's death, a new Kropotkin Library was built in his honor at the Stelton Modern School in Stelton, New Jersey (Avrich, 2006, p. 304).

Anarchists saw their libraries as vital social centers for their movement. These libraries were not simply places to collect social and political books that addressed anarchism; they were active locations for anarchism. They were meeting places and spaces to share, spread, and develop the ideas of the anarchist movement. Yet anarchists have also wanted to preserve their written propaganda and political culture for the future, and they have used and participated in the resources of more traditional institutional libraries. One of the oldest collections of anarchist material in the United States was established at the University of Michigan when anarchist and labor activist Joseph Labadie donated his personal papers and library there in 1911. This collection was later organized and further developed by anarchist Agnes Inglis, who was curator of the Labadie collection from 1925 until 1952 (Herrada, n.d.). The Labadie Collection today remains one of the most important collections of anarchist material in the United States. Emma Goldman would establish her and Alexander Berkman's archives at the International Institute of Social History (IISH) in Amsterdam in December 1938, a time when the IISH was collecting the papers of labor activists and other radical individuals throughout Europe as Nazism spread. Around the same time that Goldman was depositing her material, the IISH librarian smuggled anarchist Mikhail Bakunin's papers (as part of Max Nettlau's collection) out of Germany (International Institute of Social History, n.d.). In both of these cases, anarchists recognized the importance of preserving their collections of books, papers, pamphlets, and ephemera for future use. These collections still exist and continue to be rich sources for documenting anarchist history, though they are held within larger institutions and among other non-anarchist collections. But they are the exception; most anarchist libraries and archives are located not within the boundaries of larger university or institutional walls, but very consciously outside them.

The proliferation of anarchist libraries, infoshops, and archives in the present day demonstrates that anarchists have maintained that instinct to preserve and provide access to anarchist literature. In most major cities, one can find at least some sort of anarchist infoshop with a library attached, and there are a growing number of online libraries and archives. In many cases, these collections have developed over time both as a continuation of a historical interest in using the written word and public space as propaganda to promote and explain anarchism, and also to fill a gap missing in more traditional, mainstream, and institutionally-based library and archival collections. These collections are rooted in the belief that access to anarchist literature was an important component of the movement, and in the reality that outside of the movement, anarchist literature was difficult or impossible to find. Anarchists, by definition suspicious of the state and its institutions, have also wanted to protect their own historical writings and culture. As others have noted, "While there are of course some very notable collections in both state and university collections, the majority of anarchist materials remain in the hands of the producing communities, preserved by the people who participated in the very struggles that are being documented" (Hoyt, 2012, p. 32).

In many ways, anarchist libraries and archives today fit within the larger umbrella of independent community archives. Independent community archives should be seen as "social movements (or as elements of social movements)" that are part of the "development of subversive and counter-hegemonic social or public memories" according to Andrew Flinn and Mary Stevens (2009, p.4). Community archives can be defined broadly as the "grassroots activities of creating and collecting, processing and curating, preserving and making accessible collections relating to a particular community or specified subject" (Flinn & Stevens, 2009, p.5). These activities look different depending upon individual circumstances and communities, and often the activities that define a "community archives" may take place without the terms themselves ever being used (Flinn, 2007, p. 152). Flinn (2007) writes that "community histories or community archives are the grassroots activities of documenting, recording and exploring community heritage in which community participation, control and ownership of the project is essential" (p. 153). Collections organized and created around a shared identity and interest in anarchism and the anarchist movement situate anarchist libraries and archives firmly within the independent community archives movement.

In reviewing the development of community archives in the U.K. in working class and ethnic and religious minority communities, Flinn and Stevens (2009) suggest that these initiatives emerged out of an activist or oppositional political community or culture: "[m]ost if not all community archives are motivated and prompted to act by the (real or perceived) failure of mainstream heritage organizations to collect, preserve and make accessible collections and histories that properly reflect and accurately represent the stories of all society" (p. 6). These archives are often viewed not only as tools for education but also as weapons in struggle. Community archives should not be seen as vanity projects, nor as alternatives to active struggle, but rather as acts of resistance, consciously made. This context helps explain why many community archives projects are hesitant or resistant to giving up autonomy over the management of the archives.

However, in maintaining full autonomy outside of mainstream institutional control, independent community archives are faced with many challenges to the sustainability of their projects. Financial stability, keeping the archives open, and managing the long-term preservation of the archives become ever-present and ever-increasing efforts. In one 2011 study of New Zealand community archives, Joanna Newman (2011) concluded that in fact those archives within a local council or other government institution had the most stable funding, skilled staff, and adequate space and materials to protect and preserve the archives. She further found that some of the community archives continued to exist "only because of the passion and commitment of one or two individuals" (p. 37-45). Newman's findings are representative of community archives projects around the world. In many cases, the archives project has been developed and kept going through the deep enthusiasm and involvement of a few people; however, maintaining such a project over the long term becomes harder. As Flinn and Stevens (2009) note, "[i]f resources remain scarce and the energy of key figures begins to wane, maintaining independence from the state and its institutions may become increasingly difficult for many independent community archives to sustain" (p. 17).

Anarchist libraries and archives make up one segment of community libraries and archives. They can range from a small collection of warped and dog-eared pamphlets and books, to a carefully curated and managed collection within a university setting, to a collection of links or PDF files on a website. Whatever the form these libraries take, they share some similarities. Like the independent community archives discussed above—with a few notable exceptions—most prefer to remain outside the scope of larger governmental and nonprofit organizations, instead relying on the volunteer service of a few committed individuals. These people see themselves as keeping anarchist history alive and contributing to the body of knowledge that makes up anarchism. These projects are not seen simply as an archive or library for the archive or library's sake, but rather as part of the anarchist movement, and their work is a contribution to that movement. They are preserving the history of the anarchist movement to correct absences or mistakes in the historical record, as well as to inform and potentially help direct the future of the movement.

In preparing the research for this article, I sent out a survey in 2012 and received responses from 26 anarchist archives and libraries throughout North America, Europe, South America, and Australasia. I was interested in questions of funding and sustainability, as well as staffing—how many people were involved with a project, what their skills and experiences were, and why they did the work they did.

The results of my survey found that of the 26 respondents, 14, or a little over half, are either fully self-funded by workers in their respective libraries or archives or funded through a combination of self-funding and donations. Of the rest, seven are funded through membership or research/reading fees in addition to fundraising. Only one archives, the Archivio-Biblioteca Enrico Travaglini in Italy, received any government money, and that was less than 1500 Euros per year; as they wrote, "funding is still insufficient" and supplemented through self-funding. The four remaining respondents were smaller anarchist collections within university libraries that are financed through their institutions. Excluding those collections within university libraries, all the libraries and archives depend entirely on volunteer labor, with the exception of the International Centre for Research on Anarchism (CIRA) in Switzerland, which is formally registered with the Swiss government as an association and has in the past been able to employ one person. CIRA also uses the labor of young men completing civilian service as an alternative to the military.

The size and scope of these archives vary widely, from collections of a few hundred books, pamphlets, and zines to those with over 20,000 items cataloged. Where collections are held also greatly varies, though the majority seem to be either in private homes (seven) or as part of other anarchist or radical spaces (six). Other locations include university settings, rented locations, or online only. Outside of the university setting, few appear to have purpose-built or stable and secure long-term storage. Interestingly, a substantial number of those responding (12) had at least one member within their group who worked in a library or archives or had library or archival expertise, though the major qualification for joining any of the projects seemed to be a willingness to do the work and an inclination toward or experience with anarchism and related social movements. A number of the more infoshop-type libraries, especially those with a lending library, offer some sort of formalized training program for new volunteers. While all of those responding to the survey said that their collection's focus was anarchism and anarchist history, whether at the local, national, or international level, only about half had any kind of articulated collection or acquisition policy. Many explained that they rely largely on donations and will accept anything that broadly fits under the definition of anarchism, excluding anarcho-capitalism/libertarianism. Some also made an explicit point about trying to keep state socialist and Marxist material out of their collections, while at the same time they maintained an agnostic position on the many strains and threads within the anarchist movement.

When asked what they understood as the purpose of their library or archives, people's responses ranged from some version of "preserving anarchist history and making it available to the anarchist movement" to "spreading the revolution." One wrote, "our purpose is to offer a lending library as well as a space to archive independently-published materials." Many are interested in providing a place not just to preserve anarchist material, but to "promote libertarian thought" or to help people learn about anarchist ideas. Perhaps the Cowley Library best represents the number of different purposes that an anarchist library can have as they explain:

> We initially conceived it as a sort of collectivized living room—a resource for the community of people who use the Cowley Club—sharing books, magazines, films and computers to make them accessible to everyone instead of just sitting in individual people's living rooms. The library also functions as a meeting space for groups to use and additionally aspires to function as an archive of the history of radical social struggles, especially in the local area.

Many of these libraries start as reading rooms and small lending libraries, often with the organizers' hopes of creating a meeting and gathering space. Over time, they begin to document and collect their own and their movements' history. Most respondents saw their projects as a combination of preserving anarchist history, helping to spread anarchist ideas, giving people the opportunity to learn about them, and participating in a concrete way in the anarchist movement. As another wrote, "We want to give people the chance to read from an anarchist perspective; books and magazines you don't find in the 'normal' libraries. We want to preserve our own history. Nobody else does...We see our library as one part of all these little things that all together make a big counter-culture against the current fucked up state of affairs." In many ways, these contemporary projects are not so different from their counterparts of a hundred years ago. Perhaps a member of the Australian online anarchist archive The Bastard Archives explained it most succinctly when he wrote that he sees the purpose of his project as "[t]o not forget what's come before us, to remember both victories and failures, and to disseminate ideas that might unfuck the world."

My interest in community archives generally and anarchist libraries and archives more specifically comes out of my personal participation in the Kate Sharpley Library (KSL). The KSL is an anarchist library and archive with its own very anarchist history. It was originally founded in 1979 as a radical library to serve the anarchist community in Brixton, London, and was connected to the 121 Anarchist Bookshop. Only later, when it moved out of London in 1991, did its main purpose change, morphing from a resource center to a special collection (and eventually archives) that focuses on documenting the history of anarchism (Longmore, 2004). Since 1991, the KSL has been maintained in a private home belonging to Barry Pateman. In 1999, Pateman moved to the United States and brought along the library. Over the next ten years, the collection has continued to grow and have a home with him. The KSL is currently housed in its own space in a 1500 square foot building and includes books, periodicals, pamphlets, articles, ephemera, manuscripts, and organizational archives. The library, located in California, usually has one to two in-person visitors per month, as well as regular research requests by email.

My participation in the KSL began with my interest in anarchist history and experience working in libraries and archives. For me, it was a way to use skills I already had to help preserve what I see as important, including rare material that is not available elsewhere. Other members of the KSL collective are two people in the U.K. with library training who help collect U.K. and European items, translate writing in foreign languages, and select and edit material that is published in periodic newsletters and pamphlets. We also have members in the U.S. who help with the technical side of things, from developing an open source online catalog to maintaining our website and online collections.

At the KSL, all work is voluntary and the format for participation is loose and informal. People become involved because they want and are able to help. While people often express a desire to help in the library, there are only about five who have a long-term involvement in the KSL. I have found in my own personal experience that the nature of the work is such that it is difficult for most people to sustain regular involvement in the project for a variety of reasons. While there are some wonderfully interesting materials in the collection, anarchists are also quite good at producing terrible materials, and beyond that, quite a bit of the general care and maintenance are the rather repetitive tasks such as filing, arranging material into a predetermined order, and simple cataloging. However, we do get visitors who are happy to help with some filing, shelving, or sorting for an hour or two.

Within the KSL, there are no formal decision-making procedures, and apart from a strict policy to collect only anarchist material or material that substantially deals with anarchism, there are no formal collection policies. Perhaps our greatest collection development discussions are centered on exactly what the often permeable and porous definition of "anarchism" is, and where to draw the lines. Decisions are usually made because one member has the time and ability to carry through a project, or when a group of members has a chance to get together either in person or through email. All work is voluntary and takes place during members' free hours, after work, on the weekends, or in other stolen time. This freedom in participation is both a benefit of the project and a weakness. Work—whether it is cataloging a book or other item, accessioning an archival collection, translating an article, editing a pamphlet, or updating the website—gets done because it is seen as important and members enjoy it, but it often gets done slowly and may not be members' first priority, no matter how much they might wish it were.

Most funding for the project comes from the sale of pamphlets, duplicate books, and periodicals at anarchist bookfairs; subscribers to our bulletin; and a few sustaining members who send us $10-20 per month in exchange for receiving the bulletin and any pamphlets we may publish. These funds never cover expenses, which range from simple things like printing costs to much larger expenses, such as ensuring the physical safety of the collections, buying an adequate supply of acid free folders and boxes, paying for the shipping of large items donated to the library, and having the funds available to purchase rare or expensive materials.

From its establishment, the KSL made the conscious decision that regardless of its financial situation, it must remain in the hands of anarchists and outside the hands of state institutions. That belief was present at its inception in 1991, when one of its founders, Albert Meltzer (1991), wrote in the first issue of the KSL Bulletin:

> Real Anarchism is not the cult of a few 'well known' quasi-father figures of the past, any more than real Buddhism is the worship of Gautama Buddha as a god. Anarchists in practice do not much care about what such persons said or wrote unless they happen to have said something with which they agree. The cult of researching their acquaintanceships, personal life and influences upon them is a deliberate ploy by State-sponsored academics, but it

has nothing to do with us. The personality cult, the worship of individuals and the imposition of bourgeois ideas lead to a phony anarchism which may flourish but is not the real thing.

The KSL has embraced a collection philosophy that doesn't simply see anarchism as a theoretical idea or set of ideas but instead tries to record anarchism from the bottom up, documenting the everyday experiences and lives of anarchists. This policy tries to preserve and make accessible the history of lesser-known or forgotten anarchists and events. In rejecting "state-sponsored academics" and "the worship of individuals and the imposition of bourgeois ideas," Meltzer was alluding to the idea that while many of the ideas and theories of anarchism may have originally been articulated by a few authors, the key to understanding the anarchist movement is to see it not as the ideas of a few great men, but rather as a community that shared, lived with, and developed those ideas. Anarchism is a living movement in which ideas move and spread, and adapt and develop over time, in and through practice. In an interview, Pateman (2010) explained:

> Albert knew that anarchism was not just Kropotkin or Stirner, or whoever. It was the putting into practice of it all that was important. He knew that this could be done by people who had only a bare knowledge (if any!!) of our major writers and thinkers. He also knew that histories of anarchism excluded countless people who had been instrumental in its development and changes. Because these people often did not write theory or were prominent speakers they were ignored.

Our contention is that lesser-known anarchists and events are just as, if not more, important than the "great" thinkers. In many ways, the KSL has followed the general shift of institutional and mainstream archives in the last few decades toward developing strategies to more systematically document the undocumented, listen for the silences in the archives, and widen the scope of collections to include people's everyday lives.

Another expression of the collection policy and justification for the work of the KSL read: "We do this to preserve and promote anarchist ideas and anarchist history. Not in a vague and fuzzy 'learning is good' kind of way, but because if we don't do it, who will? [...] Anarchism is the sum of years of struggle of thousands of comrades. Ideas are honed in argument, and in practice" (Kate Sharpley Library, 2004). Trying to document how anarchism was used in discussions over time, and how ideas were put into practice, explored, used, or rejected, allows for a much deeper understanding of the political theories. This article goes on to assert that while there will always be someone interested in preserving a first edition of Kropotkin, he isn't the beginning and end of the anarchist movement. All the poorly printed, badly argued, or beautifully designed and articulate newspapers, pamphlets, books, and more that make up the anarchist movement help to shed light on anarchism as a human reality instead of a dead group of ideas.

There are a number of questions my involvement with the Kate Sharpley Library has led me to, not just pertaining to the sustainability of the KSL, but also about anarchist and community archives collections more generally. Some of this concern may simply be a matter of balancing my professional training and experiences working in larger institutions, with what is possible and makes sense when working on a volunteer-run project with little to no funding. But I worry about the proper care and handling of collections for preservation. I worry about the difficulty or lack of good recordkeeping for collections; as collections grow, institutional or personal memory isn't enough, and it won't be enough long-term. But I think my biggest worry, and perhaps the most important question, is that of the sustainability of the collections and the projects—how will they continue into the future? Will these collections of rare and important anarchist materials last from generation to generation? Or even year to year? How will they remain alive and relevant? There are anarchist libraries and archives of various kinds and at various stages of development throughout Europe, the U.S., Latin America, and Australasia, but they are small volunteer institutions, surviving through the sheer will and enthusiasm of a few individuals. Will they be available and useful to people for the long haul? I don't want them to become boutique vanity collections, open only to a small number of people in the know, but I also recognize that serving large numbers of users is often impossible with a small staff and limited time. Yet the answer for these projects is rarely partnering with or transferring the collections to a bigger institution. The anarchist movement is a diverse and dispersed one, with no large organizations or centralized organizational culture. There are no long-lasting anarchist organizations, as are often found in other social movements. There are no organizations to which an anarchist archive or library could be donated, nor any that has the ability to sponsor or support such a library or archive.

This is the tension for me. These collections hold material that can be found not in your local public library, probably not at your local university library, and perhaps only at a few major research libraries with one-of-a-kind manuscript and archival collections. There are a number of important unpublished manuscripts and archival collections in the KSL that you cannot find elsewhere, for example, the records of the long-running anarchist bookstores Bound Together Books and Left Bank Books in San Francisco and Seattle respectively, and the records of the support group for the 1979 U.K. Persons Unknown Trial. I feel strongly as both an anarchist and an archivist that this material should be preserved and made accessible to those who want to use it. As a member of the KSL, I feel equally strongly that the material in this collection should not fall into the hands of a university or state-sponsored research library. That wasn't what the donors to the collection wanted, or what those who have given so much time and effort to the project wanted. But neither do I think the collection can be given to some amorphous, undefined "anarchist movement." The responsibility is too great, and the work too important, not to have some committed individual or group responsible and accountable. But as far as I am aware, neither the KSL, nor any of the other anarchist libraries and archives surveyed, have long-range plans for survival. What happens to these collections when those currently involved in the projects no longer have the time, energy, or ability to be part of them? In darker moments, I despair. But most of the time I am hopeful that the anarchist movement will remain relevant to enough people to attract future generations who will want to take up the mantle and care for these collections—just as de Cleyre, Notkin, and Cohen have influenced generations of people to keep the tradition of anarchist libraries alive. In these moments, I believe in the spirit of anarchism that inspires people to act for themselves and each other and to protect, preserve, and continue these projects without any help from the state.

References

Avrich, P. (2006). *The modern school movement*. Oakland, CA: AK Press.

Falk, C., Pateman, B., & Moran, J. (Eds.) (2003). *Emma Goldman: A documentary history of the American years, volume 1: Made for America, 1890-1901*. Berkeley, CA: University of California Press.

Flinn, A. (2007). Community histories, community archives: Some opportunities and challenges. *Journal of the Society of Archivists, 28*(2), 151-176. doi: 10.1080/00379810701611936

Flinn, A. and Stevens, M. (2009). "It is noh mistri, wi mekin histri": Telling our own story: Independent and community archives in the UK, challenging and subverting the mainstream. In J. Bastian & B. Alexander (Eds.), *Community archives: The shaping of memory* (pp. 3-27). London, England: Facet Publishing.

Herrada, J. (n.d). History of the Labadie Collection. Retrieved from http://www.lib.umich.edu/labadie-collection/history

Hoyt, A. (2012). The international anarchist archives: A report on conditions and a proposal for action. *Theory in Action, 5*(4), 30-46.

International Institute of Social History. (n.d). History of the ISSH. Retrieved from http://socialhistory.org/en/about/history-iish

Kate Sharpley Library. (2004). The Kate Sharpley Library: What and why. *KSL: Bulletin of the Kate Sharpley Library, 40*. Retrieved from http://www.katesharpleylibrary.net/n2z41d

Longmore, C. (2004). Some notes on the founding of the Kate Sharpley Library. *KSL: Bulletin of the Kate Sharpley Library, 40*. Retrieved from http://www.katesharpleylibrary.net/rv16fn

Meltzer, A. (1991). The purpose of history. *KSL: Bulletin of the Kate Sharpley Library, 1*. Retrieved from http://www.katesharpleylibrary.net/3tx9mw

Newman, J. (2011). Sustaining community archives. *Aplis, 24*(1), 37-45.

Pateman, P. (2010). The Kate Sharpley Library then, now, and next: An interview with Barry Pateman. *KSL: Bulletin of the Kate Sharpley Library, 63-64*. Retrieved from http://www.katesharpleylibrary.net/0vt50w

Building an Archive from Below: Reflections from Interference Archive

Molly Fair

Social movements have long-standing traditions of cultural production as part of their ongoing work to create a better world. The process of self-documentation might not always be at the forefront of the minds of those involved in the moment of political struggle, but nevertheless a few of the hundreds of flyers passed out at a demonstration, a banner carried in a march, or a video shot of a street theater performance end up being saved. Some of these materials are salvaged by their creators or other movement participants, or they might end up in more traditional cultural heritage institutions.

In December 2011, Interference Archive opened its doors in Brooklyn, New York, providing access to a wide collection of materials produced by social movements. The archive was envisioned by my friends and collaborators Josh MacPhee and Dara Greenwald as a place to explore, preserve, and make accessible what they termed *social movement culture*—or the diverse forms of creative expression produced by people mobilizing for social transformation. In sharing the story of Interference Archive, its founding, its mission, and the work that we have set out to do, I hope to offer one perspective on how a grassroots archive can function, and what we can accomplish with the movements and communities with which we are connected.

All over the world, grassroots archives have emerged and are radically reimagining how archival work can reflect activist practices. The mission statements of some of these projects make clear that they are custodians, not owners, of the histories their collections represent. They are creating archival traditions in their own right, as they strive to celebrate and make visible the stories of people mobilizing for change that have been traditionally marginalized within the dominant narrative.

From Personal Collection to Public Archive

Through years of engaging in art, activism, punk, and DIY culture, Josh MacPhee and Dara Greenwald had amassed a large personal collection of thousands of posters, flyers, publications, photographs, moving images, audio recordings, banners, buttons, t-shirts, and other ephemera. The scope and uniqueness of the materials in the collection are significant, but this is more than just an assemblage of politicized objects. The collection represents their own participation in social movements and the relationships and solidarities they have cultivated with other socially-conscious cultural workers all over the world. Through conducting research for curatorial projects, they began to look critically at what happens to these types of materials after their initial time of dissemination has passed. They had the idea to turn their collection into a public archive, conceptualized as an archive "from below," which would not only house our collective material culture but also be a social space for learning about movements of the past and organizing for present-day struggles.

I was invested in the idea of creating an autonomous archive, as was another friend, Kevin Caplicki. We felt that it was important to preserve culture we were actively producing, and that an archive would be a way to have agency to tell our own stories from a radical perspective. As an archivist just entering the field, I was actively exploring how an archive could be an overtly political space. I was thinking about the ways history is controlled by those in power, and how this manifests in archival traditions—in terms of what is collected and preserved, how it is described, and how it is made accessible. Since Dara and Josh's collection was crowding them out of their small apartment, we were all compelled to act on their longer-term vision to transform this personal collection into one that was a publicly-accessible resource.

We found a space to rent for the archive in a former warehouse building in the Gowanus neighborhood of Brooklyn. The location was not far from where we all lived, and with public transportation just a few blocks away it would be easy for people coming from different places to visit. The area was once active in manufacturing but now is populated with small businesses and artists' studios, though it is mostly still known as the site of the notoriously toxic Gowanus Canal. There are some wonderful cultural resources nearby, including public library branches, a museum, and even several other grassroots archives—but there are few public activist spaces. We felt it was important for Interference Archive to fill that gap. From the beginning, we wanted to build a public space that would do more than serve as a repository to hold the collection—we saw great possibility for cultivating a social center bustling with activities like workshops, talks, movie screenings, and media production, all happening in conjunction with our archival work.

The Interference Archive was introduced to our community with an exhibition exploring punk and feminist subcultures, a world that Dara Greenwald had been intimately part of, as a member of the riot grrrl scene in the '90s and a participant in the feminist media projects that followed. We covered the walls with poster art, show flyers, and record albums. At the opening, people crowded around a table to read zines about topics like self-defense, reproductive rights, and queer liberation. Visitors browsed shelves of books while a video of bands performing at a festival Dara had organized almost two decades ago, Rocket Queen Rampage, was projected onto the stacks. The event showed us the possibilities for building community in the archive and making our shared histories come alive by interacting with the collection. The experience was amazing and extremely emotional for all of us—it was the only event that Dara would share with us, as she passed away weeks later, after battling cancer for over a year. She sent us on our way, and her spirit infuses everything we do at the space.

Making a Grassroots Archive Grow

Conducting research and working as professionals in the special collections of universities, museums, and libraries have often left us feeling disheartened and frustrated. The necessity of having academic credentials to gain entry to these spaces makes access to information exclusive to a privileged few. In some cases, we have observed a lack of concern for and focus on social movement culture by institutions (whether for political or aesthetic reasons), or conversely, these histories are tokenized to fill in gaps in collections. Even at institutions where the focus is mainly on social movements, there is often inaccurate or sparse descriptive information available. To a degree this is understandable, given the limitations of someone's body of knowledge or time to do the work. However, it seems obvious that this work could also be done by movement participants, who possess firsthand knowledge of the materials.

Throughout the process of forming Interference Archive, we have considered what makes us a grassroots archive, and how our practices are distinct from other kinds of traditional institutions that have similar collections of social movement culture. We have been inspired by other projects that have come before us and continue to thrive, such as the Lesbian Herstory Archives (also located in Brooklyn) and the Freedom Archive (in San Francisco). These archives and their collections originate with the liberation struggles of their founders and have been carried on by intergenerational movement participants. They are social places around which a collective identity is built, a sense of community is strengthened, and a feeling of empowerment may be achieved through one's participation. We invited our community to become part of this process of building Interference Archive, drawing from the wide range of knowledge and experience that surrounds us. This has meant engaging in work like devising our own organizational systems, and figuring out vocabularies to reflect culturally-specific knowledge and historical contexts. We hope this will result in a more horizontal approach to knowledge management that reflects the ways social movements are often structured, without the barriers and top-down organization of traditional institutions.

We are continuing to figure out how to build our internal infrastructure as a volunteer-operated space. Our core group of archive coordinators has expanded to include Cindy Milstein and Blithe Riley, and many others in our community have contributed to the work of building shelving for the collection, fundraising, cataloging, creating a database, designing an online interface, coordinating outreach and promotion, and organizing events and exhibitions. Together we are realizing our vision of making Interference Archive a sustainable project and devising ways for the work that is usually undertaken by professionals to be carried out by a much broader set of people.

The archive is now open to the public three days a week—Sundays, Tuesdays, and Wednesdays from noon to 5 p.m.—and we have seen a variety of ways people use the collection. Visitors from all over the world have stopped in to casually browse through our flat files or read a book for a few hours. Others have more directed research projects like documenting images of raised fists found in movement graphics, or finding out about squatted social centers for an interactive mapping project. Educators have brought groups of students to learn about radical history and DIY culture. People appreciate the hands-on approach and the opportunity to have educational experiences and access to resources outside of more formal settings.

The size and scope of the collection have also grown as other activists have reached out to us to donate their personal collections. We recognize that there are limitations to what we can accept into our collection, since we lack the resources of well-funded institutions. We do not necessarily want to have responsibility for somebody's original artwork, personal manuscripts, or incredibly fragile materials in need of preservation, since we strive to be as hands-on as possible. Nevertheless, people have expressed excitement at the prospect of taking these objects they have saved out from their basements and closets where they have been hidden, so that others may discover and appreciate their histories.

Celebrating the Production of Social Movement Culture

For those of us who are involved at Interference Archive, cultural production has been an intrinsic aspect of participating in social movements. It was through creating work collectively and engaging in different political projects that we first encountered each other, and started to collaborate. We became part of a wider network of people independently publishing, producing, and distributing alternative media. Forming an archive around these materials with participants in these communities is a natural progression of our activities.

We have seen firsthand how with few resources and little expertise, one can use various low-tech mediums for communication, such as cutting stencils or screen printing posters and wheat-pasting them in the streets. We have explored how print, audiovisual media, performance, digital technologies, and the intersections of these forms have historically been invented and innovated on, created from whatever resources are available or "liberated" from corporate and government control. This kind of cultural work is not intended for gallery exhibitions, or solely for an individual's personal artistic expression; rather it is a means to participate in a broader collective struggle. As Dara Greenwald once put it, this constitutes a form of interference, in the sense that it reflects the collective efforts of people working to disrupt the flows of power.

Interference Archive also functions as a venue for cultural production and a place for movements to devise new strategies for communication. In 2012, we hosted a series of critiques organized by Occuprint, a group in the Occupy movement, to discuss the imagery and messaging of movement graphics. Images that were developed from these sessions were subsequently printed (in quantities in the thousands!) and distributed out of our space. We served as a resource for École de la Montagne Rouge, a group of design students involved in the six-month-long strike against tuition hikes in Quebec, who turned their 72-hour visit into an artists' residency, combing through the collection for inspiration and reference. With Todos Somos Japon, a group raising awareness of antinuclear activism since the 2011 meltdown at the Fukushima Daiichi nuclear power plant, we created an exhibition of international protest culture since the '70s and designed a map of nuclear sites in North America as an informational tool. As we explore the cultural production coming out of social movements historically, it is crucial that we continue to support and raise awareness of the ongoing work of social movements today.

Through our archival work, we are tracing the trajectories of numerous social movements across time and borders. Originating from unique contexts, their histories offer common threads—such as the role that aesthetics can play in envisioning a new society, cultural production that is carried out as a collective process, and the creation of emergent new forms for communicating ideas to the public. When Sublevarte Colectivo, a group of artists who came together out of the 1999-2000 student strikes in Mexico City, exhibited their work at the archive, they explained at the opening that it is crucial to recognize that the cultural work that comes out of social movements is not just about political themes—it comes out of struggle, literally enacted at the barricades. Sublevarte member Mariana Sasso Rojas reflected that it is vital to share the stories of grassroots struggles repeatedly because of how briefly they last in our collective consciousness. It is essential to be a witness, to share this collective history, and to prevent it from disappearing.

It is not our desire to take on an objective position when it comes to telling our histories, and this informs our archival practices as well—in terms of what is collected and saved, how it is described, and how it is made accessible. We are building Interference Archive as a consciously political space in which to do this work, without the guise of professional neutrality. Together we are creating a space for our collective memory. We hope to preserve this history to which we are all indebted, and that we continue to define.

In the Community

Queer Housing Nacional Google Group: A Librarian's Documentation of a Community-Specific Resource

Shawn(ta) D. Smith

Introduction

There was a time in New York City when Craigslist was the only viable source for housing. When seeking to rent a room, with no other contacts, a queer person would often enter "lesbian" or "queer" in the Craigslist search engine, hoping that the keyword would amount to possible lodging. Aside from bulletin boards at the LGBT Community Center in the West Village, or perhaps on college campuses if one was a student, there was no community resource for queer housing.

Queer housing is a historical necessity to the queer community (I'll use the word "queer" here for lesbian, or QWOC for queer women of color, because this is the segment of the community that Queer Housing Nacional serves primarily; this isn't a footnote because it is the purpose of this essay: "Housing for Queer Women of Color!" as a necessity, a purposeful venture, a need unfilled and politically relevant, a librarian's resource). The lesbian separatist movement initiated lesbian land communities in the late '70s and early '80s where somewhere in the middle of the country, or at its borderlands, land was attained and women had the ability to construct utopian coexistences outside of the patriarchal culture. A documented herstory of lesbian land communities exists, as well as of its urban iterations such as collectively run organizations where consciousness-raising groups led women to gather and deconstruct race, gender, identity, and other political associations. Two such organizations from this time which are still in operation are in NYC: the Lesbian Herstory Archives (LHA), of which I am a collective member, where archiving and access to lesbian culture are part of the mission, and the WOW Café Theater, where performance and radical theater are at the forefront of its mission. Each of these organizations remains with volunteer-led community practice as its base.

Although these volunteer-run collectives have legal ownership of their spaces, and LHA even has a caretaker who lives on premises, neither has housing at its center. The unpaid, work-from-sweat-and-love-and-community ethic of the lesbian community is still here, yes, but the concept of a utopian existence of home life, where this culture is a possibility from the moment of waking to the moment of rest, where options for safety and shelter and uncensored living are primary—like in the separatist housing communities of the past—is gone. Instead, we have an urban population in New York City where, whether in the outskirts of Brooklyn or the buildings that line the Bronx, a queer woman of color's access to affordable and safe housing is teamed against the gentrification of working class and people of color communities, masked as hipster intentional communities where food coops, coffee shops, yoga bars, and community gardens often leave queer women of color as the last to be chosen for housing.

The housing crisis for queer women of color is an issue of access. As a native New Yorker—born and raised in "the people's republic of Brooklyn," in neighborhoods during a time when they were still filled with like faces and foods and language—as a descendent of Jamaican and Guatemalan-Belizean-Garifuna peoples, the African and the Arawak; as an American same-gender-loving queer woman; as a City University of New York student and then employee; as a legally blind rasta-man's daughter, sibling to nine brethren and sistren, eight surviving, with two mothers, two fathers, and cousins upon cousins to call home, *it is with the queer women of color (migrant) communities in mind that my work as a librarian—the ability to share resources and provide access—is made useful.* These are the communities from which I am bred, the places that have created me, and the identities that inform my work.

Where access is unattainable, librarians are necessary. As librarians, we learn that we have access to all information, and when we do not, we fight for this access and implement resource-sharing initiatives. Yet having access to information also means noting the gaps. The work is in claiming, naming, and defining the collective community in order to close these gaps. Where information does not exist for others, we as agitated and informed community members take the risk of "creating" information by noting the gaps—the missing names, forgotten institutions, and skewed language—and filling them.

As a librarian of multiple communities, however, I often struggle with these ideas of communities and information access. If community exists in spatial realms, as does information, how then can we ensure access to all information if first we do not advocate to open all spaces? Information, like a physical space, is definitively closed to some while available to others. There are contextual boundaries that limit and arrange formations of thought and space. In this new open source age we as information creators and disseminators have the power to fill gaps of information access and widen spaces, reconstructing boundaries and how information is applied and used. To provide access to these spaces, however, one must not neglect the herstoric concepts of lesbian separatism. Some communities are intentionally separate, with doors bolted from the inside, and require that these separations remain as collectively-defined community. It is the model of a closed community resource that I found helpful in grappling with the contradictory nature of open source possibilities.

Ensuring that users were at the root of information-gathering and dissemination is the core principle that I used for this constituency-based initiative. In other words, queer women of color decided how the resource was formulated and accessed. This article is meant to stand as a case study for how librarians can apply their skills of information dissemination and the theoretical tools of open access to specific community groups. An inadvertent result may be to further document the continuing journey of a queer housing movement.

In my work with Queer Housing Nacional, I have found that when community members have total power to uphold a mission, they grow stronger, share information responsibly, and ultimately find the community-based component to be the most valuable characteristic of the resource. One may, however, find that this resource complicates librarianship's promotion of open access since Queer Housing Nacional encourages closed participatory group structures, with collective distributions of power, using lesbian separatism as its guide. Nevertheless, honing the skills of my profession and allowing them to extend to those who share my own identity was a key factor in the success and depth of Queer Housing Nacional. As moderator, I received messages and screened them. Yet, as a librarian, I made specific choices to ensure that this was a useful, active, and relevant resource. Here I outline the ways in which the creation of a Google Group as a community tool benefited from the skills of a librarian as moderator. I also discuss the challenges of simple classification when applied to an intangible and fluid community. An overview of my assessment and its implications, followed by an appendix listing survey questions and notable responses from list members, conclude that efforts to create true community-specific resources are necessary and possible.

Information and Community

First, what is information? The principles of records information management (RIM) generally teach us that there are four steps to birthing information. Step 1: All existence is data. Step 2: Data in context is a document. Step 3: A document must be "managed" to become a record. To "manage" in this instance means to provide a story and attach this document to other data, or what we call in information science "metadata." Step 4: The record must be accessed to finally become information.

Although data, documents, and records exist all around us, seldom are the datasets of *all* life—to be specific, Black life, Caribbean life, lesbian life, the list is infinite, really—documented, and even more seldom are they cataloged as records and then turned into information by the above definition. My role as a librarian is to provide access to information, but my role as a community member—as a black lesbian, an archivist, and a writer—is to create new information, by providing access to various forms of community documentation. My marginal voice and multiple communities enhance my role as librarian and archivist in the information life cycle, constantly documenting, recording, naming, and making context for our existence.

In some communities, there is a stable understanding of who and what belongs inside its borders. Although if I were asked to define a completely static community, this would be a challenge: Religiously-affiliated communities? Married people? Students? Librarians? Do we know where the folks of these communities end and begin?

In the library world, "community" takes on a geographic scope for public and new media libraries, or a cohort in academic libraries. Public service librarians see the community as the boundaries for which service should stretch, and so, with this in mind, community is at times expanded to include all possible patrons—those walking through the doors, those accessing the website, the campus at large, friends' groups, and alumni. Although the library world's concept of community varies in language based on type of library, the linking factor for a library's community is based on a single characteristic: access. Those who have access to the library are the library's community. In a technical sense, every person in the nation has access to at least one library. Privileged people have access to multiple libraries—a university library, a special or private library, and, of course, one or more public libraries. Less privileged people have only their prison library, or a single underfunded public branch library with limited hours. As an example, every person with a New York State address has access to Brooklyn Public Library, New York Public Library, Queens Library, and any additional library that exists in his or her geographic territory. Consortiums such as the Metropolitan New York Library Council (METRO) and the Academic Libraries of Brooklyn (ALB) give patrons with initial library privileges continued access to multiple libraries. As a student at Queens College and a faculty librarian at the CUNY Graduate Center, I, for example, have access to all CUNY campus libraries, our METRO membership, Columbia and New York universities through a pilot program called the Manhattan Research Library Initiative, and the list continues. Furthermore, resource sharing and Web 2.0 information exchanges have blurred the lines of individual access, thereby definitively expanding the abstract definitions of community. The work that I do, whether or not I chose it, is affected by and deeply instilled in community. A career in librarianship was justified because it represented a vehicle, a tool, or a possibility for community-building in an expansive way, as well as a deeply-rooted ethic for our mission of systemic access.

As communities are tightly woven together, it is difficult to comprehend the individual and her level of access. While some people may have many access points, others have very few. A strong community focus with a targeted scope will reify the community's definition. Just as how tools that librarians develop and promote are often those meant for direct community consumption, Queer Housing Nacional was intended for the queer woman of color community. This act of community-building begins with the following actions: Compiling information—what housing resources are available for queer women of color? Defining relevant sources—how can these resources ensure applicability to the QWOC community? Constructing tools for understanding information— which tool will allow information to come to the women directly? And, finally, a practice of outreach and engagement to disseminate these resources—where are queer women of color needing and offering intentional housing space?

Google Groups: A Community-focused Tool

Long before Facebook and other social networking sites, we had email. And email continues to allow for multiple communities to coexist. Within the queer community, anonymity is respected in the blank carbon copy (bcc field), and, due to Google, advanced search mechanisms allow email to quantify and track whole interactions. Like a wiki, which allows for all participants to contribute equally, constituency-based resources such as Queer Housing Nacional require participants to self-identify as a part of the closed group prior to access.

In this act of self-identification, the individual who signs on to the list defines herself as a part of the community. Furthermore, the participant, now member, sends her own messages to the board and decides when and if to share the information with others outside of the closed group. Although this is a description of rudimentary Google Group mores, when one considers the nature of the group—a queer woman of color community—it becomes clear that moderation of such a list is necessary, and that having this moderator be an "informed agitator" is the best practice.

Queer Housing Nacional was created simply because my social network was tired of receiving forwarded emails. One lesbian woman whom I work with at the Lesbian Herstory Archives actually wrote back one day and said, "Shawn, I love you, but for God's sake, stop sending me these things." I was surprised that she felt that way; weren't we both librarians, and lesbians who wanted to spread the word about our resources? Perhaps it was because I sent three forwards in one week that she was frustrated. To solve the issue of no longer sending 50 hand-picked contacts an email that may seem solicitous, I sent one relevant email to all of my contacts. The message read:

> Hello Friends,
> Two things:
> 1) Every week, I receive an ad or a request from a friend who is seeking housing. Or, as someone who often has a room for rent. Here's where we ought to post people, this new listserv!
> 2) Summer 2010, I travelled to LA, DC, Michigan, and Toronto, and in each space, I met amazing Queer folks. And I always needed a place to stay. Let's keep our revolving doors in the community shall we? If you are interested in joining this listserv, then accept the invitation.
>
> Love,
> Group Moderator
> Shawn, Your Lesbian Librarian

Labeling myself "Your Lesbian Librarian" is something that I did in multiple contexts, and it became my signature for all things lesbian-related, and, slowly, librarian-related as well, although that was still mainly to close professional contacts. In this email, as it traveled into the inboxes of hundreds, the title bestowed on me the onus for this endeavor to become a viable community resource.

On September 27, 2010, a Google Group was born that would shift the queer community. Within the same day of sending this email to friends and close colleagues, about 50 people chose to join the group. The first message arrived the next day. It was an ad from my ex-girlfriend, who had an opening in her artist house. I wasn't sure what to do besides write "Please excuse cross postings," as is customary when forwarding a message to professional lists. *"room(s) for rent $700 Lefferts Gardens"* was the title. Although she had posting privileges, she sent the message to a list we both have access to with hopes that I'd send it to the queer housing list.

From this first message, I had to consciously manage user participation, especially because the list grew very quickly. It was important to have the people send emails directly to the list, instead of to me. For the first few posts, I worked with the limitations of Google to instruct members on how to send messages. Within one month, I received dozens of emails from queer women of color asking to be added, having been alerted by a friend. This meant that soon folks whose names and email addresses I did not recognize began to join the list. Although this was exciting, I had to consider the possibility that some of these folks might not be QWOC, and this is what actually happened. The list quickly changed from QWOC only to QWOC and our allies.

One day in February 2011, I received an email that came to me in response to a post titled *"27 year old queer female seeks room in queer or queer friendly home."* The message to me read:

Member 11:03am: Peace Shawn. Is [name removed] a person of color?

That was it. No other disclaimers, no signature, no additional reason for asking, just this one question. And this baffled me; as moderator, I was supposed to be accountable for the messages that came in, for upholding the mission of the list, for determining the rights for the members to be present. Immediately I responded, and we had the following exchange:

Me 11:30am: Peace friend,
    Let me check for you. I don't think that she is. But I'd like to confirm it before identifying someone without their consent.
    Shawn

Member 11:30am: word up thank you

I dug through the add-on prompts to see who had recommended the poster, but Google deletes this information. I used Facebook to hunt for the person via their email address and any other possible clues I found in their post: address location, style of writing, etc. I was finally able to track down the poster and report back to the other list member.

Me 12:43pm: So, I asked a friend. Who says affirmative, POC.

Member 1:00pm: Thanks friend. What's her contact information?

Me 1:54pm: I believe you should just send an email.
    No phone number was posted.
    Hope it works out well.
    Shawn

Aside from the two hours of mid-day time it took me to complete this query (while at the reference desk, hence the mild delays), this e-interaction led me to consider what necessary steps it would take to derail possible pitfalls of a community-specific resource. I began to ask myself questions like, who is an ally? Queer by whose definition? And what of this gender—"woman"—do we mean this as female-bodied, solely a gender identity, or sex? Was this language trans-inclusive? And, ultimately, I did not want to be the one to answer these questions. I chose to create a survey to inform my decisions and include user input. (See the survey questions in Appendix II.)

Although no one on the Google Group claimed separatism, throughout the years, messages came in requesting accountability from me, the group moderator and lesbian librarian, for how I was able to ensure that folks were queer women, of color, or allies to queer women of color. Initially, I added everyone who asked, but after this February 2011 e-exchange, I realized there needed to be parameters.

Survey responses allowed me to reflect on how to guard the door to this resource.

Responses revealed:

- All but one respondent identified as a QWOC.
- The majority considered a Google Group as the best way to communicate housing information, as opposed to Facebook or a website.
- The majority wanted to stay on the list, regardless of their housing search.
- Definitions of who is an ally varied. (See Appendix III: notable answers to question 4 on Community.)

The survey responses made it clear to me that folks had real opinions on these matters of community and access, and that it was my role to steer the conversation.

I added a few questions to prompt incoming members to prove their connection with the community. Folks had to self-identify as a QWOC or not, name the person who directed them to the list, and, finally, state if they were an ally and, if so, the type of ally: a white person; a man; if a man, whether they were cisgender or trans; etc. Beyond explaining yourself to enter the list, there were also parameters to post: folks had to, within their ads, mention that they were either QWOC or allies to QWOC, and, if allies, what type. This proved productive for some time, until folks of other communities began to demand access without demonstrating whether they were allies or members of the community.

Community Service or an Organizing Tool?

Retribution came in small spurts. A handful of white queer people demanded to be added and not mention race in their ads. These aggressive requests to restructure the list and its language were often rectified with a few email exchanges. Still, some posters were clear that they wanted to live with someone like them—for example, in a gay white man collective house; a house of drag queens in Park Slope, Brooklyn; a hipster commune; etc. All variations were not likely fitting for queer women of color as a primary constituent for housing goals. Not allowing these folks to post meant they would seek other outlets, except Queer Housing Nacional was the only of its kind. The Queer Commons list, with over 1000 members—largely white and academic, as it began from a City University of New York queer student organizing list—began to receive housing requests. On July 23, 2012, I sent to the Queer Commons list an announcement, by the request of the list moderator, to introduce the Queer Housing Nacional list, since Queer Commons was being barraged with housing-related messages and was meant to be an events list and discussion board. On the Queer Commons list, I posted:

"Hello all,

My name is Shawn, and I moderate the Queer Housing Nacional group. Thanks Karalyn and Adrien for sharing.

We're over 200 members now, from across the country, and I intend for it to be a resource where we can share great housing opportunities in our communities.

Before you consider requesting to join, please note the following:

1) We are a group for and by queer women of color (and our allies).

2) If shared space, all posts must state whether the people living in the space identify as queer women of color or qwoc allies, and if allies, the type (straight white allies, gay men of color, etc).

3) So not to over-saturate the group, not all allies are added, but will be put on a waiting list.

4) All messages are moderated.

Generally speaking, at this point, for every two self-identified queer women of color that request entrance, one ally will be added. Allies who are offering housing will only require a one-to-one rate. This is my current process, it was different in the past, and may change in the future. I simply ask that allies take into consideration the complexities of access when choosing to share and benefit from opportunities intended for queer women of color. Truly consider how you are an ally to the members of this list and include that in your postings and intentions.

In Housing,
Shawn
Founder/Moderator
Queer Housing Nacional

It took one day or so for Queer Housing Nacional to receive about 50 requests for add-ons, mostly from allies, perhaps one or two from QWOC. Some were offering housing, but the majority were simply interested in being a part of this needed community resource. Some, however, were in desperate need of housing. This was a real dilemma. If all allies were added, then for sure any poster offering housing would receive more responses from allies than from QWOC, thereby replicating the issue that had led to the existence of the Google Group in the first place. I had to remember the women to whom I was accountable, "the mission" of the list. I began a wait list, asking allies who were waiting to get two QWOC friends to add before they stepped in line. Eventually, because the need for housing is a real and timely one, folks went back to the moderators of the Queer Commons list and requested a new option.

In July 2012, the Queer Commons Housing list was launched. The birth of this list initially felt like a shove to the side for Queer Housing Nacional. However, having somewhere to direct interested queer folks felt as good as the resource-sharing models of libraries: "Sorry, we don't have what you need, but this space does, and I'll show you how to get there!"

The final step toward making Queer Housing Nacional an exclusionary list came when a trans man of color from the West Coast had a problem with the parameters. Because he was a trans man of color, he didn't see it necessary to name himself as an ally to women. Our conversation took place in August 2012, two years after the creation of Queer Housing Nacional:

Mon, Jul 30, 2012 at 10:50 AM

I've read your post however, it seems unclear as to whether you and your roommate are cis-men or trans-men or gay men, etc. This may make a difference to the folks of this listserv. Could you clarify and re-post/re-send?

Mon, Jul 30, 2012 at 1:32 PM

hi shawn , my roommate is gay cis male and i am trans male. I am not sure i want to live with someone who makes the decision based on someone being cis and gay verses trans and queer. I'm looking for LGBTQ community but someone more open minded and laid back than that.

The discussion continued for a few additional email exchanges. It was good fortune that the Queer Commons Housing list was available to share information and divert any potential complications of this deliberately exclusionary resource. But it is as a result of these intentional and, to some, harsh, exclusionary practices that many queer women of color have found Queer Housing Nacional to be a valuable resource. Without a QWOC focus, users would be overrun by the majority of those who often obtain access to information-sharing resources. The responses to question 4 of the survey distributed in February 2011 (see Appendix III) act as testimonies that queer women of color find it necessary to have a closed and exclusionary Google Group. Aside from the appreciation and successes that exist—one woman launched a self-sustaining business as a dog-sitter from initial contact through Queer Housing Nacional, others have responded to housesit queries and made friends and lovers, or started housing communes—the low post rate is due to the fact that many are happily housed, but excited to know that they no longer have to worry about housing if the need arises. I sent a welcome message in 2012 (see Appendix I) thanking everyone for his or her contributions while describing the list as it stands as an intentionally separate space. Love letters and appreciations were returned.

Conclusion

To date, Queer Housing Nacional still exists. Messages come in from throughout the country, plus some from Canada, but primarily from the New York City region. Since the creation of Queer Housing Nacional, what has erupted is a new way to envision queer housing. After the Queer Commons Housing list, a Facebook housing group has also appeared, starting on the West Coast, and now present in NYC. In the span of three years, a single librarian's response to a missing community entity, queer housing, has led to the development of multiple venues to find it, thereby creating multiple community resources. Community members, both allies and queer women of color, request to be added to Queer Housing Nacional at a rate of about five per week, often sent by a friend or a Google search. As moderator, I've made it my duty to stay up-to-date with the traffic of my own list as well as of Queer Commons Housing, and I find that most posts are replicated in both forums. When folks request membership to Queer Housing Nacional, standard messages are sent with instructions on how to post, and seldom are people excluded from the list. What has shifted communities and sustained itself throughout the lists, however, is the culture and language of queer housing. What I find most significant is the template for how to post to these lists. Regardless of which list you frequent, you'll find that folks announce their identities when seeking to share a space and will note whether they are an ally to queer people of color (women are often not mentioned, since in queer culture gender identity politics complicate singularities), using different terms such as "anti-racist," "inclusive," or "anti-oppressive." Soon, it may make sense to consolidate all resources in one space, which would be my personal goal, as I don't imagine moderating forever. When I pose the question to members individually, all will urge me to keep a list specific to queer women of color, yet the number of subscribers outweighs the number of posts in comparison to larger, more inclusive lists.

With consideration to librarian-specific goals and how this relates to libraries, Queer Housing Nacional calls for an open-access policy within a community-specific resource—a resource that is both open and closed at the same time, geared toward a single group, with the intention of reaching that group, and marketed specifically for the purpose of this group's access. When developing tools and programs, librarians ought to consider the limitations of communities and address these limitations, first by outlining the parameters of this designated community in comparison to the larger one that the library generally serves. Examples of this practice exist in the curation of digital archives, for example, when deaccessioning or curating exhibitions. Designated communities are often at the fore of these curation policies. Whether an instrument is for a particular department, a campus-wide demographic, a Friends of the Library group, or another audience, creating resources that are managed by these communities may allow for greater use and interaction within the communities themselves. As so often resources are underused, Queer Housing Nacional proves that making a resource open access is no longer the determining factor for maximum patron use. When materials or resources are community-focused, outreach can be targeted. This act of community engagement will allow for greater access by a small number of community-focused individuals. Once the tool is implemented, it is possible that other communities may demand access, thereby opening the possibility for additional resources to be produced. The work of claiming, naming, and defining the community closes the gaps of information access when the users are the agents generating the information; the work of the librarian is to provide these forums and aid in their dissemination.

Appendix I.

Queer Housing Nacional Initial Update

Thursday, May 17th, 2012 at 7:34pm

Welcome to the Queer Housing listserv. I'm happy to say that we have made it to 192 members, and 195 posts!

Give yourselves a round of applause. Everyone on here has helped to keep this space useful and alive, a network for us all.

Before we approach 200 members and posts, I felt it necessary to introduce myself and thank you for being a part of this possibility.

Before I share my queer housing story, I will outline where you are:

You are a member of the Queer Housing Nacional Listserv *-a listserv for queer women of color and our allies*:

- All posts will be moderated by me -whom you will meet below.
- All posts for shares/shared spaces must include identification of race, gender identity, and sexual orientation for those who will live in the space.
- Please POST! Some people have vacancies and won't post, because they are waiting for a ...seeking add. Don't wait for others to post. Post yourself!
- Use photos. Who doesn't like photos? -Specifically of the space, not yourself (these aren't personals).
- Links to C-List and other websites like airbnb.com are okay, but use this opportunity to be personal and introduce yourself while offering the add as a supplement.
- DREAM BIG, and don't be afraid to ask for what you want...In price, in space, in roommates... You can't receive it if you don't ask!
- Be cautious -I know how each and every person on here has gotten here. I screen with a magnifying glass. A handful have come from a google-search engine, but I recognized their email addresses anyhow! We are a network of friends and lovers. Still, community does not guarantee integrity, so be cautious for how you choose to open your home.
- Give me feedback by filling out the queer housing nacional survey. I read all of them, seriously!
- I am not a Realtor, only a curious librarian and faithful community participant. If you don't see what you need, then post; I cannot personally place people.
- Have fun, and be good to each other.

My queer housing story:

I started Queer Housing Nacional in November 2010 after signing a lease for a large apartment. Somehow, I needed all of my friends to know when I had a vacancy, without going through my contacts list each time. Also, I remembered when I was looking for a place, and how Craigslist often felt like a maze, and I was caught in a time-warp... Before I panicked, I made a solution: Queer Housing Nacional was born...

Speaking of born...

I was 'Born and Raised' in Brooklyn, NY, in the projects in Brownsville, and then, in a one-family house in East Flatbush. I have family throughout the city, and NY will always be my home. 18 years ago, my grandparents sold their house while I was in gradeschool, my dad bought a BedStuy Brownstone building while my mom rented a three bedroom in Kensington; it's still the same. My family housed people like Abner Louima while his court proceedings littered our house. My cousin married the landlord's niece. My dad lost $40k over ten years from tenants not paying rent, and survived two electrical fires. My mother's rent has doubled since she moved in. One aunt still lives in the projects and could never afford to leave... At 17 years old I leased my first place: $875 for a brand new 2-bdrm apt. I moved in my ex, her new girlfriend, my brother, friends going through nervous breakdowns, you name it, I moved it in. Then as a budding and in love little dyke-ling, I put my name on a lease with three others, with a dream of living in a lesbian of color household, but a soured relationship led me to be taken off of a founders list from an organization I loved, then **sued** years later by the apartment's management company...a long story, but let's just call it a bad break-up from which my housing life took a while to recover.

... Renting has been my life since I came out. And Queer women of color have specific housing concerns, which is why:

The Queer Housing listserv is for queer women of color and our allies.

- If you are offering housing, and you are a true ally, you should be excited about the possibility of housing a queer woman of color.
- If you are seeking housing, and you are a true ally, then you should be looking to give your money to a queer woman of color as your new landlord.

This listserv fails if in a pattern, non-queer-women of color, connect with other non-queer women of color, and the people for whom it serves are still seeking.

I am very much sensitive to the housing wars of NYC. Women of color who, are gender non-conforming, have women as lovers, for their own reasons (not to be questioned) choose to not live with men, are artists, are nudists, are terribly brilliant or sassy or scared, these are the people that this listserv is for. Those women who continuously search for home, always wanting a new beginning, I hope you find a home through this service.

Those people of color, that do not identify as women, but are perceived as such, I hope you find a home through this listserv.

Those people of color, that identify as women, but are not perceived as such, I hope you find a home through this listserv.

I also hope that others do not gentrify the listserv, but remain as allies. That we will continue to step up, and step back, and think about our own privileges as we seek and offer housing. From the perspective of an owner, a renter, a boarder, a native, knowing what it means to not have documentation or "on the books" income, but needing housing; knowing what it is like to compete with hipster kids who make other roommates "vibe" better and so they get chosen over you, knowing what it is like to have to be "evaluated" before a yes is given, knowing what it is like to walk into a housing interview and fear for my life, time and again,

We ALL need to figure out how to make housing work for US.

I'm sure everyone has their Queer Housing Story.

Through this listserv, I feel, even if temporarily, safe, in my housing. Since November 2010, I feel safe knowing that I can reach out when needed. I've found great roommates, and others have sent me stories of happiness, that they have found great roommates too.

Thank you for keeping this space for and about the housing of queer women of color. Allies, thank you for offering yourselves to a world with these intentions. Women of color, THANK YOU, for being brave enough to handle your own, and not settle for less in your home-life.

I had intended this listserv to be Nacional, but it seems as if in this great city, we continue to spin inside of ourselves.

Send me questions. I will gladly answer them. Or send your Queer Housing Story, maybe I'll post a few.

Appendix II.

Survey Questions - Posted February 10, 2011

1) Demographics: For statistical purpose only, please tell me how you identify, in terms of your queerness, your gender, your race, and any other identifiers that you would like to claim. Be as specific or as broad as you like. But please answer. Please use the same level of specificity that you would like to see used in posts.

2) Do you identify as a queer woman of color?

3) If you are non-qwoc ally, do you have issues or questions regarding posting? This feedback is helpful to my own wording. The goal is for you to feel confident in your posting, not hesitant or guilty.

4) Community: In terms of queerness, gender, race, and any other identifiers are there specific groups of people that you would not consider community and that you would not like to have on this listserv? *A gay boy for example? A white gay boy? A white straight boy who has a queer sister? When if at all do we draw the line (please keep in mind that the purpose of this listserv is to house queer women of color, and our allies... Folks have to consider themselves an ally to join if not a queer woman of color). Allies in my understanding are: Trans folks of color, gender non-conforming folks of color, queer people of color (some men, but not majority), and some straight people if they have a place to offer, but not if they are seeking. This is completely confidential, and as a member of this listserv, you have the right to answer these questions and moderate your space.*

5) Have you posted to the listserv before?

6) Have you contacted any poster due to their posting on this listserv?

7) Have you had a negative experience on the listserv? *This includes reading something offensive, contacting someone and having a bad experience, seeing a place and feeling unsafe, or anything else that made your day sour. If yes, please be as descriptive as possible. If no, please write N/A.*

8) What city do you live in?

9) What is your primary reason for joining the listserv?

10) To offer a room for rent

    a) Seeking a room for rent

    b) Traveling to another city for a short period of time

    c) Conference

    d) To make friends

e) To be up to date with what folks are doing

f) I'm interested in real estate

11) Are you still interested in being on the listserv if you are stable in your housing? Meaning, if you were seeking or offering, (for example) do you still find the listserv interesting?

12) Do you think the listserv would be best hosted under a different format? From a scale of 1 - 5, which do you think is the most effective format for hosting Queer Housing Correspondence. Please keep in mind, this is without funding and on a volunteer basis, so we would need to use open source software and minimal maintenance.

a) GoogleGroup (As IS)

b) Facebook Page

c) Blog

d) Website

e) Other Format?

13) Any additional comments or feedback? Knock yourself out! Be brutally honest. Tell me what you think is missing, what you'd like to see. Think big. Be unreasonable!

Appendix III.

Notable answers to question 4 on Community from February 10, 2011 – July 2012

- Male-identified people, white people.
- I'm fine with all queer women regardless of their color/whiteness, queer men of color are fine too. But I'm not sure about fun-loving white gay boy. It's fine to have a few of them, especially if they offer, but an ally is an ally so I would hate to say that a certain person is not acceptable. I don't know. I personally am hesitant of living with any heterosexual males but that is also my personal experience not too many!!
- For me, the line would be at homophobic straight people - of any color - but I guess they won't be joining anyways.
- …my primary idea of allies is those who self-identify as part of the queer spectrum regardless of sexual behavior, and those who identify as part of or intrinsically linked to the people of color spectrum, regardless of pheno or geno type. Essentially its more about who you are, than what you are – but who must be central not a side part of you.

- I would rather not see white + straight people on the list serv. A white queer ally is cool. A straight person of color is cool. But if a white straight person is a real ally then they should have one of their queer or POC friends post. I don't think that's too much to ask. Understanding still that the list serv is to house Queer/SGL/LGBT women of color...
- I am willing to have anyone here who identifies as Queer. I don't have a problem with cis men or other white people, but unfortunately there's no way of discerning whether a person is Queer in the particular way we define it or a mainstream gay with bad politics, and being the identity police would not be fair. Housing can get a little sensitive because people make a lot of casually racist remarks about neighborhoods so if we're gonna open it up to more people and risk people being offensive in the name of being fair and not policing identities, there should be some kind of statement about what kinds of things are not okay to say.
- For the purposes of this list: straight men no (no matter how many gay relatives they have. White trans or gay men -no (they are in my community but not in this part of it -perhaps in my next lifetime -- I have not really found them to be among my allies when push comes to shove although they always expect me to be theirs.)
- I think that it is good the way it is. The fact that people can't post without being a member is good.

iCommunity: Digital Media, Family Heirlooms, and a Global Audience in the Lebanese in North Carolina Project

Caroline Olivia Muglia

"History means both the facts of the matter and the narrative of those facts, both 'what happened' and 'that which is said to have happened.'"

~Michael Rolph-Trouillot

Archivists dig. They dig *toward* a beginning for meaning and context. They dig into boxes, attics, albums, and hard drives; into financial records, intimate correspondence, government documents, and home movies; into the lives of those esteemed, ordinary, scandalous, and sometimes unknown. And so do activists. They dig for truth, justice, knowledge, and unity. As an activist-archivist who worked in the labor movement organizing public employees and healthcare workers and who has been politically active for as long as I can remember, I constantly think about how people use information. Forging activism and archives is the need for transparency, access to information, and communication. Both activism and archives are rooted in a diverse public and attempt to bring attention to marginalized aspects of societal history, often for purposes of transforming them.

Knowing this, I should not have been surprised to find myself seated at a wobbly kitchen table in a dizzying apartment complex in central North Carolina, explaining to a woman through her son, who was serving as an impromptu translator, the importance of the naturalization records they had retrieved from the recesses of their storage space to the collective knowledge of the state-wide community. It would turn out that those records, the ones I later digitized and made available through the project's online archive, could not be found on commercial genealogy websites and, as a result, were quite historically valuable.

Such simple acts of historical archaeology have far-reaching implications. Archivists are the shapers and protectors of many materials that otherwise would be unknown to an eager public, and they understand that what society knows and catalogs cannot be everything that exists in this world. Thus the archival profession is connected first to human experience and second to documenting that experience—which resembles work in the arena of social justice. A combination of theory, practical experiences, and collaboration, the Lebanese in North Carolina Project centralizes community history-telling and transforms it into an archive. While it did not begin with activist intentions, this project is situated firmly upon tenets of social justice, public history, and the process of community participation. The act of digging offers an opportunity for shared authority[1] in cultivating a participatory archive[2] imperative to the cultural history of the American South.

Several years ago, as a graduate student in History, and preparing to begin a second program in Library Science, I answered a call for graduate students interested in a community-based oral history project. The project's first mission was based on research. As any good scholar would proceed with the research task before her, I looked to regional memory institutions, including libraries, archival repositories, and museums, to illuminate the historical impact of the community. But, I came up short. In fact, I came up so short that I began to question the goal of the project with which I was becoming more involved. What happens when the memory institutions are not the custodians of a state's history that is richly remembered by those who lived it? What about when the gulf between what happened and what is documented as happening is too broad to reconcile? The answer: you have to write the history. And you have to make it accessible to the widest possible audience.

Nearly a decade after the events of September 11th struck the country, the Lebanese founder of the project decided to act locally on the national feeling of

---

1. The term is borrowed from Frisch (1990). In a non-traditional cultural or historical institution, the so-called authority on the subject or context would interact with and learn from the audience.

2. Participatory archive, a controversial notion in the field, refers to the contribution from multiple channels to the larger product. In the case of this project, working with both scholars and the community that they study reflects participation in achieving the goal.

unrest among the diverse Arab community in the country. An active member of the community in North Carolina, he began listening to the stories of the local Lebanese,[3] often sitting at kitchen tables not unlike the one at which I sat. In an effort to preserve those stories as well as to publicize them and educate the public statewide, the Lebanese in North Carolina Project was born. Working alongside non-Lebanese archivists, Middle East scholars, educators, documentary filmmakers and editors, computer scientists, and graphic designers, the Lebanese-American community has become involved in the process of researching, recording, preserving, and displaying archival materials of their own heritage through open access platforms.

Since 2010, the Lebanese in North Carolina Project has centralized the community as its primary source in learning about the robust 130-year transmigrational history of Lebanese-Arabs to North Carolina, beginning in 1890 and continuing today. The project began with four cultural goals that all draw from the multilingual archive of materials donated by the community, including photo albums, documents and records, music, home movies, oral histories, and heirlooms. The goals, along with the people responsible for working on each of them, are:

- Produce a full-length documentary based on oral histories from first, second, third, and fourth generation Lebanese-Americans (documentary filmmakers and editors, Middle East scholars, archivists, community)
- Develop an online archive that houses digitized materials donated by community members (Middle East scholars, archivists, community)
- Curate a physical and virtual museum exhibition (Middle East scholars, archivists, community, computer scientists, graphic designers)
- Create educational programs to broaden the knowledge about the Middle East, Southern history, and transmigration (Middle East scholars, archivists, community, educators)

The Lebanese-American community living in North Carolina represents approximately 15,000 people of first, second, third, and fourth generations. Most of the earlier generations were Christians (Maronite) or Druze who worked as peddlers, then became storeowners. Some of those stores still exist today, with a high number of business owners in the community. Later generations included a bigger Muslim population and community members with higher education degrees who found work in the bio-medical, pharmaceutical, and computer science fields. While it is difficult to say with total accuracy, much of the popula-

---

3. To learn more about the history of the Lebanese migration to the Americas, see Khater (2003).

tion in North Carolina is middle to upper-middle class, and nearly all speak English (among other languages). For the project, this made communication through email and collaboration in digital endeavors possible, if not favorable. Many felt comfortable around technology and had digital photographs and converted DVDs and CDs in their collections. Many also used digital scanners and recorders. Certainly, some community members were not familiar with these tools, so, where possible, this was also an opportunity for skill sharing.

Because memory institutions could not provide information on the history of the Lebanese in North Carolina, this project had to sidestep formal channels of research. In the beginning, we worked distinctly outside the archive to engage a community that had not been represented in their own regional history. The first step was to continue what the founder had done and capture as many stories as possible on video and audio. Initially, three of us involved in the project in a paid, part-time capacity conducted full interviews with people identified by a few leaders in the community, which grew each day until we had about 50 interviews. After that, and once we understood the time required to conduct interviews, we engaged the community to conduct micro-interviews that normally centered on questions the interviewers wanted to ask their family members ("What was it like to take the journey to North Carolina?" or "What's your *dolma* recipe?"). The micro-interviews allowed community members to interact with each other (usually inter-generationally) and for the project to begin capturing unique moments of history.

Oral histories are the history of experience. And they are most genuine when they are captured in places familiar to the interviewees. I found myself in people's living rooms, basements, and foyers. I met with people during their lunch breaks, sitting in offices across from them as they ate sandwiches from Styrofoam shells. We met after work and before church. For one community member, the only free time she had available was when she was grocery shopping. She had old home movies bequeathed by her ailing father and wanted to donate them to the project. On numerous occasions, I met her in crowded parking lots. She handed me the box of reels and proceeded into the store to finish her errands. These meetings reminded me of my labor organizing days, when I'd meet with workers anywhere at any time just to have an opportunity to talk to them.

Making materials, including the documentary and oral histories, easily accessible was especially urgent as a portion of the contributors to and users of the project live in Lebanon. The second major step in engaging the community arose when we built the online archive, located at nclebanese.org. Using Omeka as a management platform and tool for the creation of virtual exhibits, the participation of the community was trifold: the community donated the physical materials to the project, which were digitized to create a surrogate and returned;

they submitted and managed materials in their own collection through a user upload plug-in added to the website; and, finally, they continued to perform outreach and promotional endeavors for the project, which deepened the investment of the community and broadened the base of contributors to the archive. As the materials appeared online and were featured on our blog, a natural occurrence of crowdsourcing helped to identify unknown individuals, families, and locations in North Carolina, Lebanon, and elsewhere. In a highly collaborative environment, community members are no longer distant benefactors of the preservation project. Instead, they transcend these boundaries to operate behind the curtain of digital archives. They create their own collections, identify and tag people and places in photographs and home movies, and interact with one another through social media.

The third step in engaging the community requires an extension of the idea of community to include the computer scientists, educators, and graphic designers, most affiliated with NC State University, who have been involved in an effort to curate an interactive museum exhibition. Working with a larger base of collaborators, the project continues to collect material from the community that helps in developing a large-scale exhibition. A community-supported project, this is also a community-accountable one. So, at each juncture, we meet with families to discuss how their materials will be used and to brainstorm ideas about how to widen the network of visitors to the site. The curation is decentralized, which is a difficult workflow to maintain, but it ensures that everyone who voices a perspective can contribute to the project. This project is homegrown, with NC State University as our largest affiliation. Our relationship to the institution ensures that we expand our local community base and can draw upon the expertise of people living in NC and strengthen our intellectual economy.

Throughout this process, several important principles have proven instrumental in advancing the content of the project while also empowering the community's relationship to it. Social media has encouraged individuals to get involved in myriad ways, some of which are not time-intensive roles. Contributing a short update to the monthly e-newsletter or even just forwarding it to a group of friends or family helps disseminate and promote the message of the project. So too does motivating those community members who have learned new digitization, metadata, tagging, geo-location, and blogging skills to offer informal skill share sessions, which has allowed more individuals to get involved in maintaining the archive. These daily exchanges are evidence of a democratic power structure where a community's historical project is flourishing under its own care.

As the project moves forward, there are several expressed goals. Thus far the community has become deeply involved in providing historical materials and maintaining, to some degree, the archive. However, because of the time required to make connections and the magnitude of the community, this project still has not collected materials from many Lebanese families. Mobilizing the community to reach out to new families is necessary for the project's longevity and inclusivity. This will also encourage the collaborators of this project to shape the content and programs derived from it. In addition, mounting the historical materials on various Web platforms may encourage traffic from diverse sources. If nothing else, branching out may help facilitate a change in the grammar of this project such that the rich historical materials can be used to inform other educational ventures.

As the project expands its funding sources in order to pursue bigger goals, its sustainability is constantly in question. Can this comparatively small community keep finding and producing rich content to keep the project fresh and educational? If the project broadens its parameters to include Middle Easterners in the American South, would that necessarily eclipse the work we have done to highlight the Lebanese? What if researchers are uninterested in the materials of the archive? My confidence in the project's long-term value comes from two decidedly opposing places: First, the community's investment is one that will allow it to follow the shape of the growing and shifting community, one that is collectively excited about their history in the state. The creators and custodians of these materials are our biggest advocates. Second, the Islamophobia seeping into this country's ideology attempts to reject the long-lasting historical contributions of Middle Easterners to the country. Its existence dismisses the very notion upon which the project is based. But without the Lebanese presence in North Carolina and other parts of the U.S., this country would not resemble the place it is today, and this archive documents that reality.

Our community-based project centers on information access and knowledge sharing, borrowing techniques from the field of librarianship. But it may also serve as an example of the ways in which librarians and other institutions can cultivate new paradigms of education. First, while time-consuming, using community members as primary sources alongside the holdings of an institution are invaluable in connecting people and place, and educating the entire community. Sources are no longer the resources *checked out of the library*. They are the *people checking them out*. Second, digital projects are inexpensive to create, contributions can be made from any computer, and there are always opportunities to teach computer skills in a personalized way. And third, advocacy takes many shapes. We attempt to nurture advocacy for the goals of this project no matter their source, even if unlikely.

Projects like the Lebanese in North Carolina Project resemble the heirlooms that populate the archive. They are at once durable and incredibly fragile; traveling over oceans to various continents, passed down through generations, and stored in the recesses of people's homes, those photographs and documents are the only tangible relics that exist to tell the story of the Lebanese in the state. The project's scaffolding is one of collaboration, interactivity, and historical inquiry. Using models of social justice and public history, this project is digging out a history of a community that had a significant impact on North Carolina, but was silenced by the official record.

References

Frisch, M. H. (1990). *A shared authority: Essays on the craft and meaning of oral history.* New York, NY: SUNY Press.

Khater, A. F. (2003). "Queen of the house?" Making immigrant Lebanese families in the *Mahjar.* In B. Doumani (Ed.), *Family history in the Middle East: Household, property, and gender* (pp. 271-299). New York, NY: SUNY Press.

In the Catalog

Cutter & Paste: A DIY Guide for Catalogers Who Don't Know About Zines and Zine Librarians Who Don't Know About Cataloging

Jenna Freedman and Rhonda Kauffman

The subtitle of the book containing this chapter being *Library and Information Skills in Social Justice Movements and Beyond*, this essay is about informing and empowering library workers with subject expertise in zines (or another special collections area) to do their own cataloging. DIY (do it yourself) is an ethos inherent in the anarchopunk community that produces many of the zines housed in the Barnard Zine Library. Being able to do it yourself, allows a person to take a more active role in activities others are more passive about—healthcare, home projects, crafts, and cooking, so why not cataloging? As a reference librarian, co-author Jenna Freedman could conceive and initiate a collection of zines in her library, but initially she had to turn over the cataloging to someone who had expertise in original cataloging, but no particular knowledge of or interest in zines. Eventually Freedman wore down her colleagues, requested training, and then continued learning on her own and with the help of special collections catalogers and zinester-turned-Cataloging/Metadata Librarian Rhonda Kauffman, co-author of this chapter. Kauffman was fluent in both cataloging and zine culture and greatly informed the practice this chapter details.

Before we go much further, we want to note that many catalogers work with materials about which they are not expert, and do a fine job of it. We're not dissing cataloging training and experience or catalogers themselves. It is possible, though, that by having technical skills and password-enabled power, they can have more influence, or even control, over what gets cataloged and how. Just as a reference librarian might seek out a cataloging colleague's expertise on a research inquiry in a subject about which the cataloger is knowledgeable, can't reference librarians share their special knowledge in the catalog? The answer is yes, but it takes work. You don't just jump into OCLC Connexion and start typing. That's where this chapter comes in. We hope that the following step-by-step guide to cataloging zines using the *AACR2R* (*Anglo-American Cataloguing Rules, Second Edition*) will enable both catalogers who don't know about zines and zine librarians who don't know about cataloging to do justice to zines and their readers.

Most non-catalogers tend to roll their eyes at the MARC codes and punctuation peculiarities, but it is our hope that you will be able to use this article as a guide to implement item-level cataloging of zines in your integrated library system (ILS), even for those new to cataloging. There *are* rules to follow, but there are websites that provide guidance on where and how to record information. Cataloging zines is the same as cataloging any other special library material such as posters or rare books; it requires some sleuthing to find or infer information about the publisher and author, and to create subject headings. Catalogers have been doing that since forever, so there is really no reason why you can't start cataloging zines at your library right away.

If you're reading this article, you or someone at your library might already know what zines are, why they're important, and why libraries should collect them. If you don't, we encourage you to read *From A to Zine: Building a Winning Zine Collection in Your Library* (Bartel, 2004), "Why Zines Matter: Materiality and the Creation of Embodied Community" (Piepmeier, 2008), or Freedman's earlier zine cataloging essay (Freedman, 2008) where she defines zines and provides a justification for collecting and preserving them.

We will take a moment to address why it's helpful for zines to be included in a library catalog, along with the library's other holdings, and thereby in a union catalog, if the library is part of one. In a recent discussion on the Zine Librarians discussion list, Freedman (2012b) argued for ILS cataloging for zines, versus describing them as one might describe archival or special collections materials:

> Zines can be cataloged at the item (or series) level like other library materials such as books and magazines. Archival holdings are more readily described in finding aids—or on a catablog—because they have lots of discrete and disparate bits. Also, many people who are looking for primary sources know they're looking for primary sources and have a chance of stumbling their way to the finding aids portal. They've probably already checked the catalog first. But lots of people researching topics covered in zines don't know of their existence, or that they can be used in an academic (or a leisure!) context. If zines are returned in a catalog search, though, the researcher will skip merrily to the zine stacks and write a paper informed by points of view

they've never considered before. Also the sun will come out from behind a cloud and cats and dogs will embrace and sing.

Once you or someone at your library has embraced the point of view that zines should be item-level cataloged in your institutions' ILS, you have to get down to the craft of cataloging materials that often exhibit drastic inconsistencies in authorship, title, publication location, size and content. Freedman faced these challenges as someone who had taken and enjoyed two cataloging classes in library school but had never had her hands in an actual catalog. (Why on earth don't more library schools or ILS vendors set up sandboxes so students can get meaningful experience cataloging?) She was, however, an extremely catalog-centric reference librarian who had an enormous personal stake in zines being cataloged thoughtfully and thoroughly, though perhaps not as carefully as a real cataloger might like them to be. Fortunately, she has had excellent guidance on zine cataloging from Barnard Director of Collection Services Michael Elmore; Seattle University Metadata Librarian Rick Block; and Kauffman, former Barnard Library zine intern and now Freedman's personal cataloging guru.

The Barnard College Library isn't the only library cataloging zines in its ILS. Freedman has copy cataloged records from Bowling Green State University, the Multnomah County Library and others. A WorldCat search for the beloved afropunk zine *Shotgun Seamstress* (Atoe, 2006) reveals that it is held by Barnard College/Columbia University, Brooklyn College, the Brooklyn Museum, Sarah Lawrence College, the University of California at Irvine, and the University of Connecticut, so you can see that several libraries have already gotten on board cataloging zines like their other holdings.

It should be noted that cataloging zines can be time consuming, as can cataloging musical scores, websites, or video recordings, or doing any original cataloging. At the very least, providing subject, title, author, and summaries are invaluable to a researcher. Even so, we've flagged a few fields as "core elements" that really ought to be included, even if one is forced to sacrifice the others.

Before we dive into cataloging, let's talk about zines a little.

Zines are sometimes published in numerical sequence like a serial/journal/periodical, but it is often difficult to decipher if a zine's issue at hand is part of a serial sequence, because it might not say so anywhere on the zine. A zine librarian must use detective skills to determine the "seriality" of a zine. Or, zines might be "one-offs" that can be treated like monographs, or a monographic series. They are not an issue from a series, and sometimes zinesters who publish a serial-like zine may decide to make a one-off zine.

The rest of this article will consist of our going through the cataloging fields used at Barnard, in order. You'll see that some of the practice is entirely standard, and some represents a house style informed by our specialized knowledge and patron use of zines. You'll note that Freedman has been cataloging according to AACR2R specifications and has not yet begun to explore how RDA or the metadata schema xZINECOREx might affect her practice (more on that later). The examples we give are all from zines held at Barnard and shared with the permission of the zine publishers when they could be found.

Cataloging Fields

First off, you have to decide whether to catalog the zine as a monograph or a serial because your catalog probably already has a template set up for each of these.

Leader

The leader (Library of Congress, 2010) describes the type of cataloging record you've got (look at position 7 for an "m" or "s" for monograph and serial, respectively).[1] The encoding level can vary from institution to institution, and it is best to check with your cataloging department on what to put in this field.

008   Fixed-Length Data Elements

The Fixed Fields provide information about what's in the cataloging record, a lot of which is duplication of the MARC variable fields (the text fields you're more familiar with). For example, if you have a bibliography that is recorded in the 504 field, you need to indicate that in the 008's "Cont Nature of Contents" field. Most of this field is pretty self-evident. For example, if the zine is in English, code it eng in the language field. We default everything to containing illustrations and biographical information.

100   Main Entry-Personal Name (Core element)

Even if you're not a cataloger, if you remember your cataloging class at all, you know that the 100 is the author field. An author is the person most responsible for thinking up and creating this thing in your hand. There may be other people who helped the author create the thing, like an editor, contributor or illustrator; save these folks for the added entry fields, the 7XX. We've also

---

1.   It should be noted that if you're cataloging in Connexion, OCLC confusingly combines the Leader and the 008/Fixed Fields into one section.

been known to use 110 (Main Entry Corporate Name) for items collectively published, (e.g. 110 2_ ‡a INCITE! Women of Color Against Violence Ad-Hoc Community Accountability Working Group Meeting (2005)). While, of course, a collective is far from being a corporation, one of the definitions of the field is, "According to various cataloging rules, main entry under corporate name is assigned to works that represent the collective thought of a body" (Library of Congress, 2007).

In zine land, as in other places, authors are complicated. Zinesters use fake last names, provide no last names, take the name of their zine as their last name, or change their last names due to marriage or a gender transition. They sometimes choose to use their real name eventually, or determine that they don't want their real name to appear in a library catalog even if it was originally printed in their zine.

As members of the zine community ourselves, we privilege zinesters' mores over some tenets of librarianship. We imagine that other special collections librarians identify strongly with their subjects but don't bend or ignore library rules. We won't comment on other people's practices (or maybe we will; we'll see), but we feel that putting zinesters first is particularly important because of the age and politics of many of the publishers. Many of the zines at Barnard were written by teenage girls. If they change their minds about being publicly identified with their work, either while they're still teens because the association may subject them to ridicule or abuse from peers or parents, or years later because their views or how they want to express them has evolved, it's right to honor that change. Another of our unorthodox practices is to list zine editors (not just authors) in the 1XX. Zines do not often change editors, like magazines do.

Freedman has not been empowered to create authority files for names, so she does the best she can to apply them consistently, using the author's current preference as a guide. She determines the author's preference directly from the person, as much as possible. She attempts to include birth dates with the ‡d delimiter.

On a related note, the practice at Barnard for assigning call numbers is to Cutter[2] on the author's name. With multiple authors who go only by "Erin," for example, we will use last names to derive the Cutter if we know them, even if we're not including them in the public catalog. This system doesn't give the authors total privacy, but with the extra effort required to guess the person's last name, it gives them adequate protection while also providing a form of col-

---

2. The definition of Cutter Number: "a method of representing words or names by using a decimal point followed first by a letter of the alphabet, then by one or more Arabic numerals. A Cutter number is read and sorted as a decimal number" (Library of Congress Cataloging Distribution Service, 2013a).

location for researchers someday when the zinesters and catalogers are dead and gone.

245   Title Statement (Core element)

Our practice in cataloging distinct issues of serials has changed since 2008, when Freedman published "AACR2—Bendable but Not Flexible: Cataloging Zines at Barnard College" in *Radical Cataloging: Essays at the Front*, so pay attention.

Back in the day, Freedman would have cataloged issue 36 of Corina Fastwolf and Phlox Icona's long-running serial zine *Sugar Needle: Licorice Is Sexy* as *Licorice Is Sexy* (Fastwolf, 2012), putting *Sugar Needle* only in the 830, the Series Added Entry field. We've come to conclude that divorcing the title from the subtitle is confusing to the user, so now the 245 for this record looks like:

245 10 ‡a Sugar needle. ‡n #36, ‡p Licorice is sexy / ‡c Corina Fastwolf and Phlox Icona.[3]

Previously Freedman didn't include the statement of responsibility (in this case, Corina and Phlox), out of ignorance. Now she does because titles are occasionally duplicated by other zines, as well as by other library holdings, e.g. *Muchacha* by Daisy Salinas (2011).

Whether or not to catalog a serial with a distinctive title or content is a judgment call. If the issue's content differs significantly from that of other issues (e.g. *Chica Loca* #3 [Endara, 1995], "Special report directly from the third world," was written during and about Lala's visit home to Ecuador), or if it has visual elements (e.g. a screenprinted cover) or was issued with accessories like a CD or a bag of valentine hearts, and you want to make note of the unusual elements in the record, cataloging it separately might best serve the zine and its potential readers.

If the title is inferred or gotten from a place other than the prescribed sources of information—which is typically the title page, the verso of the title page, and the colophon—then you need to put the title in brackets and make a note in the 500 field, e.g. "Cover title" or "Cataloger-supplied title."

240   Uniform Title

Zinesters love to change things around a lot, so a title may change spelling from issue to issue (e.g. *Boredom Sucks* vs. *Boredom Sux* [Martin, n.d.]). Apply-

---

3.   Although "No." is preferred to represent numbers, we like to use the # sign, since it doesn't interrupt the title in a catalog search.

ing to monographs, this field uses the name of the title that it is most known as, and you can type in the title however it appears on the item in the 245. For serials, use the 130. These fields help to collocate all the items under one uniform title, so that a user can click on the uniform title link in the search results and see all items for that title.

246   Varying Form of Title

We frequently need to add an alternate title, due to the usual things like providing access points for the use of ampersands vs. ands. There are often misspellings, abbreviations, and special characters in zine titles; the 246 is where you spell it all out, e.g. "Shivers & sparkles" (Arbabi, 2005) needs a 246 for "Shivers and sparkles." It's all about providing access. A user may also search for the title spelling out the "and" vs. using the "&," and we want to anticipate different search avenues.

250   Edition Statement

As with other materials, sometimes revised or otherwise altered editions of a zine are released. For example, in the record for the second edition of *Instigations from the Whore Revolution: A Third Wave Feminist Response to the Sex Work "Controversy"* (Koyama, 2002), we note in the summary that it contains "greater debate about working-class prostitutes" in order to show what has changed between editions.

260   Publication, Distribution, etc. (Imprint) (Core element)

This is a basic field, one we've been using since the beginning, when Michael Elmore developed the practice that Freedman eventually took over. When creating records in OCLC Connexion, we note that other catalogers make greater use of brackets [ ] than we like to. We sometimes see them applied even when the location or date is included in the zine, which we find to be delegitimizing. Catalogers use the brackets when any information is inferred or gotten from a place other than the prescribed sources of information (again, the title page, the verso of the title page, and the colophon). These are the places a cataloger knows where to look, so if the information in the 260 is in brackets, then the cataloger knows that the information was gathered from somewhere else. So, if the date was inferred from a postage mark or a date of a journal entry on page five, then that information is supposed to go in a bracket. A lot of the 260 should end up being in brackets for zines, but we've been a bit lax with this rule at Barnard.

If the place of publication, ‡a, isn't clearly identified in the zine, we will attempt to determine it from the zine's postmark or content, by contacting the publisher, by doing research online, or by reading other zines. Many zines, especially zines from the 1990s, are hand-addressed to the recipient, on the back cover of the zine. Freedman sought a solution for discerning these zines' publication dates by asking Lauren Jade Martin, who donated about 500 zines to the library, to provide a dateline of her postal addresses so that Jenna could determine from the address on a zine at least when it had been received, if not published. Martin, who began making zines in high school and who, like many zine publishers, was somewhat transient, provided seven addresses in two NYC boroughs and three states for a seventeen-year period (L.J. Martin, personal communication, November 13, 2006).

Some zines are published by a third party or list a publishing, press, or production name. In those cases, that name is listed in the ‡b, name of publisher/distributor. We do not use it to indicate a zine distro[4] that distributes, but an entity that publishes or produces the zine itself. When no publishing name is given, we use "the author." We've noted that other catalogers will give the author's name or the author's first initial and last name, as if the person is some sort of official publisher. We hope that "the author" will be useful for identifying self-publishers. When cataloging unruly materials like zines, it's a good idea to be adaptable.

Zinesters are notoriously bad about dating their work, so entering something into the ‡c "Date of Publication, Distribution, etc." subfield can be a challenge, but one well worth undertaking. Zine researchers, like researchers using any other primary sources and special collections materials, will want to know as best as they can when an item was published for the sake of context, to know how old the author was when they wrote it, and so on. The date can be an estimate; just indicate so with a question mark. If you are pretty sure, but not positive, that it was published in 1999, use [1999?]. If you estimate the decade, use a dash: [199-?].

300   Physical Description (Core element)

Nothing controversial here, though generally an effort is made to count pages and put the total in the ‡a in brackets if no page numbering exists, rather

---

4.   Distro is the colloquial name of mail and email order distributors of zines and related materials, e.g. Sweet Candy Zine Distro, at sweetcandydistro.weebly.com.

than listing the zine as "unpaginated." Nearly every zine is illustrated, so the ‡b normally gets an "ill." If it's a minicomic or art zine, we'll note "chiefly ill." If a zine comes with a CD, coloring pages, a separate map, or anything else that is not "inside" the zine but accompanies it and will stay with the zine in the collection, it can be added it in the ‡e Accompanying material subfield.

500   General Note

The 5XX fields are where catalogers put notes to let other people know about where information was obtained, or to give more bibliographic information about the work. The 500 field is the one for all kinds of information, including, for monographs—or, in zine parlance, "one-offs"—how you identified the title. Pretty often that's from the cover. We've heard conflicting arguments about "cover title" vs. "title from cover" and have chosen the former for its simplicity. We've also said "title from inside cover," "...from title page," "...from first sentence" (sometimes zines don't have an apparent title, and you have to call them something), and "...from author."

For-real catalogers probably think it's highly annoying that the 500 ends up being such a catch-all that it's practically a Misc., when the whole idea of this complicated system is that everything has its place. However, sometimes stuff ends up here because of how your ILS presents information. We wanted to put provenance in the 541 (Immediate Source of Acquisition Note), and that's perhaps where it should ideally go, but since the 541 doesn't show in the public interface, we have to add even more miscellaneous information in the 500.

We identify the donor or how/where a zine was acquired like so:

500 __ ‡a Gift of Felix Endara, donated in 2007. ‡5 NNBa.

Or

500 __ ‡a Purchased at the Women of Color Zine Symposium in 2012. ‡5 NNBa.

The ‡5 is an institution code, which can be found by searching the MARC Code List for Organizations (Library of Congress, 2011).

Notes fields that others might use, but that we don't at Barnard because of how our ILS is configured, include:

501 With Note
515 Numbering Peculiarities Note
542 Information Relating to Copyright Status
563 Binding Information (e.g. "Japanese stab binding")

We've also used the Notes field for things like, "The zine was made for Sara Jaffe's Barnard Pre-College Program writing about the arts class."[5]

504   Bibliography, Etc. Note

As with other library materials, this field is good for "Includes bibliographical references," "Includes endnotes," etc.

505   Formatted Contents Note

This is the most labor-intensive thing to do: adding tables of contents information to zine records. But the payoff, particularly for compilation zines (like anthologies), where we can enter all of the contributors' names and the titles of their articles, essays, comics, photographs, poems, etc. is well worth it.

The ‡g is for miscellaneous text, used if a descriptive text was added to let you know it's the introduction, part 1 or issue 3. ‡t is for Title, and the ‡r is for Statement of Responsibility (the ‡c in the 245). The "--" creates a hard return in the public record.

Here's what a few entries in the record for *Evolution of a Race Riot*, edited by Mimi Thi Nguyen (1997) look like:

‡t Introduction / ‡r Mimi Nguyen -- ‡t Letters -- ‡t War cries and battle scars / ‡r Helen Luu -- ‡t The grass is always greener / ‡r Mimi Llano[6]

The above coding presents like this, in the public side of the catalog:

Introduction / Mimi Nguyen
Letters
War cries and battle scars / Helen Luu
The grass is always greener / Mimi Llano

You can also do a simplified or basic contents note without the t's and r's:

505 0_ Introduction / Mimi Nguyen -- Letters -- War Cries and battle scars / Helen Luu -- The grass is always greener / Mimi Llano.

Useful, right? One can enter tables of contents whenever they present themselves, and even sometimes when they don't, as was the case with *Evolution of a Race Riot*. *Evolution* was such an important zine and had so many noted contributors that Freedman, with permission, derived a TOC herself.

---

5.   Musician and zine maker Sara Jaffe taught in Barnard's Pre-College Program and had her students make zines as their final project.

6.   The TOC was brutally truncated, for the sake of our word count.

Tables of contents are also included for multiple issues of a zine in one record, as we did for *Angry Young Woman* (Gloria, 1994):

505 00 ‡g Issue 1. ‡t Talkin' baseball: of greediness and thanklessness -- ‡t Men: I love to hate them (and hate to love them) -- ‡t Keeping abreast of it: welfare moms and the public tit -- ‡t Bobby's boys: lawless athletes with free scholarships, police immunity and a mouth, crass jerk for a coach -- ‡t What do Cathy and I have in common? We're both disgusted with ourselves.

505 00 ‡g Issue 2. ‡t Only the lonely: Chinese and Indian men are running short of pussy -- ‡t Hey whitey! Want a taco? The confusion of straddling two cultures -- ‡t Say "yes" to Michigan (and the Midwest): my boss solves the homeless problem -- ‡t The meet market: it sucks, even on the info highway -- ‡t Work is hell: when the owner of the place you work is your worst nightmare of sexism and stupidity -- ‡t Why Gloria hates to read women's magazines: a one page rant and rave.

There are three more issues, all analyzed, but we're trying to keep this chapter from getting out of control.[7]

520   Summary, Etc.

This is the field that is often used for back-of-the-book copy and other descriptions. At Barnard, student workers create original abstracts for all monographs and create or add to descriptions for serial records as needed. The students are directed to shoehorn relevant and vernacular keywords into the abstracts, and to use the summary field to describe the zinester and the physical appearance of the zine, as well as its content. This field is incredibly useful and worth the money Barnard and the work study fairy spend on paying the students to read and write about zines for five to ten hours a week. Currently Freedman is blessed to have two students who are excellent writers and have knowledge of punk, queer, and DIY cultures.

The vernacular keywords are invaluable to researchers and leisure readers who are not well served by Library of Congress Subject Headings (LCSH) as access points. More on that when we get to the 650 field!

---

7.   Too late?

588   Source of Description Note

This field identifies where the cataloger got information to create the serial catalog record. A description of a serial's first issue can be very different from the description of the fifteenth. It goes something like: ‡a Description based on : no. 1, published in [2000 or 2001]; title from cover.

6XX   Subject Headings (Core element)

The 6XX fields provide subject access based on the thesaurus or vocabulary coded in the second indicator. These could be LCSH, National Library of Medicine Medical Subject Headings, Getty's Art and Architecture Thesaurus, or other vocabularies. Subject headings should cover as narrow a topic as possible on whatever the item is about. Catalogers often say this is where we capture the "aboutness" of the work.

We mostly use LCSH, and ideally we use ClassificationWeb to search for headings. If you're not fortunate enough to subscribe to ClassWeb, you can always search the LC Authorities at authorities.loc.gov or the LC linked data service for authorities and subjects at id.loc.gov by subject. LCSH is a controlled vocabulary, so there are preferred terms for things, and directions for you to use certain words over another or suggestions to look under related or similar terms that might fit your item's subject. Generally speaking, the controlled vocabulary helps to bring synonyms or related terms together in a hierarchical, syndetic structure.

The subject of an item can be divided into types, including corporate, title, meetings, subject, and form.

610   Subject Added Entry-Corporate Name

This is the field for works that are *about* a group, what LC calls a "corporate name." Check LC authority records for authorized forms of names. If a group is responsible for authoring the item, and the item is not about the group itself, this goes under a 710 field, for Added Corporate entry. For example:

610 20 ‡a Barnard College. ‡b Library. ‡b Zine club. (Barnard Zine Club, 2012)

630   Subject Added Entry-Uniform Title

‡a My so-called life (Television program) ‡x Analysis, appreciation (*Demon Angela*, 1995).

The above heading, in this case describing a zine/fanzine called *Demon Angela* (no author listed), is so awesome and represents such a ubiquitous topic in zines from 1995 that we were tempted to type it in all caps, but we didn't want to confuse you.

650   Subject Added Entry-Topical Term[8]

The pictured quote below, taken from a webpage that no longer exists but viewable at www.screencast.com/users/jennaf/folders/Jing/media/64ea60d1-5628-4 058-bfe1-7c8c450307cd, kind of says it all, especially the "narrow and specialized" bit, when in the same month the Subject Authority Cooperative Program (SACO) approved distinct headings for thirteen different roads in Turkey (Freedman, 2012a).

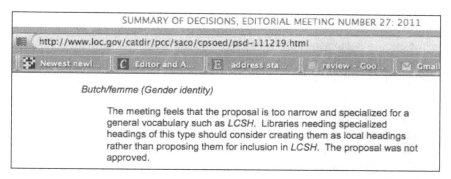

SUMMARY OF DECISIONS, EDITORIAL MEETING NUMBER 27: 2011

http://www.loc.gov/catdir/pcc/saco/cpsoed/psd-111219.html

Newest new!... | C Editor and A... | E address sta... | review - Goo... | Gmail

Butch/femme (Gender identity)

The meeting feels that the proposal is too narrow and specialized for a general vocabulary such as *LCSH*. Libraries needing specialized headings of this type should consider creating them as local headings rather than proposing them for inclusion in *LCSH*. The proposal was not approved.

It's also unfortunate that SACO rejected ‡v Zines as a form subdivision, which is an additional term you can add onto a subject heading to indicate the form of an item, for example:

650_0 ‡a Stay-at-home mothers.

650_0 ‡a Stay-at- home mothers ‡v Diaries.

---

8. We have much to say about the topic of LCSH, but we're not going to go into all of that here, other than to say the people who decide about LCSH have gone out of their way to hate on LGBTQ-related headings. Freedman blogs about it sometimes, so if this topic interests you, check out lowereastsidelibrarian.info/search/node/queer%20lcsh.

The latter subject heading with the form subdivision of ‡d Diaries yields items that are a first-person account of being a stay-at-home mother. The former can be anything about stay-at-home mothers.

So, with LC's rejection of the ‡v Zines, we can only identify items *about* zines, rather than zines themselves, in the 650. One cannot assign 650 _0 ‡a Single mothers ‡z United States ‡y21st century ‡v Zines, which would help readers find more zines about 21st century American single mothers. The only way to capture the form of a zine in a subject heading is to use it in the 655 field.

Sanford Berman (2005) notes that there is no cross-reference in the zines subject heading to fanzines or vice versa, and LC has no established headings for "zine distributors" or "zine libraries."

In an attempt to counter the U.S.-centric and other biases inherent in LCSH, we like to be specific about the country the zine is about. Our eyes are on future researchers when we include the century. It's a little awkward with the zines in the Barnard collection because they were almost all published close to the turn of the century (and millennium!). With Riot grrrl movement (Library of Congress, n.d.), however, 20th vs. 21st century makes a big difference, even to contemporary researchers.

Another perhaps unorthodox (read: inappropriate) way Barnard uses the field is to describe zine publishers, rather than just the content of the zines. We go out of our way to acquire zines by women of color. Therefore, our collection is of particular interest to people doing research on women of color. Therefore, it seems prudent to make a zine publisher's racial identity prominent in the record, e.g. *Picaflor*, by Celia C. Perez (1999):

650 _0 ‡a Hispanic American women.

650 _0 ‡a Cuban American women.

650 _0 ‡a Mexican American women.

650 _0 ‡a Graduate students ‡z United States.

650 _0 ‡a Racism ‡x Political aspects ‡z United States.

650 _0 ‡a Local transit ‡z Florida ‡v Anecdotes.

We keep a spreadsheet of the LC subject headings we've applied to Barnard zines at tinyurl.com/zinesLCSH.

651   Subject Added Entry-Geographical Name

The lovely 651 field showcases places that a work is about. A fun subdivision is the topical "Description and travel," which is just what it sounds like. From *There are not enough hours in the day for all the bitching I have to do* by Lynette Koh [ca. 1990]: 651_0 ‡a Seattle (Wash.) ‡x Description and travel.

655   Index Term-Genre/Form

This is how we conquer the form issue referenced in the 650 section. Every zine is assigned 655 _0 Zines.

One or more genre terms are assigned with a _7 indicator, which necessitates a ‡2 with the explanation "local."

655 _7s include but are not limited to:

- 24-hour zines. These are zines that were made from start to finish in a 24-hour period. Zinesters often create such zines during July, which is International Zine Month. There is a website devoted to the project, 24 Hour Zine Thing, at 24hourzines.com.
- Art zines. Susan Thomas (2009) writes, "The form of art zines may include silk-screened covers, assemblage (including inserts or attachments of three-dimensional objects like stickers, badges, patches, photographs, toys, seeds, or DVDs), or collage—either pasted onto paper or photocopied" (p. 28).
- Catalog zines. This applies to zine distro catalogs.
- Compilation zines. Edited by one or more people, or a collective, these are typically themed volumes, with writings generated from a call for submissions.
- DIY zines. Topics taught encompass cooking, crafting, graywater reclamation, and more.
- Fanzines.[9] Fanzines are devoted to science fiction, music, candy, stars of the academy, television shows, libraries, and anything else you can think of.
- Literary zines. Primarily comprised of poems, fiction, and essays, lit zines have some overlap with chapbooks.
- Mamazines. These are zines that are mostly about parenting. We call zines by people who identify as men mamazines, as well, which we probably shouldn't, but it's not relevant in the collection at Barnard since the vast majority of its holdings are by women.[10]
- Minicomics. These differ from comics in that they are most often about the author/artist's own life, rather than someone fictional. They physi-

---

9.   In direct defiance of SACO deciding to replace Fanzines with Fan magazines, which just kills Freedman. She's not kidding. More on that on her blog at lowereastsidelibrarian.info/lcsh/2009/week35/fanzines.

10.   In case this needs to be said, and we hope it doesn't, transgender women are women.

cally resemble zines rather than the average comic, in terms of size and how they're reproduced (being half or quarter-sized,[11] and photocopied).

- One-page folding-zines. These are zines folded and cut a certain way from one sheet of paper (or whatever material).
- Personal zines. Also known as perzines, they detail the author's life in essays, anecdotes, lists, journal entries, comics, photos, art, haiku, recipes, etc.
- Political zines. These can be hard to distinguish from political pamphlets. Elements that differentiate them are the same as noted above in personal zines, as well as a subjective—though not unfairly biased—perspective on the topic.
- Program zines. Zine fest organizers often create a companion zine that contains workshop schedules, maps, vendor listings, and guides to the location.
- Review zines. These zines review other zines. Some contain reviews exclusively. Others also have articles and other ziney elements.
- School zines. Any zine made for an assignment or grade and not created purely from the author's own motivation.
- Split zines. Usually made by two authors with each having its own cover and half of the zine, which the reader switches between by turning and flipping the zine.

You may notice that some of the above genres describe the form of the zine (e.g. minicomics, split zines) and others the contents (personal zines, political zines). This is a mistake Freedman made early on and doesn't know how to fix other than by assigning multiple terms to a zine as needed, like for a minicomic that is also a personal zine.

7XX   Added Entry Fields

The added entry fields provide additional access to people, groups, or meetings that contributed to the creation of a work.

700   Added Entry-Personal Name

We use this field for non-main entry authors and editors, including notable contributors and split zine co-authors.

---

11. The size is in relation to a sheet of letter paper, in the US 8.5x11". Zines are sometimes made with legal sized sheets and are then designated as "half-legal," for example.

710   Added Entry-Corporate Name

This field is used for a group that contributed to the creation of a work but is not directly responsible for its creation, sort of along the lines of "brought to you by..." or "in association with..."

780 & 785   Preceding & Succeeding Entry

Serial zines sometimes change their names. The 780 and 785 help you connect old and new titles. Indicators create "continues" and "continued by" relationships. A serial record may change names throughout its life. The current record for a title may have a link to the 780 (the preceding title), and the record for that preceding title will have a link to the 785 for the succeeding title. These links can be transferred to the catalog, so a user can see the development of the title over time. Note that the preceding record should have its volume coverage "closed" in the 362 field.

830   Series Added Entry-Uniform Title

This is the field that connects distinct titled issues of monographic series. Librarians who wish to catalog their zines as monographs can use the 830/490 to bring together all issues of the same zine under the uniform title in the 830. A monographic series is "[a] group of separate items related to one another by the fact that each item bears, in addition to its own title proper, a collective title applying to the group as a whole. The individual items may or may not be numbered" (Library of Congress Cataloging Distribution Service, 2013c). This is the initial approach we took before we branched off and decided to catalog zines as periodicals, with the "collective title" essentially being the main title of the zine.[12]

Earlier, this idea was introduced in the section about the 245 with regard to *Sugar Needle*. The 830 is the uniform title, so, like the 240, it is the one title a series is known as. "Normal" bibliographic items usually have an authorized form, that is, a uniform title that an item will now and hereafter be known as

---

12. There are advantages and disadvantages to cataloging zines as monographs or periodicals. For our collection, we found that the additional holdings fields for periodicals helped to give more information about the history of the zine, such as when we estimate it started or for how long it ran. This is a pretty personal choice for librarians to make, and all depends on the individual collection and librarian.

(check out LC authorities and search for a title). Zines, of course, have no LC-authorized form of name.

The 830 is linked to a 490 or 500 note that shows the series title as it appears directly on the item in hand, so that's why there may be discrepancies between the two fields. The 490/500 notes are as-is; the 830 is authorized. When you click on the title as it appears in the 830, you should in theory get all the items associated with that title.

That being said, we typically don't add a 490 or 500 note. Having a 490 adds an extra, often redundant note in the public catalog, and we don't know what we would even put in the 500 that would do anything but clutter the record.

We use ‡a for the title and after a " ;" either ‡n or ‡v for the number or volume, as appropriate.

856 Electronic Location and Address

You can add a URL or other electronic access points to a record, not that we've ever used the 856 for anything other than first indicator 4, HTTP (Library of Congress, 2003). For the second indicator, we've used 0 – resource, 1 – version of resource and 3 – related resource.

View the record for *Minutiae, No. 2. Wandering sweet pea* by Aijung Kim (2009) for an example: 856 42 ‡u http://aijungkim.com ‡z Website

Classification and Call Numbers

When we first started shelving zines at Barnard, Michael Elmore—who, as we wrote earlier, devised the original cataloging practice at Barnard and cataloged the zines until Freedman took over with the help of library school graduate student interns such as Rhonda—attempted to assign LC classification numbers to the zines. He convinced Jenna that determining subjects for the zines was impractical and that most of them would end up in the AC2s (we're an LC library), and instead to assign Cutter numbers based on the author, if known, or the title, if not. We're happy with the decision. We think it serves the zines and researchers best to group them by author as best we can.

Here's an example of a call number for *Yo Ridiculous: A Split Zine* by Silvia Chenault and Kelly Caplan (2007?): Zines T67y 2007. We do worry that the call numbers will become unwieldy. Some of them already are, e.g. Zines R334455u, assigned to *Ugly Mug* by RAchelle (1998).

Barnard's zine collection is housed in two locations, Barnard Special Collections and Barnard, which is for the circulating copy.[13] Special collections call number labels are applied via a typed acid-free flag, and stacks copies get a barcode and spine label. We now create an item for each issue of a serial for both special collections and stack zines. The latter always got its own item records because the barcode necessitated it. Creating an item record for each issue of a serial will help us get a better grip on the total number of zines we hold.

Adding the date to the call number is a relatively new innovation in Barnard zine cataloging, but of course it's not new for us to assign Cutter numbers.

Things to Think about

Split zines. Sometimes zine authors smash together multiple issues into a single one, which is what we call a "split" zine—for example, Stab #6 and Root #4 brought together in one issue (Edworthy & Evans, 2005). Sometimes the authors give the special issue its own title; for these, the special title goes in the 245, but access to the individual issues of each author's zines is given in a 700 added entry field:

700 1_ ‡a Edworthy, Sonia. ‡t Stab. ‡n No. 6
700 1_ ‡a Evans, Sarah, ‡d 1980-. ‡t Root. ‡n No. 4

The 505 contents would appear as: 505 00 ‡t Stab / ‡r by Sonia Edworthy -- ‡t Root / ‡r Sarah Evans.

Sometimes, there is no special (or "collective") title for the issue. In this case, we would follow AACR2 rules for items without collective titles, such as Rule 1.1G (Library of Congress Cataloging Distribution Service, 2013b), which basically says that the work is treated as a unit, that the first title listed is depicted as the first title in the 245, and that the other titles and authors are listed in the order they appear, with the information also given in a contents note.

Here is an example of a split zine record title (Dearest & Ries, 2011): Culture slut. ‡n No. 24 / ‡c Amber Dearest. Motor city kitty. No. 16 / Brianna Ries.

Because these are also serials, access is provided to the authors and titles in a 700 field: 700 1_ ‡a Ries, Brianna. ‡t Motor city kitty. ‡n No. 16

The first author is given the main entry (100) with title access in the 245 ‡a.

---

13. At Barnard, we attempt to acquire two copies of each zine. The first is shelved in the climate-controlled, acid-free archives as a special collections item, and the second goes into the open stacks, where it is available for lending to Barnard and Columbia University affiliates as well as for interlibrary loan

Finally, a Catalog Record!

After all this work, a catalog record is created! We hope this list is not over-whelming! We didn't say it was easy, but it is really, really fun. Our intention is to help you as you catalog and for this paper to be a resource.

Below is an example of a Barnard serial bibliographic zine record (Vo, 2011).

```
LDR 02100cas 22003374a 4500
001 10130128
005 20130112161931.0
008 130112u2011uuuugw_uu_p_____0____0eng_d
035 __ ‡a(OCoLC)ocn824052041
040 __ ‡a ZCU ‡c ZCU ‡d ZCU
035 __ ‡a(OCoLC)824052041
049 __ ‡a ZCUA
100 1_ ‡aVo, Anna.
245 10 ‡a Fix my head / ‡c Vo and Jamie.
260 __ ‡a Berlin, Germany : ‡b The editor ; ‡c 2011-
300 __ ‡a v. : ‡b ill. ; ‡c 28 cm.
310 __ ‡a Irregular
500 __ ‡a Gift of the author, donated in 2012. ‡5 NNBa
505 00 ‡g. ISSUE 2. ‡t The lady issue... (subtitle) -- ‡t Intro / ‡r Vo -- ‡t
Intro / ‡r J -- ‡t Christine from Deathrats -- ‡t Bryony from Good Throb
-- ‡t Sam from Lich and Battle of the Wolf 359 -- ‡t Things I love to hate
to hear / ‡r Vo -- ‡t MZ from Mellow Yellow Aotearoa -- ‡t Meghan from
Ampere and Siamese Twins  -- ‡t Pettybone -- ‡t Meghan from Punch
-- ‡t Community accountability for sexual violence interview with Vo /
‡r Transformative Justice, EU -- ‡t Andy from Agatha and the Christies.
[...]
588 __ ‡a Description based on: [No. 2], published in 2011; title from
cover.
650 _0 ‡a Women in music ‡x Political aspects ‡y 21st century.
650 _0 ‡a Punk culture ‡y 21st century.
650 _0 ‡a Punk rock music ‡v Interviews.
650 _0 ‡a Asian American women.
650 _0 ‡a African American women.
650 _0 ‡a Hispanic American women.
655 _0 ‡a Zines.
655 _7 ‡a Political zines. ‡2 local
700 0_ ‡a Jamie.
```

856   4_ ‡u http://annavo.files.wordpress.com/2011/02/fmh-2-us-paper-size.pdf ‡z No. 2, formatted for US paper size

Future Implications

Does it seem silly to write a paper on how to catalog zines using AACR2 when new standards are being adopted? Perhaps. But the guidelines discussed here are generally transferable to Resource Description and Access (RDA) records. Most important is having a grasp of the principles of basic cataloging as library cataloging and metadata move more into the collaborative spaces of the Internet, linking data and sharing and harvesting metadata between individuals and institutions. The fields discussed above may seem very MARC-specific, but understanding the difference between the 100/author field and the 700/added entry field may help you better understand the difference between Dublin Core metadata elements for creator and contributor (Dublin Core Metadata Initiative, 2011), and perhaps get you ready to use non-MARC metadata in your zine catalog.

Non-MARC metadata schema are everywhere, including the xZINECO-REx (MKE ZL(u)C., 2012) schema that will be used to create an online union zine catalog with metadata specific to the needs of zine library materials. How amazing would that be? Zine records could be entered into a collaborative database and extracted and contributed to by zine librarians all over the world, adding yet another resource that individual library catalogs can access. Information your catalog gathers is reaching beyond the ILS. Between an archival finding aids culture of "more product, less process," (Greene & Meissner, 2005), the switch to RDA, and the use of cataloging discovery layers such as Blacklight and VuFind, catalogs are returning results from not just the ILS, but also a library's federated databases, institutional repository, websites, and archives portals. It might be time to consider changing how we describe special collections items. It may be that enhancing traditional catalog records with the kind of information more typical of a finding aid isn't so far-fetched. Researchers don't always distinguish among the platforms they search, especially in a federated search environment. Inputting detailed information on item-level special collection records exposes your zine collection to more people, and it showcases the unique and far-reaching content contained within each zine.

References

Arbabi, N. (2005). *Shivers & sparkles*. Richmond, VA?: Ephemeral Mailbox Museum.

Atoe, O. (2006). *Shotgun seamstress*. Alexandria, VA: Author.

Barnard Zine Club. (2012). *Sticks & stones: May break your bones but WBAR will never hurt you*. New York, NY: Barnard College Library Zine Collection.

Bartel, J. (2004). *From a to zine: Building a winning zine collection in your library*. Chicago, IL: ALA Editions.

Berman, S. (2005). Berman's bag: Cataloging zines and widgets. *Unabashed Librarian, 137*, 23-25.

Chenault, S. & Caplan, K. (2007?). *Yo ridiculous: A split zine*. Fresno, CA: Authors.

Dearest, A., & Ries, B. (2011). *Culture slut/Motor City kitty*. Montreal, Quebec: Authors.

Demon Angela. (1995). New York, NY: Authors.

Dublin Core Metadata Initiative. (2011). User guide. Retrieved from http://dublincore.org/documents/usageguide/elements.shtml

Edworthy, S. & Evans, S. (2005). *Stab & root*. Halifax, NS: Authors.

Endara, L. (1995). *Chica loca #3: Special report directly from the third world*. New York, NY: Slanted.

Fastwolf, C. (2012). *Sugar needle, licorice is sexy*. Portland, OR: Author.

Freedman, J. (2008). AACR2—bendable but not flexible: Cataloging zines at Barnard College. In K. R. Roberto (Ed.), *Radical cataloging: Essays at the front* (pp. 231-240). Jefferson, NC: McFarland.

Freedman, J. (2012a, January 15) LC rejects Butch/Femme (Gender identity) and other queer headings but establishes thirteen different Turkish roads [Web log entry]. Retrieved from http://lowereastsidelibrarian.info/lcsh/2011/month27

Freedman, J. (2012b, July 11). Help me with my website? Message posted to http://groups.yahoo.com/group/zinelibrarians/message/2659

Gloria. (1994). *Angry young woman*. Fort Wayne, IN: Author.

Greene, M. A., & Meissner, D. (2005). More product, less process: Revamping traditional archival processing. *American Archivist, 68*(2), 208–263.

INCITE! Women of Color Against Violence Ad-Hoc Community Account-ability Working Group Meeting. (2005). *Gender oppression abuse violence: Community accountability within the people of color progressive movement.* Seattle, WA: Author.

Kim, A. (2009). *Minutiae.* Richmond, VA: Author.

Koh, L. [ca. 1990]. *There are not enough hours in the day for all the bitching I have to do.* Singapore: Author.

Koyama, E. (2002). *Instigations from the whore revolution: A third wave feminist response to the sex work "controversy"* (2nd ed.). Portland, OR: Confluere Publications.

Library of Congress (n.d.). Riot grrrl movement. *LC linked data service authorities and vocabularies.* Retrieved from http://id.loc.gov/authorities/subjects/sh2001002388.html

Library of Congress. (2003). 856: Electronic location and access. *MARC 21 format for bibliographic data.* Retrieved from http://www.loc.gov/marc/bibliographic/bd856.html

Library of Congress. (2007). 110: Main entry, corporate name. *MARC 21 format for bibliographic data.* Retrieved from http://www.loc.gov/marc/bibliographic/bd110.html

Library of Congress. (2010). Leader NR in MARC 21 bibliographic: Full. *MARC 21 format for bibliographic data.* Retrieved from http://www.loc.gov/marc/bibliographic/bdleader.html

Library of Congress. (2011). 110: MARC code list for organizations. Retrieved from http://www.loc.gov/marc/organizations/org-search.php

Library of Congress Cataloging Distribution Service. (2013a). *Classification and shelflisting manual, 2008 edition, 1: January 2013.* Retrieved from Cataloger's Desktop.

Library of Congress Cataloging Distribution Service. (2013b). Items without a collective title. *Anglo-American cataloguing rules, second edition (2002 revision with 2005 update), 1: January 2013.* Retrieved from Cataloger's Desktop.

Library of Congress Cataloging Distribution Service. (2013c). Series. *Anglo-American cataloguing rules, second edition (2002 revision with 2005 update), 1: January 2013.* Retrieved from Cataloger's Desktop.

Martin, L. J. (n.d.). *Boredom sucks.* Staten Island, NY: Author.

MKE ZL(u)C. (2012). Union catalog. Retrieved from http://mkezluc.wikispaces.com/union-catalog

Nguyen, M. T. (1997). *Evolution of a race riot.* Berkeley, CA: Editor.

Piepmeier, A. (2008). Why zines matter: Materiality and the creation of embodied community. *American Periodicals, 18*(2), 213-238.

Perez, C. C. (1999). *Picaflor.* Tampa, FL: Author.

RAchelle. (1998). *Ugly mug #6.* Allston, MA: Author.

Salinas, D. (2011). *Muchacha.* Nashville, TN: Author.

Thomas, S. (2009). Value and validity of art zines as an art form. *Art Documentation: Journal of the Art Libraries Society of North America, 28*(2), 27-38.

Vo, A. (2011). *Fix my head.* Berlin, Germany: Author.

In the World

Knowledge, Access, and Resistance: A Conversation on Librarians and Archivists to Palestine

Vani Natarajan and Hannah Mermelstein

In June 2013, 16 librarians and archivists traveled to Palestine to connect with Palestinian librarians, archivists, activists, and organizers, to learn more about their struggles and their work. We came from the U.S., Canada, Sweden, Trinidad and Tobago, and U.K./Palestine. We were public, academic, and school librarians; movement archivists; artists; and activists. We spent eight days traveling throughout the West Bank and '48.[1] In the few days that followed, participants went off on their own to participate in follow-up meetings and to connect with people we hadn't had time to meet during the first week. We reconvened at the end for a public event in Ramallah. Most of us did not know each other beforehand.

Hannah has led many delegations in Palestine over the past decade, but this was the first specifically with librarians and archivists. Vani traveled to Palestine with an LGBTQ delegation in January 2012. Both live in New York and work with Adalah-NY: The New York Campaign for the Boycott of Israel. For this article, we sat down in August 2013 to reflect on the Librarians and Archivists to Palestine delegation. We recorded and transcribed our conversation, and edited

---

1. Palestinians often refer to areas of Palestine by the year they were occupied. Israel is called "'48" or "1948 Palestine," and the West Bank is sometimes called "'67." Palestinians with Israeli citizenship, whom Israel refers to as "Arab Israelis" or "Israeli Arabs," often use the term "'48 Palestinians" to describe themselves. We mostly used this language during our conversation.

and rearranged it slightly for the sake of clarity. It should be noted that we often refer to the U.S. in our conversation, because this is the context within which the two of us work. Not everyone from the delegation lives in the U.S.

* * *

Vani: What is the significance of having librarians and archivists do solidarity work in Palestine?

Hannah: Part of what brought me to my Palestine work is what brought me to librarianship: issues of access to information and to stories. Palestine is not a place that's underreported; it's a place that's misreported and misrepresented. There's actually a wealth of information out there, but it's very hard to sift through that information, and a lot of the work I've done has been to help people sift through it. I've worked with many delegations, taking people to Palestine to experience for themselves what's happening there, to have that direct access. As librarians we have a responsibility to help people access the information they want about different issues.

V: My involvement with Palestine activism is also rooted in my belief in access to information; I also like to think about this in terms of knowledge, and how knowledge is structured. Like you said, we get so much misinformation about Palestine, and even the categories that we're given—whether on the news, in a reference book, or when you look on a map—the ways that things are named obscures so much. Giving people access to different ways of looking at history, different stories and perspectives, is really important because so much has been erased.

We've talked about the importance of access to information, but what do we do with a collection of facts and stories? How do we make sense of images, sounds, numbers, and words? I like to think of knowledge as what happens when we make meaning out of information, when we imbue it with a consciousness. I want to think of our work as beyond information access, as something deeper than just the sharing of information.

I'm also interested in the question of solidarity. It's important and it also opens up a challenge. In my training as a librarian, I've learned to try to be accountable to a community of users that I come to know well and that is directly around me. Then again, a lot of that work is about solidarity, as I've worked in communities where I'm not actually a member of that community. I don't have much of a history of librarian practices of transnational or global solidarity from which to draw, though. Solidarity still feels like more of a possibility than an existing condition.

H: A big challenge in planning the delegation was how to approach it as people who have specific skills we want to use and share in Palestine without doing so in a framework of charity. In some ways we do have more resources, and we are able to offer things that people need and want. How do we do that without imposing upon people? How do we recognize that there is a power differential and that we want to learn from people? We have a lot to learn from Palestinians that can inform our own work locally. With solidarity work, what's hard is recognizing a power differential but trying not to play into it, trying to have an equal relationship with those we work with.

Our professional identity—though we're not all paid for our librarianship and archiving work—helped us avoid some of the problems of other delegations. Sometimes people on generic human rights delegations lack focus and end up asking questions that are not relevant to the expertise or interest of the person we're meeting with. Or people get inspired in a moment, come up with ideas without consultation, and make promises they do not fulfill.

V: Did you notice many moments on our delegation when members would say, "This needs to be captured and recorded!" and when we might be imposing our ideas of documentation onto people?

H: There were definitely moments of walking through a community—Balata refugee camp in Nablus, for example—with half the delegation taking pictures and the other half cringing at the thought of taking pictures. But we worked through it. It's very difficult to avoid voyeurism when you have a large group of people walking around in a community that they are not from.

V: There are problems with witnessing as a form of activism. It's easy to forget that people who have been directly experiencing occupation, colonialism, and apartheid have been "witnessing" it all along. There is a danger in ascribing a special significance to the U.S.- or Europe-based, mostly white, non-Palestinian acts of witness. And this idea that injustices don't happen unless they are documented and observed with western eyes—why is that gaze given so much privilege? How do we acknowledge our ability to share what we have seen in Palestine, within our own communities, without intensifying these power dynamics? How do we make sure to center Palestinian expression, Palestinian narrative in our reporting back? And most importantly, how do we make the act of reporting back one that is accountable first and foremost to the Palestinians whose communities we visited?

H: Those are tough and crucial questions, especially as we try to share information. We have already put out a statement and a zine, and we're going to release a longer report, but we're trying to do it in a way that's accountable to the people with whom we're working in Palestine. Our initial statement had a mistake that a Birzeit University librarian caught, and we changed it. We had laid the groundwork for this interaction when we were there. Even before any of this production and dissemination of our experience, on our last day in Ramallah we did a report-back to share with Palestinians a bit about what we had seen in the prior couple of weeks and ask people to tell us if we were wrong about something, if we were missing things, or if we were focusing on the wrong things. So I think asking for feedback and fostering relationships with colleagues in Palestine are necessary parts of solidarity work.

V: In order to really do solidarity work, and do library work according to our values, we often need to challenge the structures within which we work. And challenge some of the assumptions that go into our profession.

H: Like what?

V: One example is the Library of Congress classification system. Many of us are familiar with this scheme of subject headings and call numbers; librarians around the world have adopted it by necessity. We've also come to know its limits—LC imposes a hierarchy on knowledge that often reflects an imperialist, sexist, racist worldview. Librarian activism has called that into question, and it came to light when we talked to librarians in Palestine. Working within this system requires a double consciousness. You have to know a system really well and also start to envision its undoing, its transformation into something better.

H: The Arabic language cataloger at Birzeit talked about using the LC system because there is no other option. He has to translate everything from Arabic into English to find appropriate descriptors, and then back into Arabic for cataloging. The terms prescribed by the LC are not the terms Palestinians would use to describe their history, geography, or culture. But they use them, and he changes a few things now and then, but he wants to be able to work in the world, and unfortunately that requires some compromise.

Hearing from the Birzeit librarians who fought to get a call number for the First Intifada was also inspiring to all of us. They were very matter-of-fact about it: it's a unique historical period that needs to get recognized. But then we heard how afterwards the LC here in the U.S. apparently created and started using a totally different call number than the one assigned to Birzeit. So most of the world uses a different call number than the one the Birzeit librarians had fought for and continue to use: DS128.4.

V: That reminds me—we talked to Palestinian librarians living and working in '48, who work in Israeli institutions and have been creatively devising ways to resist these from within. There was a conversation at Mada al Carmel[2] in Haifa, with Palestinian school librarians working in schools within '48. We had not been aware of so many of the challenges they're facing under Israeli apartheid, including the Hebraization of school curriculum. For Palestinian kids in '48, there's a growing pressure to read only materials in Hebrew and not read in Arabic.

H: And the fact that they can't access materials in Arabic. Many new children's books in Arabic are published in Beirut, and because Israel and Lebanon do not have relations, they can't get those books anywhere in Palestine. In Haifa and elsewhere in '48, most of the Arabic books in Palestinian libraries are translated from Hebrew, so they're reading Zionist stories in Arabic. This makes it even harder to get kids to read in Arabic. We had a librarian from Sweden with us who maintains an Arabic literature collection at a public library in Stockholm; she focuses on children's literature. She was shocked to find that there was less original Arabic literature in Palestine than she has in Stockholm, because she goes to Beirut and other places and she buys the stuff. When she was in Palestine, she saw more books that had been translated from Swedish into Arabic than ones originally written in Arabic. In Haifa, we also learned that the first school libraries in Jewish schools were established in 1927, and in Palestinian schools inside Israel, it was in 1992. That discrepancy was pretty shocking.

One of our follow-up ideas is to help people get materials they don't have, and a question for us is how to do that responsibly. Especially when we start to make campaigns public, we need to be conscious of our relationship with Palestinian projects and institutions. We want to avoid the model of "We have things we want to give to less fortunate people," and embrace a model of mutual struggle in response to a political problem.

V: I often hear librarians in the U.S. refer to neutrality as a core value or cornerstone of librarianship, but curiously I do not see it on the American Library Association list of the core values of librarianship (American Library Association, 2004). There *is* a value of social responsibility on that list that doesn't get talked about nearly enough. It's really interesting that neutrality is not listed as a core value, while social responsibility is.

---

2.   Mada al Carmel: Arab Center for Applied Social Research "generates and provides information, critical analysis, and diverse perspectives on the social and political life and history of Palestinians, with particular attention to Palestinians within Israel's 1948 boundaries" (Mada al-Carmel, n.d.).

H: And within social responsibility, it specifically says, "ALA recognizes its broad social responsibilities" and affirms the "willingness of ALA to take a position on current critical issues with the relationship to libraries and library services set forth in the position statement." So it's decidedly not neutral. Not only does it not mention neutrality, but it's saying we can take positions on things, so far as they are for the public good, democracy, access, and these other values.

Are there ways in which we're challenging the core values? Or are we really just challenging the core practices or the core assumptions?

V: Well, the word "democracy" carries so much baggage. For those of us living in the U.S., we're living in a country that projects itself as a democracy and proclaims democracy as a core value of its existence. Yet many of the values associated with democracy run counter to what the U.S. government is actually doing. Similarly, Israel, an apartheid state that is occupying Palestine, self-identifies as a democracy. So much mainstream reporting about Israel/Palestine refers to Israel as the "only democracy in the Middle East." There's hypocrisy in the ethos of many countries that label themselves democracies, particularly the U.S. and Israel. Our work can challenge and unpack that core value of democracy, a word that so often goes unexamined.

H: It seems like the ALA's core values are very much about the U.S. They refer to "the nation," and the one about democracy specifically talks about the First Amendment, but otherwise it seems to be more about little 'd' democracy. It says, "the publicly supported library [...] provides free and equal access to information for all people in the community." That's the idea of democracy they're talking about, which is something I think we can get behind.

V: I totally agree. Still, it's useful to look critically at the fact that the ALA cites the First Amendment. The U.S. Constitution in its inception had a very limited definition of personhood. So who even counted as a person, who counts as a person, is something that we should interrogate.

H: It's the same with Israel. Israel defines itself as a democracy, and it's able to do that only by not recognizing the personhood of Palestinians. Israel is a democracy for Jews, just not for the rest of its citizens, particularly the 20% who are Palestinian.

V: Exactly. This is a really interesting value to look at critically.

H: This isn't part of the core values, but perhaps a core tension of librarianship is that on the one hand the public library was founded as a place for free access to information. We're supposed to provide that access. At the same time, at the beginning, it was very much about assimilation into American culture. It's this whole question of whether we're trying to better people by providing them with what we think they should have, or trying to be a place where people can come and get what they're looking for.

V: This is why I was so inspired by Palestinian public libraries. The public libraries in Palestine are more public to me than ones in the U.S.—when you think about the history of American public libraries, so many of them are tied to these rich white men philanthropists, and they had this whole "civilizing" mission. That history is still there and can be very prevalent, even though many public librarians do a lot of work to challenge that ideology. From what we learned about public libraries in Palestine, they emerged as spaces of political resistance against occupation. I think about Al-Bireh Public Library near Ramallah, which was founded right before the 1967 invasion, right before Israel was dropping bombs on the West Bank. The library became a space for popular education, folklore, transmission of Palestinian culture, and politicization. How the story of public libraries is told was really moving and inspiring.

H: During the First Intifada, in the late 1980s, Israel closed the Palestinian schools, and it was illegal for people to teach in their own houses. In this context, the library by default becomes a space of resistance, as does the underground school. Libraries were in fact used for political meetings in the Intifada.

There are also libraries that come out of the prisoner movement, which within Palestinian society is not necessarily a challenging idea the way it would be in many parts of U.S. society. Within mainstream Palestinian society, everyone supports the prisoners, and it's assumed that if you're in prison you're unjustly imprisoned. In the U.S., mainstream society generally thinks that prisoners deserve to be in prison.

V: And we are often unaware of what is going on in prisons in the U.S. It's out of sight, out of mind.

H: Right. So these Palestinian prison libraries may not challenge Palestinian society, but they are challenging to the U.S. ethos and, obviously, to Israelis. So I think about the Nablus Public Library, how they have a section—almost like an archive—with materials that were in the Nablus prisons before most of the prisons were moved inside Israel. They have books from the prison libraries and books the prisoners wrote themselves. At the Abu Jihad Museum for the Prisoners Movement Affairs in Abu Dis, collections highlight the experiences and voices of Palestinian political prisoners. These include orientation manuals about prison rules and internal systems, written by prisoners for each other. They're archiving all this material. We can learn a lot from these libraries and archives.

The whole question of archives in Palestine is huge. It's like many colonial situations in that the people who are being colonized, the people under occupation, do not have access to most of their own materials. We can define archival materials a lot of different ways: legal documents, photographs, and claims to land and history, for example. Most of that information is either in Israeli archives and inaccessible to Palestinians, or in the archives of the U.K. and Turkey, previous colonial powers. Or even held by private Israeli collectors. So it's important to have archivists connect to learn how Palestinians create social history archives in the absence of a Palestinian national archive.

Many people we met mentioned the importance of digitization, both because you have a very real threat of materials physically being taken by an occupying force, and you also have a dispersed Palestinian population throughout the entire world that is prevented from entering Palestine. So there's digitization in service of access. And there are practical concerns about it: Palestinians were asking our opinions about whether PDF or TIFF is a better format for digital preservation, for example, and we had a good discussion about the relationship between access and preservation.

V: I sensed that this experience for archivists and librarians forced us to challenge our inherited assumptions about what constitutes an archive. The way we often learn about archives is tied to institutions and bodies with power ascribing significance to a collection. There is so much we learned about in Palestine and so much we didn't have time to see, including the many ways in which people collect or preserve or transmit memory, the oral tradition—which, so often in U.S. settings, gets dismissed. And then the official questions of archives and state power, the ways that the Israeli state has clearly and violently co-opted and taken by force so much of the Palestinian archive.

H: There was also a conversation among Palestinian archivists about how to create archives that are parallel to movement-building rather than state-building, as there is this new institutional interest in archives in Palestine. Some people on the ground see a potential danger of working with the Palestinian government on state-building rather than serving the people that the archive represents.

In thinking about what constitutes an archive, I'm reminded of Nabi Saleh[3], where people were both documenting their protests against settlements and land confiscation and also collecting tear gas canisters and sound grenades that the Israeli army used against them and displaying them on fences in front of their homes. We all looked at that and said, "That's an archive!" But were we ascribing a label that they wouldn't use? I guess we can say they're documenting their current reality and their resistance in a way that is similar to an idea of archives.

V: I thought of that when we were in Abu Arab's house in Nazareth[4], too. We might think of Abu Arab's collection as a museum or an archive, but he also challenges and subverts so many traditional aspects of museum and archive curation.

H: Like the fact that nothing was labeled, and he wasn't necessarily interested in documenting and labeling. Someone asked him about it, and he responded, "That would take a while"—it's all in his memory, in his brain. And when we asked him to tell us some stories about the objects, the oral tradition was there. He showed us his mother-in-law's bridal dress.

V: And the blanket under which he and his brother—the poet Taha Muhammad Ali—slept as children.

H: And their cradle. And I was thinking, "Someone should record him describing every single one of these objects!" But if that's not something that he's specifically interested in, then, I don't know. It's interesting to think about that—a really rich history that people should know about and that he wants people to know about. And at the same time, how much should we push our ideas and methods? If we want to send someone to record him—is that really something he wants or not?

---

3.   Nabi Saleh is a small village northwest of Ramallah that has been affected by Israeli settlement policy for decades. Since 2009, villagers have been holding weekly demonstrations against land and resource confiscation. For their nonviolent actions, protesters have been arrested, injured, and even killed by Israeli soldiers. For more information, see nabisalehsolidarity.wordpress.com.

4.   Abu Arab is a Nakba survivor originally from the town of Saffourieh. He and his family were expelled from their home in 1948. They fled to Lebanon for several months and returned to Nazareth, where Abu Arab has lived ever since. During our visit, he showed us the objects he has collected from destroyed villages over the years; he houses these in an apartment adjacent to his own.

V: These are crucial questions. They also make me wonder: what *is* our role? How do we act and engage in ways that are useful?

H: Part of our role started in Palestine, just in organizing these conversations. We brought together librarians and archivists—in Haifa, in Ramallah—who, because of occupation and colonialism and apartheid, are not always able to meet. So some of the discussions we had were just as much an opportunity for people from different organizations and projects to have conversations with each other as it was for them to meet with us.

Now that we've returned to our own communities, maybe our most important role is to use our library skills and a particular framework to approach this issue that, as far as we know, hasn't yet been publicly approached in this particular way.

V: Do you think this is an especially challenging time to do that? There's a sense that libraries, especially public libraries, are in a state of crisis. It seems like people are constantly asking these questions. *What is the future of our work? What is the future of our profession? What is the future of the work outside professions or official institutions?* Because it already feels like a lot of libraries are grasping at straws, do you feel like it's a harder time to push things politically? Or do you think it's easier because people are politicized around libraries and their larger meaning or goal?

H: Hard to say. I think that with globalization comes the sense that we are larger than ourselves, that our communities are larger than we have previously thought, and that, consistent with the ALA's core values, we can and should take a stand on certain issues. As a group of librarians and archivists who support access to information, we can have a unique voice in the BDS movement.[5] People are generally familiar with consumer boycott tactics, but when we talk about academic and cultural boycott, it is often misunderstood as a limit on freedom of expression and individual rights. Having librarians say that we support a boycott of institutions that are complicit in Israeli occupation can be quite powerful.

V: I totally agree. I think that our work is so much about freedom of expression and challenging censorship. What I hope we do well is to illuminate that it's the occupation, and not BDS, that is equal to censorship. The very conditions created by the occupation stifle freedom of expression and access to informa-

---

5.   In 2005, Palestinian civil society called on international supporters to impose boycott, divestment, and sanctions (BDS) initiatives against Israel until it complies with international law and basic Palestinian rights.

tion and knowledge. One thing that inspires me about the BDS movement is how multifarious and increasingly diverse it is. I hope we can help support that growth, and also sustain and nurture the connections we made with the people we met this summer.

H: I guess the rest remains to be seen. We need to keep asking in what ways our network will be a political awareness or advocacy campaign, in what ways it is about practical skill-sharing or project support, and how these connect.

* * *

Librarians and Archivists to Palestine is committed to sharing what we have seen, applying what we have learned, publicizing projects we have visited, and building a wider network of librarians and archivists to continue this work. To learn more about us and stay updated on our ongoing work, visit us at librarians2palestine.wordpress.com.

References

American Library Association (2004, June 29). *Core values of librarianship.* Retrieved from http://www.ala.org/advocacy/intfreedom/statementspols/ corevaluesMada al-Carmel (n.d.). *About.* Retrieved from http://mada-research. org/en/about/

In the Streets

Radical Reference: Who Cares?

Lia Friedman

Radical Reference in the Beginning

Radical Reference (RR) is an unaffiliated and intentionally unorganized "organization" of library workers that supports the information needs of activists and independent journalists. Its origin lies with one librarian's desire to connect with the protest movement developing around the Republican National Convention (RNC) in New York City in 2004. At the time, local activists were outraged that the Republicans planned to come to New York in what they perceived as an exploitation of the site and memory of the terror of 9/11; Jenna Freedman wanted to be involved—and came up with this:

From: Jenna Freedman
Sent: Tuesday, May 25, 2004 7:50 PM
To: plg-nyc@lists.riseup.net
Subject: [plg-nyc] radical reference

Hi All,

I went to the most recent clearinghouse meeting of the groups organizing against the Republican National Convention, and I left the meeting inspired, but also wondering what kind of role I could take. To paraphrase Phil Ochs, "Then I remembered I was a librarian."

That's when I came up with this idea of doing "radical reference." Before the Convention it could be a web-based service where people e-mail us their questions, and we attempt to answer them, or at least refer them. At the convention we could do the kind of on-the-street reference that Jessamyn West practiced in Seattle at the WTO protests. (I've got an e-mail out to her asking for more details.)

Do either of these plans appeal to anyone? I thought we could start with NYC folks, but there's no reason to limit the "virtual" part of it. In fact, I'd like to enlist some more tech savvy people to come up with an interface, and we'd definitely benefit from having some law librarians among us.

I mentioned the idea to an activist friend who is organizing with a SF Bay contingent, and he immediately submitted the questions below. They're not actually what I imagined; they're much more involved!

I'd love to hear what you think and if you'd be interested in participating.

All my best, Jenna

PS The Phil Ochs reference is to his intro to the Canons of Christianity on I don't remember which album.

Freedman received some positive responses from the NYC chapter of the Progressive Librarians Guild (PLG) and the Social Responsibilities Round Table (SRRT) of the American Library Association (ALA) which were seen as possible homes for the service. But between concerns that ALA's 501(c)(3) status might be jeopardized by hosting a project focused specifically on a political party convention, the potential inability to create a new task force or initiative between ALA meetings, and the fact that PLG and SRRT had similar leadership, it seemed best to develop RR as a separate and (we believed) short-term project. It wasn't until June 2004, after getting support from likely RR patrons at the Allied Media Conference (AMC) in Bowling Green, OH, and then librarian collaborators at the ALA conference in Orlando, FL, that the project began to take shape. Members of the NYC Independent Media Center and Paper Tiger Television were excited about the prospect of librarians serving as researchers and fact-checkers for journalists at the convergence space being set up to serve independent media reporting on the RNC, and that enthusiasm spurred the project forward.

Encouraged by AMC attendees' interest, Freedman met with other librarians, notably James R. Jacobs, Chuck Munson, and Shinjoung Yeo, at the ALA conference that June, and they began the collaboration that would inform the shape of the project for years to come. Munson put out a call to a radical tech list to solicit a Web developer for the project and was quickly answered by Eric Goldhagen from the InterActivist Network in NYC. InterActivist used free and open source tools exclusively, and the idea of code and tools that were freely shared without anyone deriving profit, other than billing for their labor, seemed in line with the values of librarianship that we hold dear. Soon after, the nascent group had a functioning Drupal website, possibly the first installation of Drupal in service of a library or library project.

Then, in July 2004, Freedman and others sent emails to activist librarian and NYC-area email lists, calling for participation in RR (which is where I came in, as a library school student looking to bring past social justice experience to present practice):

FROM: Jenna Freedman
TO:a-librarians@lists.mutualaid.org, plg-nyc@lists.riseup.net
Tuesday, July 27, 2004 9:17 PM

Sorry for the cross-posting, but please forward to other lists that you think would be interested.

RADICAL REFERENCE

Library workers are launching a project in support of the demonstrations surrounding the Republican National Convention in New York City August 29-September 2, 2004.
We will offer blog, chat, street, and news reference, responding to questions from demonstrators.
Sound ambitious? It is, so we need help.
Please contact info@radicalreference.info if you would like to:

- answer e-mail reference questions
- use your foreign language skills to answer questions and make the site more accessible
- perform chat reference
- participate in street reference
- be a news librarian, teaching and researching for independent media journalists

- help with the website
- gather "Quick Facts & Contacts" info for street reference
- rally together as library workers at the protests
- send us money (for hats to identify us, materials, technical costs)

All will be welcome to participate regardless of skill level or proximity to NYC. Indicate in your message in which areas you will participate.

NOTE: our website www.radicalreference.info is under construction. We hope to have it ready to receive reference questions by the end of the week.

And thus Radical Reference in its earliest iteration was formed. Volunteer librarians came together in the pre (for most) smartphone era to assemble "ready reference kits" that could be carried during the RNC protests and contained maps, legal information, lists of events, and more. These street reference volunteers were connected by phone to home support volunteers, who made themselves and their computers available to answer questions. Some also used the now-defunct synchronous Web-based messaging service TXTmob, which was developed by the Institute for Applied Autonomy to support activists at the Democratic and Republican National Conventions in 2004. Messages could be sent simultaneously to multiple groups that needed access to the same information at the same time. This pre-Twitter service allowed real-time reference help as well as the distribution of information on peripheral yet important updates like, "The police have cordoned off 37th Street and are arresting everyone."

So RR filled a need that perhaps we hadn't known existed. Up to this point, most modern reference was a role filled by "professionals" behind a desk. Information was selectively freed from shelves and firewalls by those trained and given the keys to do so. Other ways of gathering specialized information existed in the early 2000s, of course—outside traditional libraries—but much of it was sequestered in databases, cataloged using antique classifications and written for scholars. What RR strove to do, perhaps unknowingly in some cases, was to liberate access to information in unique ways. To take the ability to find and understand information outside of brick and mortar institutions and bring it straight to a perceived need. Protestors on the street have to know, when a police officer decides to confiscate a bicycle in a bike lane during a protest and threatens violators with imprisonment or impoundment, if that is legal or not. They can hope to come to an action having sought out and remembered potential information needs, but unanticipated experiences are part and parcel of protests. So seeing someone with a sign reading "Info Here" became an unexpected but instantly useful resource. It is hard to imagine in this hyperconnected year of

2013, but ubiquitous, at-your-fingers information just didn't exist for most, especially those in the margins. Connecting those with limited access to information (whether geographically, being on the street, or monetarily, unable to be affiliated with an academic institution or lacking an address and thus without a public library card) was a way of balancing the scales, flattening the information hierarchy and giving more power to more people.

RR's Place in Alternative Library Models

RR is not the only group of political/activist/alternative librarians in town. Within the North American anglophone context, we could place ourselves in a group that includes Ask MetaFilter (one of the first and best crowdsourcing Q&A models); SRRT and its sub-units (e.g. the Feminist Task Force); ALA's Gay, Lesbian, Bisexual, and Transgender Round Table (GLBTRT); ALA's Committee on the Status of Women in Librarianship (COSWL); PLG; library unionists, ALA's ethnic caucuses (e.g. the Black Caucus of the ALA and the Asian Pacific American Libraries Association); the philanthropic partiers of the Desk Set and Que(e)ry in NYC; the less philanthropically-minded but possibly harder-partying ALA Think Tankers (aka the Drink Tank); legislatively-focused efforts from the ALA Washington Office and the EveryLibrary political action committee; zine librarians; the Internet Archive and San Francisco's Prelinger Archive, where ephemera and documents of social importance are saved, collected, and, most importantly, arranged with the user in mind; open source coders and Code4Lib; and the librarians of Occupy Wall Street and books-to-prisoners projects around North America.

Providing a comprehensive list of alternative libraries and library models is out of the scope of this chapter, but I do want to situate RR within the contemporary library activism landscape and examine what connects us. Like many of these other initiatives, RR exists on the Web and not in a physical space. When organizing a day of working on the site and answering questions, an actual space must be found. In NYC for example, that space was often ABC No Rio, a collectively-run arts and activism center that RR allied itself with early on. We also don't "create" anything, at least in a traditional publishing sense. RR archives all of our questions and answers; creates "ready reference" guides on subjects often asked about or seen as useful by members who have a certain expertise or desire to learn about a topic; and documents our presentations, which often include detailed handouts. So the connection between RR and other alternative library projects ends up being the different modes and ideas surrounding access—access in its broadest sense, encompassing physical access, but also the examination of the ways in which information is "protected" and certain types of it are marginalized in academia.

Radical Reference, Success and Failure

So how are we doing? RR's intentional under-organization makes calling it an "organization" paradoxical. Many of those who created the group identified with anarchist tenets or at least had hopes of flattened hierarchies, with no leaders per se, and so the group has moved forward with loose ideas of leadership and power guiding us. From its beginning as a project supporting protestors and organizers out on the street, a small number of volunteers built and have maintained the RR website, added members, and monitored questions and answers, as well as moved RR forward into a group that presents nationally and worldwide, forms local collectives centered on specific work, and occasionally operates in its original form as a street reference service. As RR grew and more volunteers were added, and these local collectives formed, workshops and projects were completed and its organizational ungainliness began (and continues) to be both a natural part of a group committed to limited "leadership" and an issue to grapple with. The RR website currently lists over 15 local collectives, some far more active than others. There are approximately 200 email list members, of which a dozen or so could be considered working members. This divide, between "members"—those who have signed up for a username and been added to the list but who have never participated by answering a question—and those dozen active members who take the brunt of deleting spam, farming out questions, and moderating the site in general, is an ongoing challenge. There are also those members, who, while active in local collectives and organizing events, have not been active on the site, answering questions. Our staffing model creates a continuous problem for the core group: how to balance answering the questions we receive with the number of volunteers who are willing to give time and are comfortable negotiating the RR site. This can be further exacerbated by media or professional coverage. For example, when we present or write about RR, it results in an uptick in visibility and traffic—will there then be an adequate amount of people ready to take on this work? Historically, this sense of stability has ebbed and flowed. After members deliver a paper or conduct a workshop, new volunteers may feel excited and energized—ready to start taking on questions—but that enthusiasm typically dies down as real life and other responsibilities make themselves known. Solutions to this problem have been mulled over by RR members but not yet implemented; for instance, we have considered making it mandatory for new members to answer one question per month, but then we balk at creating strict guidelines.

Many projects taken up by local collectives over the years have been successful.

In 2009, members of the RR collective in Portland, OR, organized and created a lending library of books and other resources at Bitch Magazine, a respected feminist publication. The publisher at that time, Debbie Rasmussen, stated:

> [Radical Reference] brought skills and expertise that none of us here at Bitch had—everything from where to place the lending library, to what kind of shelves we should build, to what categories we should have and where they should go, to how we should organize them in an online catalogue ... We were pretty lost until they arrived! ... It's brought new meaning to the work we do because we'll finally have a way of connecting more directly with the community here in Portland, on top of connecting with an amazing group. (as cited in Morrone & Friedman, 2009, p. 392)

More information about the Bitch Community Lending Library is at bitch-magazine.org/library.

In November 2012, the Boston collective organized a Critical Library Symposium, "Practical Choices for Powerful Impacts: Realizing the Activist Potential of Librarians," to address librarians' roles in "mirroring and perpetuating systems of oppression found throughout the rest of society" (Radical Reference, 2012). This examination of how librarians who identify as activists in whatever form interact with patrons and students, make collection choices, maintain archives, and organize events and programs was well-attended and well-received. One of the organizers, Heather McCann, said:

> [T]he discussion with the participants [was] so rich. The breakout groups were frank conversations where people brought up issues in their own organizations that were sometimes troubling, sometimes heartening and always thought-provoking. When we regrouped to report back, people were excited to continue the conversation. I don't think that I've seen a group that large where so many people were interested in contributing (even given that librarians are a chatty bunch). (H. McCann, personal communication, March 20, 2013)

A number of presentations and workshops have been done by Radical Reference members on archives and alternative library materials. In 2010, for example, Alan Ginsberg, Matt Metzgar, and Deborah Edel presented at "Documenting Struggle Redux: Radical New York City Archives," which examined how community history is kept alive through archives, documentation, and community support. Highlighting the Lower East Side Squatter-Homesteader Archive and the Lesbian Herstory Archives, this talk made these important materials visible and allowed people to learn more deeply about how these collections are being handled, arranged, and made accessible.

RR members have also presented at conferences across the United States and Canada, including the NYC Grassroots Media Conference; the Allied Media Conference; the Mid-Atlantic Radical Bookfair and the NYC Anarchist Bookfair; the Women, Action, & the Media Conference; the National Conference on Organized Resistance; the US Social Forum; and NYC's Brecht Forum on issues regarding open source software, fact checking for journalists and activists, community needs assessments in activist work, alternative materials in libraries, and alternative libraries.

Conclusion and Future of RR

As I was finishing this chapter, RR received an email from a librarian with the subject line "are you still a group?" which is a perfect question at this time. Many of the organization's cofounders have not been actively involved for years; new volunteers and moderators have stepped in to care for the site, but the balance—between being able to answer questions, host events, flyer at protests, and create learning guides—seems always to be precarious. The original coauthor of this article dropped out due to time constraints, a recurring theme with our volunteers. We consistently sign up new librarians, and local collectives such as the Boston one do inspiring work in their community. We believe that we have value in the field of alternative library models but fear for the future of Radical Reference in its present state. How do we fit into the future of libraries and library work as we move forward?

References

Morrone, M., & Friedman, L. (2009). Radical Reference: Socially responsible librarianship collaborating with community. *The Reference Librarian,* *50*(4), 371-396.

Radical Reference. (2012, October 9). Critical Librarianship Symposium (Boston). Retrieved from http://www.radicalreference.info/PracticalChoices

Librarian Is My Occupation: A History of the People's Library of Occupy Wall Street

Jaime Taylor and Zachary Loeb

As bicyclists, joggers, and tourists looked on in bemusement, three exhausted individuals pushed a broken-unwieldy-wooden-wagon-thing-on-two-wheels across the Williamsburg Bridge. It was July 21, 2012, a hell of a day to push something heavy through Manhattan and Brooklyn. It is impossible to know exactly what the onlookers thought of those pushing the cart, but it is likely they did not recognize that what they were watching was working group members from the Occupy Wall Street People's Library moving the last remnants of the collection out of a storage unit and to, alas, another temporary home. It may be that three sweaty people pushing a giant wheeled crate does not make most people think of libraries, but the People's Library had always been dogged by others' ideas of it.

We should know. We've heard them all.

Zachary heeded the original call and was there on day one. Jaime, skeptical, didn't get there for another two weeks. Writing this just over a year later, we've faced down riot cops, stood in rain and snow, seen our library destroyed, spoken at conferences, sued New York City, gotten to know the city's jails and courthouses, lost a lot of sleep, and been (further) radicalized. Granted, that we were there at all implies certain political leanings. And that we have in large part participated in Occupy Wall Street as librarians suggests a certain view of our profession, both internally and as we relate to the rest of the world. Let's call this a case study, then. We will relate the history of the Occupy Wall Street People's

Library (OWSL) as we experienced it, while interspersing this recounting with broader theoretical observations.

We certainly do not claim to speak for all librarians, or even for all of the members of OWSL, but this is our analysis of what it meant to be People's Librarians in our limited free time while being "actual" librarians during our "work" time (though we often felt that it was the other way around).

September 17, 2011, to October 13, 2011

For two months, Occupy Wall Street (OWS) held off a paramilitary police force, a billionaire mayor, and the combined ire of the world's biggest, baddest global corporations. And it was done with bandanas, tarps, apples, and books. But it started small, on September 17, 2011, when rabble-rousers unrolled their sleeping bags in New York City's financial district.

It is hard to pinpoint an exact moment at which OWS exploded into something large enough for the news media to declare it was of no significance while simultaneously covering it. Perhaps it was when a video of a police officer pepper spraying young women cordoned off in orange netting went viral, maybe it was when hundreds shut down the Brooklyn Bridge, but trying to discern the exact moment is pointless. The very nature of social movements, and of protests, is their fluidity. It is impossible to truly know what will happen next. Nobody foresaw the pepper spraying going viral until it did, nor could those who marched on the Brooklyn Bridge know the impact of that march (or that they would still be going to court over it a year [and then some] later).

And the library? It started with a pile of books. Really. Maybe it was mitosis, or some other unseen process, but the pile of books kept growing. The pile became a hill, which became a mountain, which garnered the attention of a few individuals who took it upon themselves to try to keep the books dry, mark them "OWSL," put them in boxes, and begin thinking about how to keep them safe and organized. In those early days, managing the books was haphazard, the working group was new, and just tagging the books "OWSL" was an accomplishment.

Rain was a perpetual threat, and much attention was devoted to basic protection: getting plastic tarps to cover the boxes (which the police continually confiscated), and switching out the cardboard boxes for plastic bins with lids. Access to the library was at its most open in these early days: the books were at times unsupervised, and the working group struggled just to keep fiction and nonfiction separate. If a patron was looking for a particular book or topic, it was up to them to forage through the collection. As the working group grew and the library found itself more consistently staffed, actual organization began taking place; the books were sorted into an ever increasing number of categories, and the collection began to be cataloged (a process that involved jotting down ISBN numbers on scraps of paper and inputting them into LibraryThing when an Internet connection was available [this is not the most efficient way to catalog {or the most fun}]). In this early phase, the following interaction was not atypical: "Are you the librarian?" "I am today." "Do you have any Marx?" "We did an hour ago."

Sunday, October 2 marks the date the working group was recognized by the General Assembly (GA). As more librarians—professional and otherwise—came to the occupation, some of those with a sense of how the occupation functioned took the step of proposing the working group to the GA. The proposal was for "formation of the People's Library Working Group for the organization, maintenance, and promotion of the People's Library" (New York City General Assembly, 2011). The GA gave consensus through "up-sparkles"[1] and the library became an official working group. This easily-reached consensus foreshadowed the love many occupiers consistently showed for the library; even during the most contentious weeks of the GA's existence, the library rarely had trouble gaining consensus for its (albeit modest) proposals, receiving support from even suspected agents provocateurs.

While much of the working group came whenever they were available, a handful of occupiers became live-in librarians (the number of live-in librarians peaked during the second phase of the library). The demographic of OWSL members was varied, consisting of full-time activists, artists, retirees, college professors, poets, students, parents, punks, wandering Canadians, and professional librarians (with many fitting into several of those categories at once). About half of the regular librarians were professional librarians or archivists—those with master's degrees, whether employed in the field or not—or in a similarly scholarly profession. Many of the drop-in librarians were also professionals, paraprofessionals, or LIS students; we had visitors from Radical Reference and the Pratt SILS program, among others. Professional or not, many ended up in the library working group in order to have something concrete to do; the library was one of the sites where there was always work. Some of us who are professional librarians felt the same way about OWSL as we do about hewing to the profession as a whole—a need to create order, perhaps a certain curmudgeonliness, a love

---

1. A note on Liberty Square dialects—the general term for the finger-wiggling motion used to express opinions in meetings is "twinkles"; Library, however, has always used "sparkles." At this point, no one can remember how or why this divergence happened, but it probably reflects the fact that the librarians were often too busy to leave the library.

of old things and dry paper, as well as a desire to be useful. In those first weeks there was an atmosphere of excitement, where even cataloging seemed like a revolutionary act.

Yet this was all disrupted in the run-up to October 13.

Brookfield Properties, which owns Zuccotti Park, the location of the OWS encampment, wanted to clear the park and used the pretext of "cleaning" as a cover.[2] Working groups within OWS were divided over how to respond, with some thinking that occupiers would be able to return after the cleaning, while others declared they would not leave. It soon became evident that the prevailing sentiment was for people to stay, but for infrastructure and possessions to be removed. At this point the active collection was between one and two thousand books, and the entire day and night (when the part of the collection still in the park had to be evacuated to an "undisclosed location" [an apartment in New Jersey]) saw the working group furiously acting to get the books and infrastructure to safety before the expected "cleaning."

It took the working group nearly 24 hours to get the books out, and, as members of the working group stood—exhausted—in the park on the morning of October 14, waiting to see what would happen, we felt the joy from the announcement that Brookfield had backed down...but also the recognition that we would have to move all of the books back into the park.

We did not yet realize that moving books was to soon become a major activity for OWSL.

Some Thoughts on Guerrilla Librarianship

Our fellow librarian Mandy Henk wrote in her blog post "A People's Digital Library and Prefigurative Politics":

> The Occupy movement, and the People's Library, are, in part, prefigurative movements. That is, they are attempts to create and embody the kind of society we want to see....We can't change the world, rebuild it into a place of justice and equity, if we can't reflect the values we support in our internal dynamics and operations. (2011)

She was writing about digital resources and their vendors, but her point is extendable to OWS, as well as to the many other sites of protest that people have created worldwide in the last few years: the means of our protest directly reflects the world we want to live in. We carry with us the good parts of the current world, try to leave behind the parts that don't work, and envision and create the

---

2. "Cleaning" is a well-worn repression tactic, as is labeling protestors "dirty."

parts we don't already have. For the occupation in New York City, as well as for our predecessor at Puerta del Sol in Madrid, Spain, and for the occupations across the world that followed us, having a library was an instance of bringing along the best of the world we already inhabit.

Librarianship and library theory is a rich source for prefigurative politics. As libraries and librarians step out of their dusty ways of being, we find that many mainstream practices in libraries are well in line with radical undertakings, though we at OWLS are perhaps more sincere in our praxis. As Jaime said at the American Library Association's 2012 Midwinter Meeting:

> The Library Working Group works on consensus. When I was in library school, we talked about horizontal structures and consensus as a cutting edge way of organizing library work and staff...The meaning of "consensus" used in my library school classroom and the meaning of it at the Occupation and in radical politics generally are not the same. For us, consensus requires that nearly everyone support a decision...Degreed librarians have no more weight in making decisions than an 18-year-old college student, an underemployed actress, or a crusty traveling kid. (Fagin, Henk, Loeb, Norton, & Taylor, 2012)

Consensus as taught in that library school course was definitely not what was used at the occupation. Horizontal organization was all the rage in that course, the flattening and (somewhat) equalizing of power and reporting structures in the library-as-workplace. But it was never a complete flattening—there were still bosses and supervisors; people with more power (and a higher salary) and people with less; and class-like divisions between types of workers such as administrators, librarians, paraprofessionals, and physical plant staff. At the occupation, temporary moments of authority and leadership were created by recognition of knowledge, skill, or ability held by one person that others might not have. Those moments fluctuate—the "real" librarian's knowledge and experience of cataloging is important in one instance, and another person's ability to run a generator is essential the next, and both are valuable. In a flattened system, those points of leadership are allowed to happen; even if a conventional system has had some of its levels removed, it remains in important ways vertical. Aside from whatever structural benefit a horizontal system may contribute to an institution, the human cost of lack of control must also always be kept in mind—we, as human beings, should be the sole power responsible for the conditions of our labor. The traditional library allows for only so much autogestion; the People's Library ran on nothing but. Working group members were (and remain) responsible only to ourselves, our fellow librarians, and our patrons.

Drawing again from the edges of library theory, OWSL built on some of the practices of existing radical librarianship. Radical Reference was formed to provide reference services at the exact point of their patrons' needs—on the ground at protests. This is the bleeding edge of the "embedded" librarian, who in a university library might dare to keep her reference desk in departmental offices instead of in the library proper. If we are to "save the time of the reader," (a central point of a librarian's responsibility), then a park full of protestors looking to brush up on their theoretical underpinnings (or just looking for some fiction) should have those resources at their fingertips.

Visitors to OWS were both surprised and then comforted by the presence of the library. It was perhaps the most normal part of the occupation, something recognizable from the regular world, a concept and a space that hardly anyone struggled to understand. So many features of the People's Library were the same—or nearly so—as those at any public, school, or college library, from the children's section to a reference collection, the visiting authors, the poetry readings, and the occasional pencil skirt or cardigan or tie on a bespectacled librarian. But the surprise always preceded the sense of familiarity, and the farther away on the political spectrum a visitor was, the more surprised they were.

OWS was supposed to be a bunch of dirty stupid hippies who needed a shower and a haircut (haven't we moved on from the late '60s yet?), to get a job, to grow up and be responsible for ourselves (never mind the unemployment rate or the cost of tuition). But then there was this organized collection of books—serious books, well-known books, books about anything and everything, books with opposing viewpoints, popular fiction, books one might have read in school—staffed by articulate and knowledgeable people, some of whom have master's degrees and maybe even a job in a "real library," (and over there, a kitchen with people wearing rubber gloves and hairnets, like in a school cafeteria; and past that, basic medicine being practiced by people with certifications). And then, when the library, along with everything else, was thrown in the trash, people who didn't much care about any of the other horrid things that happened to the occupation (before that or since) were outraged at the brazen and callous actions of the mayor's office, NYPD, city sanitation, and Brookfield. And surprisingly (not so surprising), until media from Twitter to cable news lit up with the story of it, all those people and organizations probably thought they'd get away with it.

And why wouldn't they think that? It isn't hard to make the jump from the quick and violent destruction of the People's Library to the slow burn of both anti-intellectual conservatism and neoliberal privatization destroying conventional libraries. The creation of the camp at Zuccotti Park (called Liberty Square by the occupiers), library included, was, while often ad hoc, built prefiguratively;

we created there the things we value, while trying to leave out the things that harm us. Free access to knowledge was in, while vertical and authoritarian organizing structures were out. Given that we were librarians, our general principles of consent and community, and our professional positions, which include equal access, privacy, and anti-censorship (which are fairly mainstream in the library world; see the American Library Association's statements [2011]) all supported the creation and curation of the People's Library. It is exactly because those principles are the bedrock of libraries as we know them that libraries from OWSL, to every little branch of every little public library, to major public and private research libraries are being dismantled.

More on that later.

October 14, 2011, to November 15, 2011 (1 a.m. [give or take 10 minutes])

Spurred by the emotions (good and bad [mostly good]) coming out of Brookfield's retreat, the librarians realized that something had to change. There had been precious little discussion or coordinated thought regarding what the library was really doing, or what it really was. The library was swelling, not by fives and tens but by hundreds. People donated dozens of books at a time, authors dropped off boxes, publishers sent cases, and the working group did its best to keep pace, trying to categorize and catalog as items arrived. This was the time when the library began to better serve the patrons: stability of location and systems for processing the collection allowed the librarians to know what was in the collection and enabled them to provide reference services. There were a few thousand books, and while they were not filed under Dewey or Library of Congress subject headings, they were sorted and cared for by a devoted and knowledgeable team of librarians.

The library consisted entirely of donations. Every book in the collection came from either an individual or a publisher (most came from individuals). The library functioned on the honor system: anybody could take any book (except for those in the reference collection [although asking people not to remove the copy of *Steal This Book* was rather foolish]), and patrons were trusted to return books or to lend them to a friend and in this way keep the library flowing. After all, wherever there was a book marked "OWSL," the library was alive. The collection included everything from Milton Friedman to Karl Marx, from Ann Coulter to Al Franken, from the Constitution to *T.A.Z.*, from rare artist books to Dr. Seuss, and from Mayor Bloomberg's autobiography to books about inspirational political figures. The library was settling into a steady track of sorts;

it would open in the morning, things would be straightened up as occupiers awoke, new books would be processed and shelved, patrons would be assisted, and so forth.

The daily activity of keeping the library open and functioning was a constant source of pressure for the working group, particularly as members sought to engage in other activities. When members of the working group were in the library, they were overwhelmed with its demands; it was not that the working group was uninterested in other matters, it was simply that they were too preoccupied with the tasks at hand to think at length about the theoretical implications of the occupation. On the plus side, this meant that the working group was largely (though not completely) spared from inter-group ideological squabbling.

We outlasted the police telling us that we couldn't use tarps (even clear tarps) to cover the books when it rained (because "there might be a bomb" under our tarps). We weathered Snowtober, the unseasonable snowstorm on October 29. We got on board with town planning (yes, there was a town planning working group), who were trying to figure out how to best use the limited space in the growing camp. We had a generator providing electricity (until the police took it [after which we got another {which the police took}]), half a dozen laptops and wireless Internet, lights, chairs, and thousands of books. Weekends featured a poetry assembly and film screenings; we were visited by authors, we provided a relatively quiet (meaning you only had to kind of yell to be heard) spot for occupiers and visitors to read and think, and we updated our catalog on LibraryThing on an almost daily basis.[3] We functioned like a traditional library, only with better air circulation, a less reliable roof, and a distinct lack of walls (real and metaphorical).

In early November, once the police moratorium on tents eased (and after they'd absconded with our first attempt to put one up [and the second]), Patti Smith kindly sent us a big grey arc that gave us two walls and a roof, with openings at either end. Inside the tent, the library looked even more like a real library—there were even shelves. The walls were covered in original posters brought to the occupation and left behind for display; the donation bin was overflowing; the work table was cluttered with librarians cataloging books; and the tent was filled with the sounds of laughter, song, and impassioned arguing. To look at the tent in this time was to think that OWS's future was promising, and the park was filled with optimistic talk about weathering the winter.

Alas, that was not the storm that came.

---

3. The catalog, at www.librarything.com/catalog/OWSLibrary/yourlibrary, contains every book ever accessioned by the library, including post-11/15/11 volumes.

The Library as Place and Space

Anybody who has ever helped a bibliophile move, pushed a book truck, or walked around carrying a stack of books knows two things: books are heavy, and books take up space. The first can be handled by a sturdy shelf. The second is of greater import. Books come in thousands of different shapes and sizes, and their space requirements vary accordingly. A problem arises once the quantity of books requires more area than can be casually given over to them.

Throughout history, libraries have sought many solutions to the problems presented by large quantities of books: from floors of densely packed shelves to compact shelving, from providing aisles for browsing to cramped closed stacks into which only the library staff may go, and on to the current trend of having physical books off-site while potentially granting access to digital versions of some texts. All of this is to say that libraries require space. Real physical space. The New York Public Library needs space for its collection, and so does OWSL. If this space ceases to be an accessible reading room and becomes a storage unit, the library vanishes except as an idea.

But this formulation is simplistic. While there is some merit in describing a library as a space that houses books, it fails to recognize the other aspects of libraries. To deploy a horrible poker metaphor (we think this is a poker metaphor; it might just be a cards metaphor [we do not play poker {really}]): libraries hold a pair of aces. One ace by itself is potentially useful, but not really; it's the pair that has value. The first ace is what has been described thus far: space—the real-world physical space that is required and occupied by the library. Every time a person walks through a library's door, or picks a book off the shelf, they are encountering the library as space. And when a library is closed, or books are sent off-site, the library space is impacted. But the other ace, which is of equal if not greater import, goes beyond simply thinking of the physical locale: the library as place.

Some of the frustration directed at a definition of a library as "a space filled with books" is that it misses out on the other things offered by a library, and it misses out on the larger meaning of a library. Libraries (particularly public libraries) present a rather unique place in contemporary capitalist society: somewhere a person can go regardless of employment status, race, gender, class, disability status, or age, and have access to a variety of important resources without having to pay for them (though tax dollars are a form of paying). Furthermore, the offerings at a library appeal to a variety of needs: access to books (for those with little disposal income, books can be expensive), access to a safe space, access to computers (something frequently taken for granted), access to the Internet (see previous parenthetical), and much more than can easily be listed here (we have to stick to a word limit). While some of the services offered by libraries seem to be offered elsewhere (think of corporate bookstores with inviting seats spread throughout), the factor that sets libraries apart—vitally—is that they are public spaces. Or to use a somewhat antiquated term, libraries function as commons.

We purport that the value of libraries exists not only in the books they lend, but in the commons that they represent. While public parks offer citizens access to green areas (ideally), libraries offer citizens access to intellectual areas (and an inside location). The idea of libraries, as places, is that people should have access to informational resources, and though this undergirds the fact that a library takes up physical space, it can go unnoticed if all that is seen is the physical space. When people thinking about libraries think first of books, they are taking a logical step; however, it falls to librarians to remind patrons that the library represents much more. Access to a library is important, not simply because it provides access to information, but because access to a library represents access to an information commons as well as a belief that people have a right to such access. Thus a cut in library hours is as problematic (if not more so) than a cut in the acquisitions budget, and libraries that are closed represent commons from which the public has been driven.

OWSL always had to hold both aces while trying to construct a full hand. When visitors to OWSL expressed delight at the sight of the library, they were reacting to the manner in which OWSL reminded them of the place that a library represents. After all, OWSL did not take up much physical space, but the presence of an information commons being set up in the heart of a—already-enclosed—private park demonstrated that a library cannot simply be a physical space; it must resonate with a societal and mental place.

Libraries are rather odd in a society obsessed with free market ideologies. In a world where everything has a price and where we are constantly told that only the free market can solve the world's problems (even if the free market created many of these problems [and free for whom?{but we digress}]), a library is one of the few spots where people can enter for free, access materials for free, and stay without being expected to buy anything. Libraries frequently get caught up in the matter of physical space—especially now when e-readers call into question how much space is really needed—and it is an important consideration, but unless libraries (and librarians) can make a compelling case based out of both space and place, then they are stuck holding just one ace, when really they have a pair.

Showing what libraries fully represent empowers us to fight for not just the physical spot but the mental real estate as well, and it further allows us to name our enemy. These are not budget cuts we face, but enclosure. And in what ways have people sought to fight enclosure in the past? Why, through occupying the commons, of course!

November 15, 2011 (2 a.m. [give or take 10 minutes])

As Jaime recalls:

At 12:53 am on [November] 15th...I got a text message from one of the half dozen live-in librarians, saying, "Police are here."...By ten after 1 [a friend in Jail Support] confirmed that it was for real this time. I rolled out of bed, and started calling and texting the other librarians.... I got on a train, and got to the financial district at 2 am.

Even making it in that quickly, I couldn't get within two or three blocks of the park. There were barricades and cops—whom Mayor Bloomberg has since called his "private army"—on every street. As we quickly learned, there was a general media blackout. Reporters were not allowed within sight or hearing of the park, supposedly for their "safety," which is belied by the fact that news helicopters were also grounded.

It hardly mattered what our emergency plan had been. Of the five librarians who were inside the park that night, two elected to stay, and the three others were only able to remove what they could carry in one trip....

The two librarians who stayed ended up being beaten, pepper sprayed, and arrested with more than 150 other Occupiers....Within a couple hours, the library, along with the rest of the camp, had been torn down, loaded into city Sanitation dump trucks, and carted away. In video from that night you can see tents being taken down with chainsaws.

As the sun came up, those of us still free gathered in Foley Square...[W]orking groups and friends tried to figure out who was missing. Around 8 am we heard that the park was cleared and we could go in. A couple of us walked back down, where we met up with a handful of other librarians. We put the books we had on our person back on the bench where the library had been just a few hours earlier and declared the People's Library open once again. We were there only a half hour or so before the cops completely barricaded the place off and kicked us all out. For the rest of the day, the park was closed off, the mayor and the police department directly ignoring a court order to allow access to the park. (Fagin et al, 2012)

Since then, there have been several abortive attempts to occupy new spaces, the working group's membership has dwindled, and the library moved from an accessible collection to boxes in storage—a problem that was only exacerbated once OWS lost its official storage space, forcing us to relocate the books to an 8x10 storage unit. OWSL tried to make appearances at major (and minor) Occupy happenings. The mic check of "The People's Library is open" was consistently met with cheers, yet those who came up to the library at such events came with lamentations over the loss of the library proper rather than with book donations.

Where once patrons had several thousand organized books to browse through, OWSL now struggled to bring more than a few hundred to any event. Indeed, much of the attrition in the working group was a result of members wanting to actively participate in events rather than perpetually guarding and lugging crates of books. Responding to this challenge, a working group member even saw fit to construct a magnificent "mobile library" (a sort of shelved cart that could be rolled) but the logistics of using it resulted in the cart spending most of its time in storage (fortuitous, seeing as the front wheels broke off on its first prolonged outing ["prolonged" means two blocks {it was terrible (and awesome), we almost died (really), see the beginning of this chapter}]).

The working group survived, indeed survives, yet its activity had, and has, changed. Presenting at ALA's 2012 Midwinter conference, several members of the working group spoke at length about the ways in which the daily tasks associated with staffing the People's Library were not unlike those performed at a more traditional library, but these aforementioned functions have largely ceased. While the People's Library has found some temporary homes, the operative word is "temporary."

The history of the Occupy Wall Street People's Library runs parallel with the history of Occupy Wall Street: it arrived unexpectedly, triggering excitement and interest amongst those who had not anticipated such an occurrence, and now it continues, less visibly, driven largely by those who recognize that resistance is not something you can rely on others to do.

You have to do it yourself.

Cassandra and King Canute Apply for Library Cards

As the occupation in Zuccotti Park drew more attention, it was common to hear people declare, "they even have a library." The library was—generally—spared the ridicule that was directed at other working groups. It is doubtless that would-be naysayers' arguments were undermined by the number of "actual librarians" participating in the working group. There was a sense that this was a "real" library.

People like libraries and tend to think positively of them even if they do not personally frequent them, and people find the destruction of libraries abhorrent. Thus, in the outcry following the raid on Zuccotti, amongst the most frequent comments were those mourning the destruction of the library. The volume of these denunciations was of sufficient force that the Mayor's office even felt the need to tweet an image of supposedly safe books (NYCMayorsOffice, 2011). Sadly, this image did satisfy some people, even as the working group realized how much was really gone.

The larger point is this: the destruction of the People's Library was shocking for a very specific reason—it was not subtle. The People's Library was literally thrown in the trash. This was too frank an image for those who have a positive view of libraries and books. People found it disturbing to think of a metropolitan police force acting on orders from the mayor—in a democracy—destroying books.

The grim irony was that it was nothing new. It was just that usually politicians are a bit less open when they are destroying libraries.

Despite "The Protestor" being named *Time* magazine's person of the year in 2011 (the accompanying article mentioned OWSL), *The Village Voice* put out a different sort of end-of-year list (Thrasher, 2012): an enumeration of the most powerless New Yorkers. "The Occupy Wall Street Crust Punks" came in 40th, and beating them by 6 points of powerlessness was the "Occupy Wall Street 'People's Library'" (34th). This is what *The Village Voice* had to say about the library:

> One of the most fun aspects of Zuccotti Park this fall was the "People's Library," a wide selection of books that sparked free-wheeling discussions. Volunteer librarians (like Bill Scott [who was on the cover]) guarded it with professional care. Although they protected it from Mayor Bloomberg's first threatened raid on the park (by taking the books away via Zipcar to an "undisclosed location" [New Jersey]), the librarians were rendered utterly powerless after the city launched its surprise raid and returned the collection looking like shit. (Thrasher, 2012)

Many members of the working group felt indignant about being called powerless. Yet the really significant thing about the list was not that OWSL came in at 34; what was significant was who was ranked 13th. Can you guess? The librarians of the New York Public Library (you guessed that, didn't you?), about whom *The Village Voice* wrote:

> Perhaps the only people less powerful in the library system than the homeless patrons are the librarians themselves. Gone are the days when a master's degree in library science and a job in the nation's largest public library system meant that you would spend your days helping writers to research and mesmerizing people with your encyclopedic knowledge of the Dewey decimal system. Today's NYPL librarian needs to be a social worker, a specialist at dealing with the homeless and the severely mentally ill, a computer tech wiz at solving people's Wi-Fi problems and a job (and suicide-prevention) counselor helping people look for jobs that simply don't exist... (Thrasher, 2012)

The quote goes on, but it does not suddenly become positive.

The moral of the story is that librarians in New York City are powerless.

But what does NYPL's appearance in 13th place mean in a broader context? Surely, NYPL is one of the most respected library systems in the country, if not the world. If the NYPL librarians are powerless, then what about those in Chicago? Or California? Texas? Missouri? Or [insert the name of the state you live in]? Librarians have organized; they have fought back; they have rallied; they have hugged their libraries; they have organized petition drives; they have held read-ins; and they have seen budgets cut, staffing disappear, and hours slashed. This is not just a siege mentality. It was not the American Library Association decrying the powerlessness of librarians, it was *The Village Voice*, and the library section on *The Huffington Post* is called "Libraries in Crisis." Not "Libraries in Transition" or "Libraries Evolve," or "Libraries are Awesome." Libraries, we are told, are in crisis (with article titles like "More Bad News for Librarians" and "Can the American Library Survive?"). A recent *New York Times* "Room for Debate" (December 27, 2012) was titled "Do We Still Need Libraries?" as if there actually was room for debate on this topic.

After the raid on the park, we heard from many who were shocked by what had happened, but what Mayor Bloomberg did to OWSL is not altogether different from what he (and other mayors across the country) have done to other libraries. The main difference is that generally they do not literally throw the books into garbage trucks. When a public library has to cut its hours or its acquisition budget or its staffing, it does not provoke the same visceral reaction that people have to seeing books being thrown into a dumpster. Yet the thousand cuts are every bit as bad as the brutal boot kick, if not worse, as they are only visible if you are looking for them. As might be predicted for a sector "in crisis," the discussion around libraries tends to be about cutting, about how deep to cut, about where to cut, about who to cut, all bolstered by the question of "Do we still need libraries?" And those librarians—pesky public workers (some of whom—gasp—are in unions [the devils])—are just another group trying desperately to do more with less. If librarians are feeling powerless, it is with good reason.

So, why did the NYPL librarians come in 13th and the OWSL librarians come in 34th? After all (at least as of this writing), there are still NYPL librarians trying to fight the cuts, while OWSL is still trying to recover from being cut in half. Perhaps it has to do with the librarians' view of their foes. Most public library systems seek to negotiate with those doing the cutting; they accept that they must be slashed but try to go for a two-inch gash rather than a five-inch gouge, figuring that they will be able to cope with the unsightly scar that is left behind. OWSL knew that it had no negotiating ability but refused to accept the power of those seeking to destroy them. New York City did not cut our budget; they cut our throat, but we got back up again because OWS is the bastard creation of the money-mad Dr. Frankenstein. We weren't getting paid in the first place.

People are powerless precisely in proportion to their willingness to sit quietly and think positive thoughts. Librarians are powerless to the extent to which they silently read the memos saying that there are cuts coming, they are powerless to the extent that they hold read-ins at the library instead of sit-ins at the mayor's office, they are powerless to the extent that they allow a mayor to make cuts and then allow that same individual to attend a gala at that same library. A common organizing cry amongst librarians is "we will not be shushed," but then we are shushed. It is past time to get loud. And if we wish to keep our reading rooms quiet and civil, then perhaps we need to take this noise to those who are trying to shush us.

Unless librarians are willing to stand up and genuinely fight, there is a chance that the only libraries around will be the renegade ones set up in public parks. But at least that way the librarians will be 21 positions less powerless.[4]

Conclusion

The Occupy Wall Street People's Library's life has been characterized by its heyday, the shouts of mayday, the thrill of May Day, and the frequent grumbling of oy vey, and just like any activist construction or incipient institution, it has had highs and more than its fair share of lows.

When patrons would ask members of the working group, "So how does this work, do I bring the book back?" they were told that they could certainly return the book so that others could use it, or they could donate some of their own, but a favorite answer amongst members of the working group was to tell those borrowing books to keep passing the book along, thus allowing the library to continue spreading. And so it is, that today, on any bookshelf that holds a book stamped with the library logo or bearing the letters "OWSL" on the edge, it is there that the library lives on in spirit.

But as for the actual library?

It's waiting to return.

But it needs you for that.

So…meet us later for some civil disobedience? Don't worry, you can wear a cardigan.

---

4. The above several paragraphs are adapted from remarks given at the ALA 2012 Midwinter conference in Dallas, TX; see Fagin et al, 2012.

Epilogue

After Zuccotti was purged, and after members of the working group recovered what they could from the sanitation garage (about 20% of the collection [a portion of which was unusable {and all of which spent the next year or so in boxes in Jaime's apartment}]), the working group started tossing around ideas for legal action. The task seemed rather daunting; luckily, we were approached by Norman Siegel, former head of the New York Civil Liberties Union, and his colleagues, who wanted to represent the library *pro bono*. After a press conference at which we displayed the destroyed books, we filed a lawsuit against the city, Mayor Michael Bloomberg, police commissioner Ray Kelly, sanitation commissioner John Doherty, and unidentified city employees, in federal court on May 24, 2012.

The saying is wrong—you can in fact fight city hall, but it takes lawyers who know what they're doing, as well as patience and fortitude (five points if you get the reference). The city's actions against the library were so egregious that we were certain that if we held fast we'd eventually win. We think the city knew it, too. They offered us a settlement early on, which we rejected as insufficient. In August the city started trying to pass the blame to Brookfield (the company that owns Zuccotti), naming them as a third-party defendant; the city knew someone would have to take the blame, and they didn't want it to be them.

Finally, on April 9, 2013, almost a year and a half after the eviction, we received a settlement offer that perfectly matched our demand. The city gave us the $47,000 at which we valued our destroyed books and equipment; they also paid out lawyers' fees (two other groups from the occupation [Times Up! and Global Revolution] had brought similar suits over their lost equipment, and they were also given the amounts they'd demanded, plus lawyers' fees). We suspect the city was trying to avoid going to trial, sure of bad publicity, questionable information coming to light, and an eventual loss.

It was never about the money. We asked for money because that's the language spoken by the government and the court system. For us, it was about getting an admission of wrongdoing from the city. And we got that, if expressed in the formal, wishy-washy language of lawsuit settlements (we had refused the previous settlement offers that had not included an admission of responsibility).

And now, writing in April 2013, we are just about done with this chapter of the library's history. We no longer have the capacity to rebuild the People's Library as it was, besides which we'd probably find our collection in the garbage again and ourselves in jail in short order if we tried. We plan to use the settlement money to empower other groups that do the kind of library and education work we did. Many of the librarians continue to do this type of work in other venues, both in our professional lives when possible, and also in our "spare time," (though we still aren't quite sure which is real life and which is the thing we do on the side).

The books recovered from the sanitation garage will go back into circulation, now that they are no longer needed as evidence, and the letters "OWSL" written on the edges of the text will always stand as evidence of what the library once was.

And what it can be again.

References

Adbusters. (2011, July 13). #OCCUPYWALLSTREET: A shift in revolutionary tactics [Blog post]. Retrieved from http://www.adbusters.org/blogs/adbusters-blog/occupywallstreet.html

American Library Association. (2011, November 17). ALA alarmed at seizure of Occupy Wall Street Library, loss of irreplaceable material [Press release]. Retrieved from http://www.ala.org/news/pr?id=8568

Fagin, B., Henk, M., Loeb, Z., Norton, D., & Taylor, J. (2012, January 21). A library occupies Occupy Wall Street [Presentation at ALA Midwinter 2012; text also available at http://peopleslibrary.wordpress.com/2012/01/24/peoples-library-presentation-at-ala-midwinter/].

Henk, M. (2011, December 8). A people's digital library and prefigurative politics [part 2]. Retrieved from http://peopleslibrary.wordpress.com/2011/12/08/a-peoples-digital-library-and-prefigurative-politics-2/

New York City General Assembly. (2011, October 2). NYCGA minutes 10/2/2011, 7:30PM. Retrieved from http://www.nycga.net/2011/10/02/308/

NYCMayorsOffice. (2011, November 15). Property from #Zuccotti [Tweet.] Retrieved from http://twitter.yfrog.com/nzdr7ndj

Thrasher, S. (2012, January 11). 100 most powerless New Yorkers. *The Village Voice*. Retrieved from http://www.villagevoice.com/2012-01-11/news/100-most-powerless-new-yorkers/

"Why archive?" and Other Important Questions Asked by Occupiers

Siân Evans, Anna Perricci, and Amy Roberts

As the Occupy Wall Street (OWS) movement began to take shape in Zuccotti Park—also known as Liberty Square—in New York City, an archives working group formed as a collective interested in preserving the physical and digital documents created by activists in the movement. Members of the Archives Working Group (AWG) were faced with a unique set of challenges, as well as the opportunity to address these challenges in an independent, non-hierarchical, non-institutional setting. Consensus-based decision-making drove the actions of the group, but competing visions also needed to be reconciled. Some of the most common questions about the role and function of archives required explanation, both within and beyond the working group.

The desire and need to interact with the archives' creators was integral to the establishment of the OWS AWG's collection. Managing relationships with any set of living donors is inherently complicated, and the occupiers we found ourselves working with represented a dynamic group of content creators and contributors. Activists ask a lot of questions. By definition activists are challenging the status quo. As members of the AWG, we were asked a lot of very valid questions including:

- "What is an archive? Is there a difference between art and archives?"
- "What are you collecting?"
- "Who will have access to what you are collecting?"

- "Where is this stuff going to be kept?"
- "Are you trying to collect all the archives produced in the movement?"
- "Why collect this?" and "Why not this?"
- "What do archivists do and why?"
- "Why should archives matter to people in the movement?"

These questions and how we answered them serve as the foundation for this chapter. We will elaborate on our answers to activists' questions and put forth an analysis of archival theory as related to some of the questions with especially complex implications. The formation of a digital archive also brought up some issues that are beyond those most relevant to the discussion of management of and access to analog archives. Part of this essay is dedicated to the ways in which we addressed these particular concerns. We will conclude with lessons learned in the process of creating a collection of physical and digital archives coming out of Occupy Wall Street in 2011-2012.

For the Occupy Wall Street Archives Working Group, Archiving Is Activism

The OWS AWG, online at owsarchives.wordpress.com, is a working group recognized by the New York City General Assembly of Occupy Wall Street. The task of the AWG initially focused on the acquisition of materials created by activists and the short-term stewardship of these objects. But from the outset, the ideal was always long-term preservation paired with a consistently high level of access. Explaining the balance between access and preservation became central to the answers the working group members needed to provide, especially to those interested in borrowing archives back for exhibition or even reusing signs for future protests. We also always intended to remain an independent working group that was part of the OWS community. While collecting can be done with and by institutions, we have an OWS working group for archives because we want to represent what is going on with Occupy from inside the movement. There are a lot of other people recording the movement and telling its story, but we want to empower occupiers to help preserve what is being made while their story is unfolding. While some archivists aim to be dispassionate and "objective," our intent was to be more involved in the movement and open about the inherent influence of our actions.

The OWS archives officially began when two participants with a mutual interest in archiving met each other on September 24, 2011, in Liberty Square a week after the occupation began. The fluid nature of the movement and its rapid evolution made it both essential and challenging to archive the movement as it unfolded. In the following weeks, as it exploded into a national and international phenomenon, it became clear that it would take more than two people to archive the different types of media that the movement was producing, from the cardboard signs that lined the perimeter of Liberty Square to the Livestream footage online. The working group that subsequently formed consists of professional archivists, students enrolled in archives and preservation programs at universities, and interested individuals who share the conviction that archiving is important. The members generally see ourselves as both participants in and supporters of the movement, and we emphasize the role that archives could play in strengthening activists' and scholars' knowledge of Occupy Wall Street in the future. As such, one of the group's initial endeavors was to draft a mission statement:

> Our mission is to collect ephemera, signs, posters, audiovisual materials, digital files, photographs, oral histories, and artifacts that were created and distributed in and around Liberty Plaza and at actions that Occupy Wall Street participates in. It stands as an evidence of how participatory democracy can work, how culture and politics connect, and how the 99% can come together to generate social and economic change. Its mission is to keep OWS historically self-conscious, and guarantee that our history will be accessible to the public.

Collecting Physical and Digital Art and Archives, in the Midst of Blurred Boundaries Between Art and Archives

In defining what archives are, we quickly ran into difficult questions about the distinction between what is considered art versus what is considered an archive. Many participants in the Occupy movement are artists, though not all of them identify themselves as such. Even those creating signs on discarded pizza boxes were in fact committing a creative act and expressing themselves. However, even occupiers who readily call themselves artists do not automatically presume that everything they produce should be considered art. The inability to draw clear lines separating artworks from archival material both enriches and muddies the discourse about how one defines art, archives, and the creative process through which they are created. Actually defining the term "art" is well beyond the scope of this paper, but let us work under the widely-held assumption that art and archives are not synonymous but may in fact be more related than one might at first realize or acknowledge. For example, the blurring of the boundaries between art, activism, and archives has been a topic of numerous publications over the past decade (Spieker, 2008). Furthermore, since the media attention surrounding OWS, there have been a series of public exhibitions on the topics of art, activism, and information science, including *Collect the WWWorld: The Artist as Archivist in the Internet Age* at the 319 Scholes space in Brooklyn; *Required Reading: Printed Material as Agent of Intervention* at the Center for Book Arts in Manhattan; and *Disobedience Archive (The Parliament)* at Bildmuseet, a museum of contemporary art and visual culture in Sweden.

The majority of the ephemera collected by the AWG could be regarded as art, both in digital and physical formats. As the movement unfolded and the group grew, its members collected and saved hundreds of cardboard signs that we felt had a significant visual and symbolic value. During the occupation, new signs were made on a daily basis and displayed on the sidewalk around the perimeter of Liberty Square to greet people who were visiting and wanted to learn about it. The physical archive currently includes over 300 of these cardboard signs, which represent the cornerstone of the physical archive because of their intrinsic value to the OWS movement.

The archive also consists of a number of other objects. In the physical archives, we have a banner for the media and information station in Liberty Square. Each station of the occupation—from the kitchen to the information and media station—was marked by an orange mesh banner. These banners did not just announce the location where someone should go to obtain food or information, they also told a story about the occupation. Much of the ephemera that the working group collected reflect the themes of resisting, reclaiming, and recreating, which are at the heart of the movement's principles. For example, the media and information banner can be read in multiple ways; the sign itself has a story, and some of its physical characteristics are especially significant. It is made out of fabric from an orange net used by the police to confine protesters in one area during a mass arrest. This material was taken from the police during the march in solidarity with the October 2011 attack on the Oakland occupation. Appropriating physical materials that symbolized repression was a common tactic among occupiers. Several protesters made jewelry out of zip ties, which are made of the same type of plastic and have a similar design to handcuffs used by the New York Police Department. Black and yellow tape styled after the archetypal police tape used to block off sections of Liberty Plaza after the eviction was also created with the word "Occupy" printed on it.

The Screen Printers Cooperative, Occuprint, and Occucopy were all creative cooperatives that came together during the occupation, producing many shirts, buttons, flyers, and posters for actions and events. The Screen Printers Cooperative printed pieces of fabric with different images and phrases that became popular for occupiers to wear pinned on their clothing. While these items are uneditioned multiples, rather than one-of-a-kind objects, they are a limited quantity of artists' work. Other materials in the ephemera collection are hand-made and unique, such as letters of solidarity from across the country, many of which were handwritten.

Our digital collection includes Livestream footage, digital video, animated shorts, digital photographs, audio files, mailing list messages, email announcements, articles, spreadsheets, and other correspondence. We have also been periodically saving data being used in the #OccupyData Hackathons, including a large number of tweets pertaining to OWS. We are not archiving websites right now, because the Internet Archive is regularly harvesting hundreds of websites, including Facebook pages, related to the Occupy movement worldwide. We have contributed to the Internet Archive's Web archiving project by sending over 200 URLs to use as seed sites for the collection, including several dozen Facebook pages that were heavily used to organize occupations throughout the world.

One remarkable thing about the Occupy movement is its embrace, development, and use of technology, from mobile apps such as Obscuracam and "I'm getting arrested" to hardware designed to meet the needs of people engaging in public protest, notably the FreedomTower (a robust mobile hotspot) and Amelia Marzec's community phone booth project (viewable online at www.ameliamarzec.com/phonebooth). An event to highlight this technological innovation, Demo Day, was held at the contemporary arts space Eyebeam in New York City on January 28, 2012. At Demo Day, a variety of tech tools made for and/or by activists was presented. The organizer, artist Taeyoon Choi, was also a co-organizer for Share Day, an event in which we invited activists to bring in their digital archives to share with one another and donate to the AWG if they so chose. Choi's Demo Day website, at demo-day.org/projects, gives more information about these initiatives.

So, What *Is* an Archive?

When this question came up, we would begin the conversation by noting that archives are traditionally defined as collections of records with ongoing evidential value to an organization and subsequently to society at large. Records (or items) can be a variety of different things, including text, images, ephemera, and digital content. Furthermore, a single item can also be called an archive. Archives document the activity of people or organizations and are often associated with other institutions like libraries, museums, or universities.

This basic working definition is only a small part of the answer. The term "archive" has been a flashpoint for critical discussion over the past few decades, and as such the term itself has been expanded to mean a variety of different things. This is partially a product of what Pierre Nora (1989) calls the "imperative of our epoch"—that is, to preserve any vestige of memory and, in the process, to produce archives (p. 14). According to this logic, archives—alongside museums and libraries—are society's memory tools. Or, as Nora puts it, "modern memory is, above all, archival" (p. 13). But if this helps us understand why we archive, it does not explain what the archive actually is. A specification of the function of an archive is an early step but not a comprehensive answer to the initial question about what an archive is.

In the process of more richly defining an archive, let us consider the history of our context and practice as archivists. While archives have been maintained since antiquity, the modern conception of the archive was developed in revolutionary France. The National Archives were founded in 1789 and the Archives Department in 1796. Similarly, in England, the Public Record Act of 1838 assembled the management of all public repositories (Ferreira-Buckley, 1999, p. 578). The institutionalization of archives is generally associated with 19th century Europe, when the archive (and especially the national archive) played into a general sense of Positivism typical to the era. By Positivism we refer specifically to an understanding of the world, derived from the philosophy of Auguste Comte, that assumes the universe is governed by natural laws that are observable, therefore implying an objective reality that is "knowable" (Harris, 1997, p. 132). Under this premise, archival science as a discipline assumes the inherent neutrality of the archivist and posits the archive as an accurate reflection of historical fact.

As Joan M. Schwartz and Terry Cook (2002) have argued, both scholars and archivists have had a vested interest in perceiving and promoting the archive as a neutral historical repository of information (p. 6). According to them, the archive is not a passive receptacle of historical information; it actually shapes and controls the way history is read, which in turn shapes our contemporary political reality. As Derrida (1994) so succinctly points out in an oft-quoted footnote at the beginning of *Archive Fever*: "There is no political power without control of the archive, or without memory" (p. 4).

The lack of clarity in the term "archive" is also a product of the expanding of the word itself in critical theory. Terry Cook (2011), for example, distinguishes between the "archive" (singular) and "archives" (plural) (p. 600). If the term "archives" refers to the development and processing of historical documents over time, the "archive" is a much more flexible term that has come to mean a number of different things and is, at times, collapsed with the term "memory" itself. While this loosening can be attributed primarily to the writings of Michel Foucault (1991, 2010) and Jacques Derrida, a series of theorists and critics including David Greetham (1999), Pierre Nora, Andreas Huyssen (2000), and Hal Foster (2004) has taken up this expanded "archive" and the relationship between archives and institutional power in a variety of ways.

We ask ourselves and our contemporaries what this means for archivists and for alternative archives. There is a small but growing community of archivists—including Verne Harris, Terry Cook, Joan M. Schwartz, and Eric Ketelaar (2002)—who have taken the postmodern critiques of archival Positivism to heart and have championed increased discussion between archivists and the historians, journalists, and scholars who use archives in their work. This has led to what Verne Harris (1997) calls "a transformation discourse" in which the role of the archivists and the process of archivization have come under increased scrutiny (p. 132). Harris and Cook, among others, have argued compellingly for greater transparency in the process of archivization. Harris' call to respect the "other," and to "invite every other into the archive," is perhaps a tall order, but it is a necessary one in a heterogeneous and horizontal movement such as OWS.

Why Should Archives Matter to Occupiers?

When we reflect on why archives should matter to activists, "Baby Pictures of a Revolt"—a section of Rebecca Solnit's poetic letter to Mohammed Bouazizi—comes to mind. Bouazizi, a Tunisian street vendor, self-immolated in protest of the poverty and humiliation in which he was living, and his death contributed to the beginning of the Arab Spring. When we think about archives coming from OWS, we could consider them documentation of a tender and formative period of a worldwide movement that has lasted far beyond the two-month occupation of Liberty Square. While "baby pictures" is too sentimental a term for wide use by the working group, the value remains: this is evidence of how things were at the beginning of something larger, and its future form was only hinted at by the manifestations recorded as it began to take shape.

These archives should matter to occupiers both because they are the result of their own ingenuity and creativity, and because these materials are representations of what happened that will outlive us if handled properly. Occupiers taking responsibility for their own archives enables us, as a culture, to preserve voices that could otherwise be silenced.

We contend that archives are not dead and instead help stories live on, sometimes giving voices to the voiceless. Through the preservation of these records, we have a chance to make sure the memory of OWS is maintained with as much accuracy as possible. Many people outside the movement have asserted what it entails and means to them, so why should we not make sure occupiers' own stories are told and preserved?

What Is a Digital Archive? Why Archive Digital Materials?

When asked what a digital archive is, the explanation starts by specifying that there are at least two ways one can define a digital archive. The first is that it is an organized collection of digital files. Digital files themselves can also be referred to as digital archives as they are archival materials (archives). To us it's important to note that nearly any kind of digital file could be saved in an archive, but the long-term preservation of the files involves more than just keeping a copy or two in a safe place.

The perception that digital archives are secure if they are posted online is one that we encourage people to question. Digital preservation is a multifaceted, long-term strategic process through which files are cataloged and managed in the short term, then stewarded on an ongoing basis. Content on the Web can disappear without a trace at the volition of the account holder who posted it, or the service provider such as YouTube, Facebook, Twitter, Flickr, or Tumblr.

The AWG collects digital materials from activists and select datasets used by Occupy Research (www.occupyresearch.net), including a large collection of tweets that were analyzed as part of the #OccupyData Hackathons in New York City and elsewhere. As mentioned earlier, for Web archiving, members of the working group submitted over 200 websites, including many Facebook pages and websites for occupations worldwide, for the Internet Archive to periodically harvest (these archived websites can be viewed at archive-it.org/collections/2950).

One of the AWG members came into the group specifically because she wanted to archive digital materials. She started her work with a needs assessment. This process was undertaken within a two-week timeframe and resulted in a flexible project plan to establish a digital archive for OWS. To determine the needs of the activists, two working group members referred the digital archivist to Livestreamers, videographers, photographers, people in the technology centered working group (Tech Ops), and avid social media users. Through conducting user interviews and encouraging collaboration between groups, several questions about digital archives frequently came up (examined below), and we made some decisions about how we wanted to approach creating and maintaining a digital archive.

The interviews made it clear that some activists knew already that they needed help managing their files and were interested in a Digital Asset Management (DAM) system. We struggled to find a robust tool that would let people manage their files and ensure ongoing access. There was no free system that was easy to use and simple to maintain that would meet the needs of the activists. Ultimately, we chose to work on a preliminary basis with Omeka, a free, open source Web publishing platform created for museums, libraries, archives, and scholars to create Web exhibits. Omeka has several very useful plug-ins, and we are using it on a test server to try out different ways to upload and catalog digital archives. Part of why we chose Omeka is because it is open source and built using a programming language called PHP, which several computer programmers in the movement know. We recognize the prospect of identifying features that would make Omeka more effective for our purposes and requesting their development by activists or other technologists who would like to help us.

Digitization Isn't the Same Thing as Preservation, and It's Not Simple

The digital archiving efforts at first were very reliant on cooperation and support from OWS's technology working group, Tech Ops. Our conversations with Tech Ops largely revolved both around our hardware and bandwidth needs as well as our reasons for requiring a digital archive at all. To get any support from Tech Ops, we first needed to answer some typical questions and explain how digital archiving is more than having a back-up and that the assignment of non-technical metadata is not a process that can be automated.

Parallel to our work, Tech Ops was looking into options for a DAM, so it was not hard to explain the value of managing files in the immediate future, although we needed to convey how a DAM is only part of the way digital archives will persist in the long run. There was a perception that digital materials would survive if they continued to be useful and were likely to be maintained by the creators of the file. A simple reminder of the ephemerality of websites usually did a good job of starting the conversation of the fragility and fleeting nature of digital works online. Almost everyone we spoke to about how easy it is to accidentally lose important data admitted that they, like most of us, have lost files or even had hard drives crash. The possibility that files would be seized by law enforcement as evidence was also openly acknowledged, as was the possibility that materials stored in the cloud could be rendered inaccessible rather easily, particularly if a paid service proved to be unaffordable.

Tech Ops members and many other people in the movement assumed that the AWG would be digitizing the physical archives in short order and then making these materials available online. There was a common belief that if a file is not available through a Web-based interface, it is not really accessible. While widespread access was a goal, immediate needs revolved around simply gathering digital and physical archives, then keeping them safe and in reasonable order.

In February 2012 at Judson Memorial Church in Manhattan, a discussion of the challenges of digitization came up at an open forum intended to determine the future of the archives held by the AWG. Some of the attendees, including a few members of the working group, pushed for immediate access to archives through the Web, albeit without having the time or expertise to contribute to the effort of doing so themselves. At first it was not easy to succinctly explain how digitization entails a lot more than taking a picture with a good quality digital camera, and how a database-driven website with a decent user interface involves a lot of work. Over time, we gained the ability to help people understand the limits of quality to rough and ready output such as unedited scans or digital pictures of ephemera in the collection. We also became more adept at explaining that while there are very robust tool sets available, it would take a lot of time and expertise to customize the kind of content management system we needed before we could even think about the front end that users would see. The ability to search the collection would also be contingent on adequate metadata assignment, which requires a significant amount of work.

Ultimately, our server space was set up and maintained by someone who had originally come to the movement as a participant in Tech Ops but joined the AWG to help us move forward with the digital archive. Having an enthusiastic and very skilled technical expert in the working group significantly reduced our reliance on Tech Ops. That said, we kept up an informal dialogue with Tech Ops to coordinate our groups' respective efforts.

Licensing to Encourage Reuse

The potential for use and reuse of digital archives was at the forefront of our thinking as we began to plan for a digital archive. There was a pragmatic need to ensure that materials would be cleared for access and reuse, particularly for multimedia files, and we wanted to be very transparent about the fact that these archives would not be private or held in confidence. We opted to require that digital archives taken into the AWG's collection be licensed under Creative Commons. Since we were not interested in supporting commercial work with our efforts, we specified that the license associated with the assets in the collection must limit the use of the materials to non-commercial purposes. Donors are always to be credited (attribution). At the time of donation, creators were asked to specify if and how editing or remixing their materials is permitted (derivatives allowed, no derivatives, or Share Alike). We also tried to reassure creators that assigning a Creative Commons license did not amount to a resignation of their right to grant additional permissions and further use, including for commercial purposes. The Creative Commons licensing is meant to serve only as a baseline for future use, with the rest being up to people beyond the working group.

Another common licensing question that came up was, "Isn't the stuff made by people in the movement in the public domain?" Works created in conjunction with OWS may physically have been in a public domain or existed on the open Web, but the works are not in the public domain in legal terms. The duration before something is legally released into the public domain is the lifetime of the creator plus 70 years (Copyright Act of 1976). The people who created these works are most likely still alive, and even if they are not they were living as of the fall of 2011 and therefore did not die decades ago.

Why Collect _____ and Not _____? Or Inviting Every "Other" into the Archive

The content of the physical and digital collections is very much contingent on donations from activists involved in OWS. While we cannot collect everything—especially given limited staff, funds, and space—we are trying to find a way to gather a representative sample of archives created through OWS.

Harris's call to invite every "other" into the archive is perhaps problematic here in that it defines the non-archivist as "other." Because the AWG has sought to dismantle the distinction between archivist and activist by establishing dialogue between the two, this boundary becomes blurred in the context of a highly participatory movement. Nonetheless, in his desire to invite everyone in, Harris gets at the principle of "total archives." The total archive is one that seeks to collect everything and does not distinguish between valuable and invaluable content. If we had more time and resources, we would have tried to determine which objects have intrinsic value and which don't. In many cases, these decisions could be judgment calls by archivists who considered themselves part of the movement. Instead, the decisions were made based on limitations of space and staffing. Ideally, it would be wonderful to be able to collect everything and anything and then thoughtfully appraise it, but with a small, all-volunteer staff and limited physical (and server) space, this was not possible.

Where Will the Archives Be Kept and Who Will Have Access to Them? Engaging the OWS Community: Open Forums for Occupiers to Share Their Visions for the Future of the Movement's Archives

Where the archives would reside in the short and long-term was very contentious within the working group and beyond. As is the case with most records, the significance of the OWS archives could be strengthened when held in the context of a rich, representative sample or reduced by the abject absence of other records from the movement. The value of having many items from the movement in one place was disputed by one of the working group members, who insisted the archives should be distributed widely rather than held centrally. However, compiling a representative sample of the works coming out of Occupy would be nearly impossible if the collection were intentionally divided and spread out in the way that he repeatedly proposed.

Maintaining collection materials in one location is very powerful and gives researchers the ability to see a range of the works that were produced and collected. How one would be able to get to and use the archives was and continues to be a contentious issue. We very much needed to explain the purpose of archives as well as highlight the value of aggregation, archival processing, and subsequent access in a safe space. Security of the materials inevitably entails some barriers to access, but there were concerns about overly protecting the records to the point that they would no longer be accessible to anyone. There was a fair amount of misunderstanding about the balance between security and access, typified well by this online exchange. On OWS's primary website for discussions within the movement (NYCGA.net), an activist who identified himself as David Everitt-Carlson wrote in a forum discussion about the future of OWS's archives:

> I fully understand your want for the work to be accessible, but having it stored in the room at the end of the film Indiana Jones does not to me constitute it being shared with the public. Initially, I had created the work to share an experience, but it certainly was not donated to anyone including the Smithsonian, NYU or the New York Historical Society.

We wanted to ensure that the experiences that made up the Occupy movement were in fact shared, rather than locked away in a private storage locker. Ultimately, attempts to safeguard the archives outside of an institutional setting amounted to simply making them inaccessible to anyone. The collective spirit of the movement, though outside of any formal institution, will likely become dependent on one for the persistence and access to the materials. That said, some institutional settings are more appropriate than others.

Issues around access were debated in weekly working group meetings, and we held two broader meetings where other OWS activists were invited to gather as a larger group to discuss the archives. During the first meeting, held on February 5, 2012, at Judson Memorial Church, many of the questions that became the basis for the FAQs on the website were posed to the working group and the other archivists in attendance. The meaning of some archival vocabulary and practices were not necessarily clear to many activists. Some criticized terms such as "intellectual control" and "materials" because they connoted concepts that conflicted with the anti-materialist and horizontal nature of the movement. One occupier, for example, asked why preservation was needed—did OWS need to be "mummified"?

The idea of preserving the longevity of documents produced by the movement seemed unsettling for some activists who viewed what they were doing as "happening now." Many occupiers expressed the desire for an online presence so that the archives would have a more participatory and decentralized feel in harmony with the ideals of the movement. One of the suggestions offered in this discussion was that participants might swap and share their personal archival collections. "Share Day," described above, was organized by Taeyoon Choi and two AWG members partly in response to this desire to engage occupiers and others in the community.

During Share Day we also had the opportunity to see a documentary in progress about Campaign 99 (online at www.99campaign.com/p/all-narratives_17.html) that was being made by an Iranian activist, Ali Abdi. This project focused on an exchange of inspirational tributes between Occupy activists and Iranian prisoners of conscience. We also learned about the work coming out of the #OccupyData Hackathons, which started with a wide harvesting of relevant data and then processed it into visualizations and other accessible abstractions.

The second movement-wide meeting to discuss the future of the collection gathered by members of the AWG was organized by the working group and held at the Interference Archive in Brooklyn on August 5, 2012. The Interference Archive was chosen because it is a do-it-yourself archive created by activists, and it is also where Occuprint—a collective of activist printmakers—is based. The purpose of the meeting was to involve OWS participants in the decision of where the archives should be donated. At the time, the archives did not have a permanent stable location where they could be accessible, secure, and safe from the elements. It had become clear that the working group did not have the resources to create and sustain an independent archive, and members had begun looking for alternatives. As of winter 2013, we are working on an agreement with the Tamiment Library and Robert F. Wagner Labor Archives, an organization that has a long history of working with activist and labor movements and is housed at New York University (NYU).

Much of the discussion at the second movement-wide meeting was around the issue of associating with an NYU affiliate. One occupier expressed concern that although Tamiment was independent, NYU could use the archives to promote their institution. The distrust of NYU was understandable given that some participants in OWS have also been protesting NYU's expansion into Greenwich Village and backing NYU graduate students' years-long struggle to have their union recognized. Nonetheless, the Tamiment Library has been supportive of the union, and a number of archivists there had been active in our working group or within the broader movement.

Institutional Partnership and Visions of Alternate Models for Archiving OWS

Finding a situation in which access and safekeeping are both considered to be adequate by occupiers is not simple, and at the time of this writing, the analog archives collected by the AWG are not settled. Work with the Tamiment Library is in progress, but establishing the terms for the deed of gift has revolved partially around the ability to communicate the necessary elements of compromise inherent to the preservation of archives in—or out of—an institutional setting.

Community archives require an ongoing sustainable effort by individuals who are committed to extended stewardship. Occupy Wall Street is a fluid and transient movement; activists' participation can wax or wane depending on other circumstances in their lives, and movements historically tend to split off into different directions. OWS is not an organization or a nonprofit, nor does it represent a particular section of society that has a shared identity and/or history. While the continual evolution of the movement made archiving in real time important, it means that maintaining an ongoing physical archive is particularly challenging.

For independent and alternative archives to survive, they require people committed to staffing it long-term and securing some type of financial sustenance, which most likely entails continual fundraising. Though the members of the working group saw an independent archive as a goal, a stable and cooperative institution that both preserves and provides access to the collection is a more attainable option. At both of the open forum meetings that the working group organized, occupiers felt quite strongly that the archives should be kept independent but were not able to firmly grasp how difficult this is to do in practice.

Although the intention to keep the archives independent might not have been achieved in this instance, consideration of alternative models of archives are valuable in current archival practice. Currently, several institutional archives in the United States are being dismantled or coping with extreme budget cuts, which impedes public access to the collections. As we have pointed out earlier in this essay, archivists and historians have a vested interest in perceiving the archive as a neutral space. However, professional archivists are to some extent unconsciously contributing their own views on the subject matter in the process of collecting and processing records. In the case of a social movement like OWS, standing apart and simply observing from a distance does not necessarily make the archivist any more objective, as archivists are also participants in the society being critiqued by the movement. Nonetheless, neutrality is an especially fraught concept for archivists documenting a social movement as well as for archivists who are also activists. An activist within a movement like OWS has gained insights that can influence how she or he processes the collection; likewise, a sympathetic (or unsympathetic) observer brings her or his own experiences to the table.

How Can Archivists Work Productively with Activists?

Even archivists who do not consider themselves activists can work productively with activists by being respectful and empathetic. There are different challenges with living creators, especially ones with concerns about privacy, sometimes stemming from the fear that archives will be used against them by law enforcement. The AWG decided that we would not try to keep closed archives or dictate who may or may not consult them. We can see how keeping certain materials closed for a set duration can be useful, but it is not something we are equipped to do. Trust and openness are integral to maintaining legitimacy and being considered safe, sympathetic collaborators.

Some activists were very concerned about the destination of the archives and wanted assurances that they would be entrusted to people within the movement or their allies. This partially illustrates one potential caveat to the total archives approach; not all marginalized groups want to have their experiences recorded, especially in official government archives. As Rodney G.S. Carter (2006) has said, "it is essential that archivists not undermine the right of groups to remain silent" (p. 227). Carter uses the example of feminist writers who have argued that silence should not be equated with absence. By this logic, choosing not to be archived can be a political tactic. Carter recommends, however, that archivists be willing to invite community members into the planning and administrative processes of archiving, allowing them to help in the decision-making around use and access of the records (p. 231). This would enable marginalized groups to make an educated choice about whether or not they would like to keep their silence.

It was this principle that guided a lot of the work we did in the OWS AWG. Because the group consisted of occupiers and sympathetic professionals, we embodied a mixture of archivists, activists, and archivist-activists. As such, we were careful not to impose an authoritarian, unified archival voice on the decision-making process. Our decision-making process was consensus-based; not only did we hold weekly meetings, but we also created an open forum Google Group in which those who could not attend could voice their opinions. The discourse on the Google Group mailing list was tense at times, but it did provide a venue for people to speak freely in writing.

Conclusion: Lessons Learned and Closing Thoughts

In this chapter, we have discussed some of the most salient questions that have come up since the group's formation in September 2011. We have faced some unique challenges in attempting to archive a movement from within it. In the construction of traditional and even independent archives, particular narratives are often adopted. All too often, while archives should represent a multitude of identities, the focus is on the stories of the privileged and powerful. By highlighting the particular questions that came up in the course of our work, we hope to educate other activists on the importance of archives as well as help other archivists work with activists.

The working group learned a number of important lessons while working both *as* and *with* activists within OWS. We learned that consensus-based decision-making is imperative in activist environments, but it requires organization, alliance building, compromise, and educational outreach. Activists and archivists need, at the very least, to understand the principles behind each other's thought processes. Archivists need to learn the proper channels for communication and organization within a horizontal movement like OWS, and activists need to be educated as to the basic principles of archiving in order to engage in productive conversation. These are not small tasks, and we hope others will continue this type of work and share their solutions to some of the questions raised in this chapter. We contend that a lack of clarity in some contexts makes room for exploring nuances in the definitions of archival terms and lets us interrogate the role of archivists in our society. This ambiguity can enrich the work of archivists among activists and all the "others" who need to be heard and represented.

References

Carter, R. G. S. (2006). Of things said and unsaid: Power, archival silences, and power in silence. *Archivaria, 61*: Special Section on Archives, Space, and Power, 215-233.

Cook, T. (2011). The archive(s) is a foreign country: Historians, archivists, and the changing archival landscape. *The American Archivist, 74*, 600-632.

Copyright Act, 17 U.S.C. § 302 (1976).

Derrida, J. (1996). *Archive fever: A Freudian impression.* Chicago, IL: University of Chicago Press.

Ferreira-Buckley, L. (1999). Archivists with an attitude: Rescuing the archives from Foucault. *College English, 61*(5), 577-583.

Foucault, M. (2010). *The archaeology of knowledge and the discourse on language.* New York, NY: Vintage Books.

Foucault, M. (1991). *Discipline and punish: The birth of the prison.* London, England: Penguin Books.

Greetham, D. (1999). "Who's in, who's out": The cultural poetics of archival exclusion. *Studies in the Literary Imagination, 32*(1), 1.

Foster, H. (2004). An archival impulse. *October,* (110), 3-22.

Harris, V. (1997). Claiming less, delivering more: A critique of positivist formulations on archives in South Africa. *Archivaria, 44*, 132-141.

Huyssen, A. (2000). Present pasts: Media, politics, amnesia. *Public Culture, 12*(1), 21-38.

Ketelaar, E. (2002). Archival temples, archival prisons: Modes of power and protection. *Archival Science, 2*, 221-38.

Nora, P. (1989). Between memory and history: Les lieux de mémoire. *Representations, 26*, 7-24.

Schwartz, J. M., & Cook, T. (2002). Archives, records, and power: The making of modern memory. *Archival Science, 2*(1-2), 1-19.

Solnit, R. (2011). The occupation of hope: Letter to a dead man. In S. van Gelder and the staff of YES! Magazine (Eds.), *This changes everything: Occupy Wall Street and the 99% movement* (pp. 77-82). San Francisco, CA: Berrett-Koehler Publishers, Inc.

Spieker, S. (2008). *The big archive: Art from bureaucracy.* Cambridge, MA: MIT Press.

Author Biographies

Siân Evans is a librarian and feminist. She earned an MA in Art History from the University of Western Ontario and an MSLIS from Pratt Institute. Since completing her graduate work, she has been published in *The Serials Librarian* and *Art Documentation* on issues around open access politics and art historical research. She lives in Brooklyn and works for ARTstor.

Molly Fair is an archivist, activist, and artist. She is a co-founder of Interference Archive in Brooklyn, NY, a public study center and collection of materials produced by social movements (interferencearchive.org). She is also a collective member of Justseeds Artists' Cooperative (justseeds.org).

Jenna Freedman is the Director of Research & Instruction Services and Zine Librarian at Barnard College in NYC and a member of Radical Reference. She publishes and presents on zine librarianship and other themes of library activism and publishes the zine Lower East Side Librarian.

Lia Friedman is a gardener, ocean lover, and librarian based in southern California. Director of Learning Services at UCSD Library, Staff Librarian for *make/shift* magazine, and a member of Radical Reference, Lia was named a 2009 "Mover and Shaker" by *Library Journal*.

Taneya D. Gethers is a writer, editor, and librarian who proudly serves the community of Bedford-Stuyvesant, Brooklyn, where she resides with her husband, Yusuf, and their three daughters. She holds a BA from Spelman College and a MSLIS from Drexel University. She believes that libraries can help transform lives and propel positive action in the world.

Dan Grace lives and works in Sheffield, U.K. He is a library and information assistant in a public library the first half of the week and an information adviser in an academic library the second half. When not working, he digs his allotment and writes. In September 2013 he will begin a PhD investigating the effect technology has on public libraries' capacity to promote community resilience.

Jens Hoyer loves libraries, grey literature, and pancakes. Jen has worked in public libraries, school libraries, special libraries, and rural African villages. She is passionate about equitable information access and new ways to create an information-literate society. And maple syrup.

Rhonda Kauffman is the cataloging/metadata librarian at Lehigh University in Bethlehem, Pennsylvania. She first wrote a zine in the 1990s as a high school student and has just recently reentered zinedom by authoring a mamazine, Bloom.

Moyra Lang is Project Coordinator and Manager for the Living Archives on Eugenics in Western Canada. She received her MLIS from University of Alberta, Canada, in 2009, and a BA (with Distinction) in 2007. Moyra is deeply involved in community organizing and volunteers extensively with local organizations to address issues of poverty, prostitution, literacy, queer arts, and community building.

Zachary Loeb is a writer, activist, librarian, and terrible accordion player. He earned his BA somewhere, his MSIS somewhere else, and is pursuing an MA because he loves debt. A Reference Librarian and Occupy Librarian, he co-captains the blog librarianshipwreck.wordpress.com, where he writes using the moniker The Luddbrarian.

Stephen MacDonald is the Resource Coordinator for the Edmonton Social Planning Council in Edmonton, Alberta. He holds a Master of Library and Information Studies degree from Dalhousie University in Halifax, Nova Scotia. Stephen has a passion for social justice and is interested in ways that library workers can use their skills to bring about social change in their communities and beyond. He is also interested in initiatives designed to address poverty and homelessness.

Hannah Mermelstein is a school librarian and Palestine solidarity activist in Brooklyn, NY. She has led 30 delegations in Palestine, including Librarians and Archivists to Palestine, and is the author of the *Jerusalem Quarterly* article "Overdue Books: Returning Palestine's 'Abandoned Property' of 1948."

Jessica Moran is Assistant Digital Archivist at the Alexander Turnbull Library, National Library of New Zealand. Prior to that, she worked in government, special, and university libraries and archives. She has a BA from UC Berkeley, a MLIS from San Jose State University, and an MA in History from San Francisco State University. She was the assistant editor of the first two volumes of *Emma Goldman: A Documentary History of the American Years* and is a member of the Kate Sharpley Library Collective.

Caroline Muglia is an archivist, which allows her to be professionally curious. She works with manuscripts at the Library of Congress and serves as the Assistant Director of the Lebanese in North Carolina Project, where she helps to build digital history tools.

Vani Natarajan works as a Research and Instruction Librarian in the Humanities and Global Studies, at Barnard College Library, New York. She is also a member of Adalah-NY: The New York Campaign for the Boycott of Israel. She writes fiction and essays. Her interests include feminist and queer politics, the spatialization of knowledge, and independent publishing.

Anna Perricci is an archivist, installation artist, and educator. She earned an MSI in Archives and Records Management at the University of Michigan. Since completing graduate research on the preservation of the Atari 2600 and highly ephemeral artworks, she has collaborated with artists and activists in New York City to preserve their work.

Barbara Quarton is coordinator of library instruction in the John M. Pfau Library at California State University San Bernardino. Her research interests are active learning, critical information literacy, and writing across the curriculum.

Amy Roberts created the Occupy Wall Street archives after being an activist for many years. Her experiences have given her insight into how archives can be a tool for activists seeking to shape their own historical narrative. She is currently finishing her Masters of Library Studies with an emphasis on archives and works at a public library in New York.

Gayle Sacuta is a promoter of libraries and literacy, writer, fiddle player, fiber artist, and mom. She completed her MLIS from the University of Alberta in 2012 and currently works as a library director in Drayton Valley, Alberta.

Maggie Schreiner is a digital archivist and community organizer based in Brooklyn, NY. As an academic and an activist, she is interested in the creation of historical memory in social justice organizing. Maggie has worked on food justice issues and in solidarity with anti-colonial struggles.

Béatrice Colastin Skokan is the Manuscripts Librarian at the University of Miami Libraries Special Collections. Ms. Skokan received her MLIS from Florida State University. She also holds an MA in International Studies from the University of Miami. Ms. Skokan is co-chair of the SAA Human Rights Archives Roundtable. Her research interests include the documentation of oral, immigrant, and peripheral cultures.

Shawn(ta) Smith is a lesbian separatist, writer, archivist, librarian. Her essays blend lesbian storytelling with documentation. For Library Juice Press, she's also written "Patricia's Child, Patrick's Penis & the Sex of Reference: A Lesbian Librarian's Log of Perverse Patronage" in *Out Behind the Desk: Workplace Issues for LGBTQ Librarians* (2011).

Jaime Taylor earned her BA at Smith College in 2006 and her MLS at Simmons College in 2009. She is the librarian at the International Poster Center in New York City and was one of the Occupy Wall Street librarians. Along with Zachary Loeb, she co-captains the LibrarianShipwreck blog. While her sweater collection is growing by leaps and bounds, she is currently catless and most days wears contact lenses rather than glasses.

Vince Teetaert lives in Montréal, Québec with his girlfriend and their two young boys. He enjoys gardening, controlled vocabularies, science experiments, and cataloging the forgotten, ignored and unappreciated. Vince is still involved with QPIRG Concordia's Political Poster Archive, working to one day have it online.

Cynthia Tobar, founder of WRI Oral History Project, has collaborated with the Occupy Wall Street Archives Working Group, conducting interviews with

OWS occupiers, as well as with Brooklyn Historical Society's "Crossing Borders, Bridging Generations" project, which analyzes mixed-heritage issues and identity. Currently, Cynthia is an archivist at The Winthrop Group.

Jude Vachon is a public librarian and health care advocate. She lives in Pittsburgh with her animals.

Scott Ziegler is a founding collective member of the Radical Archives of Philadelphia and works with a number of other community collections, including the Soapbox: Philadelphia's Independent Publishing Center and Zine Library. He holds an MLS from Drexel University, is a member of the Academy of Certified Archivists, and works as a professional archivist during the day. For the current article he is not expressing the views of his employer or of his other professional associations.

Index

CPSIA information can be obtained
at www.ICGtesting.com
Printed in the USA
LVHW04s0031110718
583279LV00005B/791/P